"Gerald Bray accomplishes an improbable task with this remarkable book on Augustine's view of the Christian life. Bray surveys the voluminous and brilliant contributions from the bishop of Hippo and presents them in a readable and understandable manner. In doing so, he provides us with an edifying, informative, and helpful resource for students, historians, theologians, and church leaders alike. It is a joyful privilege to recommend this excellent addition to Crossway's Theologians on the Christian Life series."

David S. Dockery, Distinguished Professor of Theology, Southwestern Baptist Theological Seminary

"Gerald Bray gives us a richly informative and richly edifying introduction to Augustine and his teaching on the Christian life. It will enable those who have read very little of Augustine, as well as those much more familiar with him, to see Augustine as he would have wanted to be seen: a sinner saved by grace seeking to teach faithfully what he found in the Scriptures. Augustine's specific devotional teaching is placed in the context of his mammoth contribution to Christian theology and Western civilization more generally. The accessibility of this introduction belies the depth of scholarship, which becomes evident in the footnotes and bibliography. Here is a sure-footed guide to the thinking of one of the greatest minds in the history of the Christian church."

Mark D. Thompson, Principal, Moore Theological College

"Augustine told us that only God can be enjoyed for his own sake; all others must be considered as they relate to God. How fitting that Gerald Bray leads us to consider Augustine not for his own sake, but as a gateway to a vision of the one true God and the life lived more deeply in his triune presence. With a teacher's wisdom and a scholar's facility with the primary texts, Bray helps guide readers more deeply into the Christian life through the great bishop's interaction with a host of challenges—real, cruel threats to Christian faithfulness—ranging from the Manichaeans to the Donatists and the Pelagians. Take up and read, and let Bray take you to school."

Michael Allen, Associate Professor of Systematic and Historical Theology, Reformed Theological Seminary, Orlando

AUGUSTINE

on the Christian Life

THEOLOGIANS ON THE CHRISTIAN LIFE

EDITED BY STEPHEN J. NICHOLS AND JUSTIN TAYLOR

AUGUSTINE

on the Christian Life

TRANSFORMED BY THE POWER OF GOD

GERALD BRAY

CROSSWAY

WHEATON, ILLINOIS

Augustine on the Christian Life: Transformed by the Power of God

Copyright © 2015 by Gerald Bray

Published by Crossway
        1300 Crescent Street
        Wheaton, Illinois 60187

Cover design: Josh Dennis
Cover image: Richard Solomon Artists, Mark Summers

First printing 2015

Printed in the United States of America

Trade paperback ISBN: 978-1-4335-4494-1
ePub ISBN: 978-1-4335-4497-2
PDF ISBN: 978-1-4335-4495-8
Mobipocket ISBN: 978-1-4335-4496-5

Library of Congress Cataloging-in-Publication Data

Bray, Gerald Lewis.
   Augustine on the Christian life: transformed by the
power of God / Gerald Bray.
      pages cm.—(Theologians on the Christian life)
    Includes bibliographical references and index.
    ISBN 978-1-4335-4494-1 (tp)
    1. Augustine, Saint, Bishop of Hippo. 2. Theology—
Early works to 1800. 3. Christian life. I. Augustine, Saint,
Bishop of Hippo. Works. Selections. English. II. Title.
BR1720.A9B68   2015
248.092—dc23   2015010886

Crossway is a publishing ministry of Good News Publishers.

VP		30	29	28	27	26	25	24	23	22	21	20
14	13	12	11	10	9	8	7	6	5	4	3	2

For M. R. W.

CONTENTS

SERIES PREFACE

Some might call us spoiled. We live in an era of significant and substantial resources for Christians on living the Christian life. We have ready access to books, DVD series, online material, seminars—all in the interest of encouraging us in our daily walk with Christ. The laity, the people in the pew, have access to more information than scholars dreamed of having in previous centuries.

Yet for all our abundance of resources, we also lack something. We tend to lack the perspectives from the past, perspectives from a different time and place than our own. To put the matter differently, we have so many riches in our current horizon that we tend not to look to the horizons of the past.

That is unfortunate, especially when it comes to learning about and practicing discipleship. It's like owning a mansion and choosing to live in only one room. This series invites you to explore the other rooms.

As we go exploring, we will visit places and times different from our own. We will see different models, approaches, and emphases. This series does not intend for these models to be copied uncritically, and it certainly does not intend to put these figures from the past high upon a pedestal like some race of super-Christians. This series intends, however, to help us in the present listen to the past. We believe there is wisdom in the past twenty centuries of the church, wisdom for living the Christian life.

Stephen J. Nichols and Justin Taylor

PREFACE

Augustine is, by any standard, one of the giants of world civilization. His writings continue to be read and studied from every conceivable angle. New editions and translations of his Latin works appear with great regularity, and the amount of secondary literature about him is more than any one person can hope to master.

This book is part of a series that focuses on the Christian life, a subject that was dear to Augustine's heart and motivated his preaching and teaching ministry but has been curiously neglected in recent years. For whatever reason, scholars have concentrated on his philosophy, his theology, and increasingly his biblical interpretation, but have had relatively little to say about his spiritual development and devotional teaching.

It is impossible to write about him without touching on the different aspects of his life and work, including the controversies in which he was engaged and that did so much to draw out the depths of his thinking. But as far as possible, these things are kept in the background here so that the man and his all-important relationship with God can occupy the center stage that he himself wanted it to have. In this book, every effort is made to let Augustine speak for himself and to understand him on his own terms, however uncongenial they may seem to many people today. Sympathy for him grows out of understanding, and that understanding can only come with listening to his voice and putting ourselves, as much as we can, in his shoes.

The selections from his writings that are quoted here have been freshly translated into contemporary (and as much as possible, colloquial) English. Augustine himself used the spoken word to teach his congregation at Hippo and put effective communication with them ahead of any literary pretensions. I hope that readers who are approaching him for the first time will be encouraged to go further and learn more about this fascinating man, while those who are already familiar with him may be challenged to see him in a new light. Above all, I devoutly desire that all who come to Augustine may be led through him to a deeper understanding and closer relationship with the God of Jesus Christ, to whom he was drawn and in whose service he spent the greater part of his life. It is for that, above all, that we remember him today, and it is only in the light of Christ that his career and his writings can be understood as he meant them to be.

The details of Augustine's life are known mainly from what he tells us himself, or from what his disciple and biographer Possidius has told us. Modern scholars generally accept this information as factual, and it is seldom if ever questioned. For more precise details, see Allan Fitzgerald, *Augustine through the Ages: An Encyclopedia* (Grand Rapids: Eerdmans, 1999), and Peter Brown, *Augustine of Hippo: A New Biography* (Berkeley, CA: University of California Press, 2000).

AUGUSTINE'S LATIN TITLES AND THEIR ENGLISH TRANSLATIONS

It is customary to refer to Augustine's works by their Latin titles, a practice followed in the notes to this book. One reason for this is that a number of his works do not have English titles, and some have more than one, which can cause confusion. On the other hand, the Latin titles are standard and universally recognized. Many of them are similar to their English equivalents, as can be seen from the following list of works referred to in this volume. Note that the Latin *de* (on) is often omitted in English translation, as is the word *liber/libri* (book/books), which is usually found in the full Latin titles, as for example, *De Trinitate libri XV* (*Fifteen Books on the Trinity*).

Latin	English
Adnotationes in Iob	*Notes on Job*
Ad Simplicianum	*To Simplician*
Bibliotheca Casinensis	*Library of Casiciacum*
Confessiones	*Confessions*
Contra academicos	*Against the Academics*
Contra Adimantum	*Against Adimantius*
Contra epistulam Parmeniani Donatistae	*Against the Letters of Parmenian the Donatist*
Contra epistulam Manichaei fundamentalem	No English equivalent (*Against the Teaching of the Manichees*)
Contra Faustum	*Against Faustus*

Latin	English
Contra Iulianum	*Against Julian (of Eclanum)*
Contra litteras Petiliani Donatistae	*Against the Letters of Petilian, the Donatist*
Contra Maximinum Arianum	*Against Maximinus the Arian*
De anima et eius origine	*On the Origin of the Soul*
De baptismo	*On Baptism*
De beata vita	*On the Blessed Life*
De bono coniugali	*On the Good of Marriage*
De catechizandis rudibus	*On the Elements of Christian Instruction*
De civitate Dei	*On the City of God*
De correptione Donatistarum	*On the Punishment of the Donatists*
De correptione et gratia	*On Punishment and Grace*
De doctrina Christiana	*On Christian Doctrine (Teaching)*
De dono perseverantiae	*On the Gift of Perseverance*
De fide et symbolo	*On Faith and the Creed*
De Genesi ad litteram	*A Literal Commentary on Genesis*
De Genesi adversus Manichaeos	*On Genesis against the Manichees*
De Genesi liber imperfectus	*Incomplete Commentary on Genesis*
De gratia	*On Grace*
De gratia Christi et de peccato originali	*On the Grace of Christ and Original Sin*
De gratia et libero arbitrio	*On Grace and Free Will*
De libero arbitrio	*On Free Will*
De mendacio	*On Lying*
De moribus ecclesiae catholicae et de moribus Manichaeorum	*On the Customs of the Catholic Church and Those of the Manichees*
De natura boni contra Manichaeos	*On the Nature of Good, against the Manichees*
De natura et gratia	*On Nature and Grace*
De ordine	*On Providence (Order)*
De peccatorum meritis et remissione et de baptismo parvulorum	*On the Merits of Sinners and Forgiveness and on the Baptism of Infants*
De praedestinatione sanctorum	*On the Predestination of the Saints*
De sancta virginitate	*On Holy Virginity*
De spiritu et littera	*On the Spirit and the Letter*
De symbolo ad catechumenos	*On the Creed, for Those Preparing for Baptism*
De Trinitate	*On the Trinity*
De unitate ecclesiae	*On the Unity of the Church*

Latin	English
De urbis excidio	*On the Fall of the City (of Rome)*
De utilitate credendi	*On the Benefits of Believing*
De utilitate ieiunii	*On the Benefits of Fasting*
De vera religione	*On True Religion*
Enarrationes in Psalmos	*Expositions of the Psalms*
Enchiridion	No English equivalent *(Handbook)*
Epistulae	*Letters*
Epistulae ad Romanos inchoata expositio	*Unfinished Commentary on Romans*
Expositio epistulae ad Galatas	*Commentary on Galatians*
Expositio quarundam propositionum ex epistula ad Romanos	*Exposition of Some Statements from the Epistle to the Romans*
Homiliae decem in Iohannis Evangelium	*Ten Sermons on the Gospel of John*
Locutiones in Heptateuchum	*Expressions in the Heptateuch*
Post collationem contra Donatistas	*Against the Donatists after the Council*
Quaestiones Evangeliorum	*Questions about the Gospels*
Quaestiones in Heptateuchum	*Questions about the Heptateuch*
Retractationes	*Retractions*
Sermo ad Caesareae ecclesiae plebem	*Sermon to the People of the Church of Caesarea*
Sermones	*Sermons*
Sermones Wilmartiani	*Wilmart Sermons*
Tractatus in Evangelium Ioannis	*Treatises (Sermons) on John's Gospel*
Tractatus in epistulam Ioannis ad Parthos	*Treatises (Sermons) on 1 John*

CHAPTER I

THE LIFE AND TIMES OF AUGUSTINE

Augustine's Life

Aurelius Augustinus, the man we call Augustine, was born on November 13, 354, in the small North African town of Thagaste, known today as Souk Ahras (Algeria). Then, as now, it was inhabited by Berbers, tribesmen who were the original inhabitants of North Africa and who have blended in with their various conquerors over the centuries without being totally assimilated by any of them. In the Roman Empire, the Berbers of Thagaste spoke Latin and lived like Romans, but they remained attached to their native soil and to customs that would survive after the empire disappeared. Augustine himself was brought up as a Roman—Latin-speaking and imbued with the culture and values of the imperial city. But he was detached enough from Rome that when it fell to the barbarians in AD 410, he was able to see it for what it was—a passing phase in human history that would vanish just as Nineveh and Babylon had disappeared centuries before.

Augustine was the son of a pagan father called Patricius and a Christian mother by the name of Monica. They were most likely of Berber origin, though there may have been an admixture of Italian stock in their background, and they were certainly Romanized. We do not know how they met and married, but most likely they were betrothed by their families at a young age. Whether Monica was a Christian when that happened we do not know, nor can we say what led her parents (if they were Christians) to give their daughter to a pagan husband. What seems almost certain is that it was not a love match but a social calculation. Patricius was a civil servant, a respectable and well-paid position that made him a man of some importance in a small agricultural village. Monica's family no doubt thought it was a good idea for them to have connections to the government, and they knew that their daughter would be well provided for. They could also hope that in time Patricius would be converted to Christ.

Christianity had been legalized in the Roman Empire in AD 313, not long before Patricius was born, and its influence was steadily growing. There was as yet no requirement that government officials should be Christians, and many were not, but the church was no longer persecuted, and Monica was free to practice her faith. What she could not do was pass it on to her children (and especially not to her male children) because in the ancient world a boy followed the religion of his father. But as Augustine tells us himself, that did not prevent her from bringing him up in a way that made him familiar with Christianity. She took him to church with her and even enrolled him as a "catechumen" (apprentice) in what was the fourth-century equivalent of Sunday school. However, she could not have him baptized without his father's permission, although she almost did when the young Augustine developed a fever and seemed to be close to death. At that point he himself cried out to be baptized.

> You saw, my God, because you were already my guardian, with what fervor of mind and with what faith I begged for the baptism of your Christ, my God and Lord, urging it on the devotion of my mother and of the mother of us all, the church. My physical mother . . . hastily made arrangements for me to be initiated and washed in the sacraments of salvation. . . . But suddenly I recovered. My cleansing was deferred on the assumption that, if I lived, I would be sure to soil myself; and . . . my guilt would be greater and more dangerous.[1]

At home Augustine's mother sang hymns to him and prayed over him, leaving an indelible impression on his mind. In later years he would recall his early upbringing and praise his mother for the teaching and example she gave him even when he was too young to appreciate what she was doing.

But strong though his attachment was to his mother, Augustine was a man who was expected to live in a man's world. For the son of Patricius that meant getting a good education and rising in the imperial administration,

---

[1] *Confessiones* 1.11.17.

which was the most secure and prestigious form of employment known to him. Augustine could not get what he needed in Thagaste, so when he was eleven years old he was sent to board in Madaura, a larger town about twenty miles to the south, which was known for its excellent schools. He stayed there for about four years, but had to return home when his father died. Patricius had accepted Christ as his Savior shortly before his death, but although in later years Augustine rejoiced at that, it made little impression on him at the time. There was nothing for him to do back home, and after a year he was sent to Carthage for further education, paid for by a certain Romanianus, who was a wealthy friend of the family.

Carthage (now a suburb of Tunis), was the capital of Roman Africa and the second city in the western half of the empire. It could not compete with Rome or with the great urban centers of the East, like Alexandria and Antioch, but it had a famous history and had long been an important center of Latin culture. The education Augustine got there was as good as any that could be had in the ancient world, and there was no need for him to go elsewhere. He was already well versed in the classics of Latin literature and had mastered the art of rhetoric (public speaking) that was essential for anyone who wanted to make a career in the ancient world. He had also studied Greek, but that language was not spoken in North Africa, and Augustine was not a gifted linguist. For him, Greek remained essentially a textbook language, which was a disadvantage to him as a Christian theologian. He had no trouble establishing himself as a teacher of philosophy and rhetoric at Carthage, but in later years his weakness in Greek would be held against him by men like Jerome (ca. 330–410), who was a brilliant linguist and translated the Bible into Latin, not only from Greek but from Hebrew as well. Augustine could not compete with that and remained dependent on translations of the Scriptures that were often of poor quality, which is surprising considering how central the Bible was to his preaching and teaching ministry.

But we are getting ahead of ourselves. On arriving in Carthage, Augustine quickly settled into student life. He spent much of his time at the theater, where he reveled in the romantic lives of the stage characters. He had an exceptional love of music and drama, and his appetite for romance was whetted as well. Before long he acquired a mistress—her name is one of the few things about his life that we do not know—who bore him a son before he was eighteen years old. It is interesting to note that although he was not even formally a Christian at this stage, he called his son Adeodatus ("given by God"), the Latin equivalent of the Greek Theodoros (Theodore). Years later, after his conversion, he sent his mistress away but he kept his son, who was very precious to him.

Not long after this, as he was honing his rhetorical skills by reading Cicero's *Hortensius*—a work now lost—Augustine was struck by the beauty not only of Cicero's language but also of his ideas, and he fell in love with philosophy. Among the many religious and philosophical groups that competed for attention in Carthage was the sect of the Manichees, named for a Persian prophet called Mani who had lived in the borderlands between the Roman Empire and Persia about 150 years before Augustine's time. Mani was eclectic in his tastes, borrowing a lot from the Persian religion of Zoroastrianism, various strands of Greek philosophy, and even Christianity. He was the "New Age" guru of his time, and his ideas suited the young Augustine perfectly. They were black-and-white in a way that the more sophisticated philosophies of the Greeks were not. Like Zoroaster, Mani believed that the world was divided into absolute good and absolute evil—two equal powers that did battle for the soul of man. He claimed to be rational, offering an explanation for every problem, but he skated over contradictions and untidy facts that did not fit his scheme of things. For someone who wanted intellectual assurance without taking the trouble to become truly educated, Mani offered the perfect belief system, and there were many who joined the Manichees for that reason.

The Manichees prided themselves on their knowledge of natural science and thought that they could use it to fight the power of evil. Regarding spirit as good and matter as evil, they claimed to have a higher form of knowledge, but at the same time they indulged their fleshly appetites in what Augustine later came to see was hypocritical debauchery. Far from achieving a balanced approach to life, they swung from one extreme to another because they were unable to judge good and evil for what they really were or cling to the former in order to subdue the latter.[2]

Augustine spent nine years in the company of the Manichees but became increasingly disenchanted with them when he realized that their great teacher, a man called Faustus, was unable to answer his most pressing questions.[3] He grew restless in Carthage, having reached the summit

---

[2] See *Confessiones* 3.6.10, 8.10.22–24.
[3] *Confessiones* 5.6.10–5.7.13.

of what it had to offer, and began to feel the pull of Rome. Eventually he left for the imperial capital, much against his mother's wishes, and tried to set himself up as a teacher there. Unfortunately for him, nothing seemed to work out as he intended. No sooner had he arrived in Rome than he fell seriously ill, and it was some time before he could establish himself as a teacher. He was mocked for his provincial accent, and although the students he attracted were better than those in Carthage, they suffered from a fatal defect—they were reluctant to pay their fees. Intellectually, Augustine was still moving in Manichaean circles, but he was attracted to the so-called New Academy, a group of skeptical thinkers who questioned everything and claimed that the search for truth was a waste of time because absolute truth did not exist. This appealed to Augustine's disillusionment with the Manichees and helped him to escape from their clutches, but it did not provide much of a substitute. Like skeptics in every age, the New Academics knew what they were against but not what they were for, so they could never provide an honest seeker after truth like Augustine with the peace of mind that he craved.

Before long, Augustine left Rome for Milan, which was then the seat of the Roman emperor in the West and a city of great importance. Augustine arrived there in 384 and soon came across the local bishop. This was Ambrose (ca. 339–397), a former prefect (mayor) of the city who had been chosen by popular acclaim to be its bishop ten years earlier, even though he was still a layman at the time. Ordained deacon, presbyter, and bishop overnight, Ambrose had quickly established himself as the leading moral and spiritual authority in the Latin world. He did not flatter those in power but castigated them—something that nobody had previously had the courage to do. Even the emperors were shamed into doing his bidding, so strong was his personality and sense of mission. Moreover, Ambrose was a master of rhetoric whose command of logic impressed even Augustine. Before long, Augustine found himself going to hear Ambrose preach. For the first time, Augustine came to see that Christianity made sense and had answers to the questions he had put to the Manichees in vain. He was gradually coming round to Christianity, but two things stood in his way: his inability to think of God as a spiritual being who had created a world that was fundamentally good, and his unwillingness to adopt a moral lifestyle.

The first of these problems was largely resolved by Platonism, which

Augustine now encountered for the first time though the translations made by Marius Victorinus, a Platonic philosopher who had become a Christian. Platonism went back to Plato, who had lived at Athens in the fourth century BC,[4] but it had been revived in a modified form about a century before Augustine was born by an Alexandrian called Plotinus (ca. 204–270) and his disciple Porphyry (ca. 234–ca. 305). Plotinus is credited with having turned what was essentially an academic philosophy into a kind of religion that would enable those who pursued it not only to understand but also to experience the supreme being. Whether Plotinus was influenced by Christianity has been debated, but in the marketplace of ideas there is no doubt that his Neoplatonism (as we now call it) competed with the gospel for the hearts and minds of men. This is especially clear from the writings of Porphyry, many of which were direct attacks on Christianity. For that reason, they are now almost entirely lost because Christian scribes of later times saw no reason to copy them (and every reason to destroy them); but they circulated freely in Augustine's day and made it easy for intellectuals to look down on the faith taught by Jesus. Augustine was in no mood for that, though, and it seems that what he took from the Neoplatonists was the positive teaching of Plotinus rather than the critical views of Porphyry.

Plotinus solved the problem of evil for Augustine by persuading him that it had no real existence of its own.[5] According to him, every created thing is good in itself because it has been made by the supreme being, which cannot make or do anything that is foreign to its nature. Evil is therefore a defect—the absence or perversion of what is good—not a power or substance in its own right. While absorbing this doctrine, Augustine was also reading John's Gospel, which to Augustine's mind sounded very much like the teaching of Plotinus. The big difference was that John spoke of the nonmaterial Word of God becoming flesh, something that a Platonist could not contemplate.[6] Plotinus also taught Augustine the value of self-examination. Rather than look for answers in the stars or in nature, a man should look into his own soul and test the witness of his conscience. This was to become one of the most significant ways in which Augustine would discover truth as a Christian, and so it is important to understand how it first came into his life.

---

[4] Augustine believed, as many early Christians did, that Plato knew the Hebrew Bible and had been influenced by it. See *De doctrina Christiana* 2.28.43; *De civitate Dei* 8.11.
[5] *Confessiones* 7.10.16–7.13.19.
[6] *Confessiones* 7.9.14.

Augustine was now well on the way to joining the church, but there were still hurdles that he had to surmount. His mother persuaded him to abandon his mistress, but she wanted to find him a suitable wife instead. She managed to identify a ten-year-old, underage girl who was more than twenty years Augustine's junior, and he was understandably unenthusiastic about her. Instead of that, Augustine tried to persuade some of his friends to set up a kind of commune where they could study philosophy in peace, but his mother objected to the idea, and it foundered when the others pulled out because they did not want to abandon their wives or potential wives. Augustine was torn between what he saw as incompatible alternatives: either he could marry and settle down like everyone else, or he could live a solitary life, which he did not want to do. He even took another concubine, impatient with his mother's drawn-out plans for his future marriage, but that was no solution and the arrangement did not last long.

At this point in his life Augustine needed someone to talk to, and he found help from one of Ambrose's assistants, an old man called Simplicianus. Simplicianus listened as Augustine recounted his doubts and fears, and was able to share experiences of his own, including the remarkable conversion of Marius Victorinus, which he had witnessed some years before in Rome. Another powerful influence on him at this time was that of Ponticianus, who was also from North Africa. Ponticianus introduced Augustine to monasticism, which was only then making its appearance in Italy, although it had been flourishing in Egypt for more than a century. Thanks to him, Augustine met people who had given up great careers and positions in the world and sought peace of mind in the simplicity and renunciation associated with the solitary life. What others saw as madness, they thought of as heroic self-sacrifice, and Augustine felt ashamed that he was unwilling to follow them in this.

Filled with a growing sense of his personal inadequacy and realizing how empty his life had so far been, Augustine fell into a state of despair. He was torn between the monastic ideal, on the one hand, and the pleasures of this world, on the other—wanting to embrace the former but finding it too hard to abandon the latter. It was when he was in this condition that he heard a child's voice say: *Tolle, lege* (Take up and read). Somewhat confused, he reached for a portion of the Scriptures that he had to hand and read: "Let us walk properly as in the daytime, not in orgies and drunkenness, not in sexual immorality and sensuality, not in quarreling and jealousy. But put on the Lord Jesus Christ, and make no provision for the flesh, to gratify its desires" (Rom. 13:13–14).[7]

The dam of his pent-up emotions broke and he surrendered his life to Christ. The change was immediate and long-lasting, but the implications took time to sink in. He enrolled in baptismal preparation classes, intending to be baptized at the next Easter baptismal ceremony (in 387). He still had several months to prepare for that, and during that time Augustine went into retreat at a place called Cassiciacum, where he began to write a series of treatises that would help to define his later life. One of the most interesting of these is the first account of his conversion, written while it was fresh in his memory and reflecting the simplicity of a man who was still absorbing the implications of the experience.[8]

After being baptized, Augustine decided to return to Africa with his mother, who had come to Italy sometime before in search of her son. As they were waiting for the boat, Monica caught a fever and died, content that she had been privileged to see Augustine finally won for Christ. Augustine postponed his departure for a year and used the time to write against the Manichees, to whom he had previously been so close.[9] Then in 388 he went back to Thagaste with a few friends, determined to make amends to those whom he had previously misled with his Manichaeism and to establish a monastic community in his birthplace. It was shortly after he got home that Adeodatus died, at which point Augustine's life changed again. In 391 he went on a short visit to Hippo Regius, a coastal city now known as Annaba (Algeria). He went to church, where the bishop, an old man called Valerius, spotted him and began to tell people that he, Valerius, needed an assistant. The congregation knew that Augustine was the right choice, and they thrust him forward for ordination, something that he had never sought. Augustine gave in to their wishes and was soon ordained. Valerius was a Greek who spoke poor Latin, so he asked Augustine to preach in his stead, while at the same time permitting him to establish a small monastery next to the cathedral.[10]

Augustine soon established a clergy training school and created an office for himself, where he quickly turned out a whole series of tracts de-

---

[7] See *Confessiones* 8.12.29 for the full account.
[8] *De beata vita* 4.
[9] This was his *De moribus ecclesiae catholicae et de moribus Manichaeorum*, a work in three books.
[10] Some people have thought that Valerius spoke better Latin than he was prepared to admit. He wanted Augustine to succeed him and may have used the language question as a means of compelling him to stay in Hippo.

fending mainline Christianity against the Manichees and the Donatists, a schismatic sect that had broken away from the church two generations before because of its stricter views on church discipline. The Manichees were relatively easy to refute, and they had no real following outside intellectual circles in the big cities, but the Donatists were another matter. They had penetrated very deeply into the countryside, where they had split the church, even in small towns like Thagaste. In order to combat them effectively, Augustine had to develop a doctrine of the church that accounted for imperfection within it without giving the impression that sinfulness should be tolerated. Like the Manichees, the Donatists were black-and-white people who found any kind of subtlety difficult, and their appeal to rid the church of its corrupt members was often welcome to those who felt they were being forced to tolerate low standards of spiritual life. Augustine did not condemn Donatist beliefs (which were theologically orthodox), but concentrated on the negative impact their separatism was having on the wider church. He wanted them to come back into fellowship with the main body of believers, though his success in this endeavor was somewhat limited. In 411 he attended a council held at Carthage whose main purpose was to reconcile the Donatists to the mainline church. In theory it was successful and many Donatists returned to the fold, but by then antagonisms had gone too deep to be eradicated overnight. Donatism limped on in a weakened state, but it did not finally disappear until the entire North African church was engulfed by the tide of Islam in the late seventh century.[11]

In 395 Valerius, fearing that some other city would get Augustine as its bishop, persuaded the church at Hippo to consecrate Augustine to that office, even though Valerius was still alive. Augustine hesitated but finally gave in to the pleas of the people, who did not want to lose him. When Valerius died the following year, Augustine was already in post, and he remained there until his death on August 28, 430. He is called Augustine of Hippo (not Thagaste) because that is where he was bishop, a practice that is almost universal when speaking of the fathers of the early church who held episcopal office. His first few years as a bishop were fairly uneventful (apart from the ongoing controversy with the Donatists), but in 410 Rome was sacked by the Goths, and once again Augustine's life changed forever.

As refugees poured into Africa from Italy, bringing lurid stories of the

---

11 On Donatism, see W. H. C. Frend, *The Donatist Church* (Oxford: Oxford University Press, 1952); Maureen A. Tilley, *The Bible in Christian North Africa: The Donatist World* (Minneapolis, MN: Fortress, 1997).

destruction they had witnessed, Augustine became alarmed by the readiness of some to blame the disaster on Christianity. Had the old gods been kept, these people argued, they would have protected Rome, which was now suffering the consequences of having abandoned them. Augustine could hardly sit back and let such a challenge go unanswered, and so he began writing the greatest book of his career—*The City of God*, a massive work in which he reconstructed the history of the world. In it, Augustine tried to show that current events are the outworking of God's eternal plan. In the end all earthly powers will collapse and fall, but the city of God, the kingdom of heaven, will go on forever. The fight between good and evil takes different forms, said Augustine, but Christians know what side they are on. They are neither Romans nor barbarians, but citizens of the heavenly Jerusalem that will descend on the last day when Christ returns to establish his everlasting rule.

Among the refugees in Carthage were some who had imbibed the teaching of Pelagius (ca. 354–ca. 418), a British monk who had gone to Rome, where he had been preaching that the human race was not entirely sinful. According to Pelagius, there was a residue of uncorrupted goodness in every man that, if it were properly nurtured, could win a soul back to God. In response to this, Augustine developed his ideas about grace and predestination, which have remained fundamental for Western theology ever since. Augustine spent many years warning the world of the dangers of Pelagianism, which soon attracted widespread condemnation, but Pelagius also had his defenders, the most articulate of whom was Julian of Eclanum, who had been banished from Italy because of it. Julian attacked Augustine quite openly and viciously, and Augustine replied by refuting his treatises one at a time, leaving only two of them still unanswered at his death.

In 426, sensing that his days were numbered, Augustine chose a certain Heraclius as his successor, and the two men governed the church together for the next few years. During that time, Augustine went over his earlier writings, correcting them and noting where he had changed his mind since first writing them. It was a remarkable performance, and like so many things in his life, it was an exercise that was without precedent in the ancient world.

Augustine died when Hippo was under siege by the Vandals, a Germanic tribe that had crossed through Spain into North Africa. A few days after he passed away, the city surrendered, and by the end of the year the

Vandals had set up a kingdom of their own in Carthage. It survived for just over a century, until the Roman general Belisarius, acting on orders from Constantinople, retook the city and the province. The empire came back for a further 150 years, but in 698 Carthage fell to the Muslim Arabs who have ruled it almost uninterruptedly ever since. But long before that happened, the Africa that Augustine knew had disappeared. His colleague Heraclius seems to have been the last bishop of Hippo, and after his time the whole area went into decline. Fortunately for us, there was a brief respite in the decade following Augustine's death, when one of his associates, a man called Possidius, was able to write a biography of him, using materials that were still extant in the library there. By then, Augustine's writings were being copied and circulated all over the Latin world, so the eclipse of Roman culture in North Africa was not the end of his influence. But the world he knew had changed forever, and it is no exaggeration to say that with his death, the great days of the North African church came to a close. Augustine would become the teacher of western Europe, not of Africa, and it is in that role that his historical importance was to lie.

Augustine's Writings

No ancient Christian writer has left us a larger corpus of writings than Augustine. His only rival in this respect is Origen (ca. 185–ca. 254), who may have written more than he did, though on a narrower range of subjects. But Origen was condemned as a heretic three hundred years after his death, and his books were either destroyed or no longer copied; so what we now have is only a small portion of what he actually wrote. That fate never befell Augustine. Some of Augustine's works have been lost, and there is a small amount of material that circulates under his name but is probably (or certainly) not his. But that still leaves over a hundred books that have survived and are undoubtedly his, plus 307 known letters and 583 sermons, which were transcribed for publication by those who heard them. An average of three books a year is a remarkable output for anyone to have achieved over a lifetime, and quite outstanding when we realize that they had to be written and copied out by hand and that Augustine had none of the modern scholar's resources at his disposal. That he should have made occasional mistakes or written something rather unmemorable is hardly surprising. The truly astonishing thing is how much he got right and how much of his work is still influential today. Whether you like him or loathe him—and Augustine has had his detractors as well as his admirers—there can be no doubt of his greatness or of the very long shadow he has cast over European culture down through the ages.

In cataloging his many writings, it is best to subdivide them according to the type of literature they are, as follows.

Autobiographical

Augustine was one of the few people in antiquity who wrote at great length about himself. In the Christian world, only the apostle Paul revealed as much of his own spiritual journey as Augustine did, and Paul only did so in passing as the subject came up in his epistles. Augustine, by contrast, sat down deliberately to write his autobiography, which no Christian and relatively few pagans had ever done before him.

His first foray into this field came immediately after his conversion, in the *Dialogues*, which he wrote between his conversion and his ordination in 391.[12] Intended as philosophical works, the *Dialogues* nevertheless contain much introductory autobiographical material that helps us to understand his mental and spiritual state when he was processing his conversion and preparing himself for baptism.

His most important autobiographical work was his *Confessions*, which he started writing soon after becoming a bishop and finished around 400. The *Confessions* are the most popular of his writings and are still widely read today because of the deep insight they give us not only into his character, but into the process of religious conversion in general. They are structured as a meditation offered to God, a kind of extended prayer in which Augustine confesses his many sins and failures. In that sense they are a searing self-examination in which outwardly trivial events (like stealing pears from a tree when he was young) become important episodes in his spiritual journey, revealing to him the depth of his sinfulness and the overwhelming need he felt for the grace of God to forgive and restore him.

The *Confessions* cover his life from birth to the death of his mother, shortly after his baptism, and they are a major source for our knowledge of his spiritual development. To them must be added his *Retractions*, written late in life (426–427) and reexamining his work in the light of his growth as a Christian. They are as close as we can come to an understanding of

---

[12] Ten separate compositions make up the dialogues. For a list and brief explanation of them, see Angelo Di Berardino, *Patrology*, vol. 4 (Westminster, MD: Christian Classics, 1986), 356–61.

his motives in writing and of the influences that shaped his thinking over time.[13]

In addition to these important works, there are two letters (nos. 355–356) that give us some details of his life in Africa after his return in 388 until he became a bishop eight years later. As I have already mentioned, there is also the *Life of Saint Augustine*, written by his disciple Possidius between 431 and 439, which draws on personal reminiscences and archival materials in order to provide a clear picture of Augustine's activity as bishop of Hippo.

Philosophical

Augustine was a professional philosopher before his conversion, and the effects of that can be seen in his earliest works. The *Dialogues* he composed at Cassiciacum addressed philosophical themes of different kinds. He wrote a long work against the skeptics of the New Academy, from which his conversion had rescued him.[14] He was also preoccupied with the immortality of the soul, on which he wrote a good deal. He was especially concerned to reaffirm its spiritual nature and examine how it could rise to the contemplation of God, something that he regarded as foundational for living the Christian life.

Other treatises of a philosophical nature included two books in which he sought to classify reality according to hierarchical principles that he believed were inherent in things.[15] He also wrote several more that ranged across all the arts known to man and tried to show how each of them could become a pathway into the knowledge of God. In addition to these he composed lengthy treatises on the question of free will, trying to explain the origin of evil, the nature of human freedom, and divine foreknowledge.[16] The three books dedicated to these and similar subjects are of particular importance for the light they shed on Augustine's beliefs about predestination before the outbreak of the Pelagian controversy, when his position on the subject hardened and its finer points were clarified.[17]

---

[13] Though they are fairly short and can be read in a few hours, there are two important commentaries on them. See James J. O'Donnell, *Augustine Confessions*, 3 vols. (Oxford: Oxford University Press, 1992); and John M. Quinn, *A Companion to the* Confessions *of St. Augustine* (New York: Peter Lang, 2002).

[14] *Contra academicos*, in three books.

[15] *De ordine*.

[16] *De libero arbitrio*, in three books.

[17] There are sixteen surviving works against the Pelagians among Augustine's writings. See Di Berardino, *Patrology*, 4:386–92 for a complete list.

Also to this category belongs a charming treatise on music, which was something dear to Augustine's heart. He was deeply touched by Christian singing even before his conversion and believed that music could lead people to God if it were understood and used in the right way. Finally, there is a treatise couched in the form of a dialogue with his son, Adeodatus, which is an interesting study in the educational methods he thought ought to be used with children.

Exegetical

Considering the volume of his works, Augustine was not a great commentator on Scripture, but given the centrality of the Bible for the life of the church, it would have been hard for him not to have written at least some exegetical treatises, and on certain matters he could wax very eloquent. He was especially interested in hermeneutics, and one of the most important books ever written on the subject belongs to him. It is called *On Christian Doctrine*, because as far as Augustine was concerned, the Bible was the only real source of Christian teaching. It had to be read in the right way of course, and in this short but important treatise he outlined what that was. Augustine made a fundamental distinction between things meant to be used (*uti*) and things meant to be enjoyed (*frui*), and he tried to demonstrate how the Bible leads us from the former to the latter because it is a means to an end, which is to glorify God and enjoy him forever. The book is also important for the way in which it develops the idea that words are signs for things and can therefore be used in different senses, both physical and metaphorical. If it were not so, finite words could not help us know the infinite God, but of course they do, and nowhere more so than in the Bible.[18]

In dealing with the Old Testament, Augustine concentrated to an unusual degree on the creation story in Genesis 1–3. He commented on it no fewer than four times—twice allegorically and twice literally. His allegorical commentaries were directed chiefly against the Manichees, whom he accused of having too narrowly literalistic an interpretation of the text, and they were written first, shortly after his conversion. He later interpreted the creation account literally, but his first attempt at this, which went back to about 393, was a failure and he abandoned it. Later on, he took it up again

---

[18] See Duane W. H. Arnold and Pamela Bright, eds., De doctrina Christiana: *A Classic of Western Culture* (Notre Dame, IN: University of Notre Dame Press, 1995).

and over a period of about fifteen years (401–415) he composed a major exposition of the deep themes of the creation that still ranks among the more important of his works.[19]

Beyond his many interpretations of Genesis 1–3, Augustine also wrote on the so-called Heptateuch (the seven books from Genesis to Judges), though his two works on the subject were not so much commentaries as a series of answers to difficult exegetical questions raised by the text.[20] He did something similar with the book of Job.[21] But by far the most impressive of his works on the Old Testament was his enormous *Expositions of the Psalms*, the only complete commentary on them that we possess from ancient times, which occupied him for almost a quarter of a century (392–416). The *Expositions* are not a unified whole but a mixture of exegetical notes, some longer expositions, and a huge number of sermons, including thirty-two on Psalm 119. It should be pointed out that Augustine used Latin versions of the Greek Septuagint (LXX) translation of the original Hebrew, which in the Psalms (in particular) is often quite different from the Greek. That unfortunately reduces the value of the *Expositions* as pure exegesis, but as a source of spiritual nourishment it is unparalleled in his writings. Even if what he says is not always securely grounded in the biblical text he is commenting on, the points he is making can usually be substantiated from other parts of Scripture and therefore have a genuine spiritual value in spite of the defects of the translation he was using.

In writing on the New Testament, Augustine more or less confined himself to the Gospels, Romans, James, and 1 John. He devised a harmonization of the four Gospels in order to show that they did not contradict one another, and also wrote two books on the Sermon on the Mount. His two attempts to write a commentary on Romans both failed, though fragments survive and we have a good idea of how he interpreted the epistle. His exposition of James is unfortunately lost, but his ten sermons on love, based on 1 John, are among his most appealing works.[22] He also preached (or at least composed) 124 sermons on the Fourth Gospel, which, taken together, form a remarkable commentary on it that is full of rich spiritual meditation and counsel.[23]

---

[19] *De Genesi ad litteram*, in twelve books.
[20] *Locutiones in Heptateuchum* and *Quaestiones in Heptateuchum*, both in seven books.
[21] *Adnotationes in Iob.*
[22] *Tractatus in epistulam Ioannis ad Parthos.*
[23] *Tractatus in Evangelium Ioannis.*

Doctrinal

Much of what Augustine wrote concerned questions that arose from his study of Christian doctrine. Apart from the treatises dealing with particular controversies, which we shall look at a bit further on, he wrote a short exposition of the baptismal creed that was eventually standardized as the Apostles' Creed that is still in use today, along with several occasional pieces dealing with specific questions that had been put to him. One of the more important works of this kind is his *Handbook* or *Enchiridion*, which is an exposition of faith (the creed), hope (the Lord's Prayer), and love (the Ten Commandments). It was to become the basis for the education of the clergy in the Middle Ages, and in that capacity it played a major role in shaping the spiritual outlook of the Western church for over a thousand years.

The most important of his purely doctrinal writings however is his fifteen-volume work *On the Trinity*, which became the starting point of all future reflection on the subject in the Latin-speaking world. The first four books deal with the biblical evidence for the Trinity, followed by a theological construction and defense of the doctrine (bks. 5–7), an introduction to the mystical experience of God (bk. 8), a search for the image of the Trinity in human psychology (bks. 9–14), and a concluding summary of the whole treatise (bk. 15). Augustine was the first to develop the idea that the image of God in which we are created is an image of the Trinity, which he compared to the memory, intellect, and will inherent in the human brain. Because of this, Augustine is often regarded as the founder of modern psychology, as well as a theologian of the first rank, and his ideas on the subject are widely studied even by people who have no particular interest in Christianity.[24]

It should be pointed out before we move on that Augustine never wrote a systematic theology in the way we understand that now. This was not because he never got round to it, but because systematic theologies were unknown in his time. The first person to write anything resembling one was John of Damascus (d. 749), who wrote in Greek. No Latin writer attempted anything similar until Peter Lombard (ca. 1090–1160) composed his famous *Sentences*, which became the textbook of the medieval schools and did much to popularize Augustine's teaching, from which Peter made copious extracts. From then until the widespread dissemination of printed editions of Augustine's writings in the sixteenth century, Peter Lombard

---

[24] See Lewis Ayres, *Augustine and the Trinity* (Cambridge: Cambridge University Press, 2010).

was the gateway through which most students learned about him, and so Augustine acquired a reputation as a systematic theologian without having been one!

Apologetical

Augustine was always concerned to win the pagan world for Christ, and in pursuit of that aim he wrote a number of evangelistic treatises designed to expound Christianity to unbelievers and to overcome their opposition to its teachings. By far the most important composition in this category is his massive twenty-two volume work *The City of God*, which is one of the most important books in world literature. It is a well-constructed defense of Christianity against its pagan detractors based on the theme that there are two "cities," the city of God and the city of the world, which are in conflict with one another. Its length and encyclopedic comprehensiveness are such that it is useful to have a breakdown of its contents as follows:

> First part (books 1–10): A refutation of paganism
> > Books 1–5: Paganism, useless for human society
> > Books 6–10: Paganism, useless for knowing God
> Second part (books 11–22): A defense of Christianity
> > Books 11–14: How the city of God and the city of the world came into being
> > Books 15–18: How the two cities have developed over time
> > Books 19–22: What the final destiny of each of the cities will be

In the course of expounding his theme, Augustine ranged over just about every subject imaginable, and there are frequent digressions dealing with subjects that occurred to him in the course of writing and that he thought were of sufficient interest to warrant special comment. Perhaps most important for the long-term future was his rejection of millenarian prophecy, especially as an interpretation of the book of Revelation. Augustine was what would now be called "amillenarian" because he rejected the literal interpretation of the thousand-year reign of Christ that was common in his day. Instead, he believed that Revelation was an allegory of the conflict between good and evil and not a prophecy that would be worked out in human history more or less as recorded in the biblical text. Many movements have tried to revive a purely historical reading of Revelation, but many churches have adopted the Augustinian position on the matter, and it is now the one which, broadly speaking, commands the assent of most academic theologians.

Pastoral and Monastic

As the head of a local church and leader of a monastic community within it, Augustine had to deal with a number of pastoral matters, many of which are to be found in his letters and sermons, or scattered through other writings. However, he also found time to write about specific subjects affecting the Christian life, the most important of which were connected with sexual questions. He wrote on matrimony, widowhood, and singleness, the last of these being especially relevant for monks. In addition he composed a rule for life in the monastery, which was revived in the late Middle Ages and is still in use today. Both Desiderius Erasmus and Martin Luther were monks in the Augustinian tradition, giving his writings on the subject a considerable impact on the Renaissance and Reformation of the sixteenth century.

Polemical

Some of Augustine's most important works were those written against heresies of different kinds. Like all Christians of his time, he regarded heresy as a spiritual disease to be fought in order to safeguard the health of both the individual soul and the body of Christ. As many others had done before him, he wrote a treatise against heresies in general, as well as one against the Jews. He also wrote against Arianism, which was creeping into North Africa toward the end of his life and would become the state religion under the Vandals, although it had been condemned many times in the East and was rapidly dying out in its Egyptian homeland. He also wrote against the followers of Marcion, a second-century heretic who had rejected the Old Testament; against Origen, who was accused of denying eternal punishment and believing in a form of reincarnation; and against Priscillian of Avila, who taught a form of Manichaeism. But by far the most important of his antiheretical writings were directed against three groups in particular.

The first of these was the Manichees, with whom he had associated before his conversion. In fact, a blistering treatise against Manichaeism may well have been the first thing he wrote.[25] In the years before 400 he returned to the same theme on several occasions, even engaging in public

---

[25] This was his *De moribus ecclesiae*, mentioned above.

debate with Fortunatus, a Manichee who visited Hippo in 392. The main themes of all these works were the same: good and evil are not competing powers; the Creator God of the Old Testament is good, one, and sovereign over all things; and evil is an absence of good and not a power in its own right. Several of the tracts were directed against particular individuals: in addition to Fortunatus, there was Faustus, who was widely regarded as the sect's chief theologian; Secundinus, who tried to persuade Augustine to return to the Manichaean fold; and Felix, who turned up in Hippo at the end of 404 and engaged in debate with the bishop. As far as Augustine was concerned, the battle lines against the Manichees were clearly drawn, and he had little difficulty in defending his position. Dualism was inherently unstable and implausible. It made much more sense to see the world as a single coherent universe under the control of one sovereign God, even if that made it difficult to explain what evil was and why it was tolerated.

The second group against which Augustine directed his polemic was the Donatist sect, which had developed out of a controversy in 311 over the honor that should be paid to the relics of martyrs. This was a sensitive issue in North Africa, where persecution had always been regarded as a badge of sanctity and running away from it had been condemned. Over time, this had led to a cult of martyrdom with its unhealthy extremes. It was believed that if the church had ceased to suffer, it was because it had compromised the gospel, and so the legalization of Christianity in the fourth century was treated as a form of apostasy. Donatism also led to the belief that the church was contaminated by the presence of sinners within it. Donatists believed that only the most rigorous discipline could protect the church's purity, but since it was they who decided what "impurity" was, they could easily target people for unworthy reasons under a cloak of sanctity.

Augustine wrote as many as twenty tracts against the Donatists, but only thirteen still survive. The loss is probably not very serious though, because (as with his anti-Manichaean polemic) the main themes repeat themselves over and over again. In the case of the Donatists, Augustine's line of argument was that the visible church is not and never can be "pure" in the absolute sense; the wheat and the tares must be allowed to grow together until the harvest.[26] By claiming to be perfect themselves and then judging the sins of others, the Donatists were falling into spiritual pride and self-deception. Once again, many of Augustine's works addressed

---

26 See Matt. 13:29.

particular individuals, like the Donatist bishop Petilian, whom he saw as key to resolving the controversy. After the Council of Carthage in 411, which sought a way to reintegrate the Donatists into the mainline church, Augustine penned a passionate appeal to them that is usually regarded as his best anti-Donatist writings. (It was also his last.)[27]

Donatism was a uniquely North African sect, a limitation that told heavily against it. If the Donatists were right, why could they find nobody elsewhere in the world who shared their views? Their localism offended against the principle of "catholicity" or universality, which was one of the marks of the true church. By no means everybody was persuaded by this logic, of course, and it is doubtful that Augustine's anti-Donatist tracts would have been preserved at all if he had not used them for a more positive purpose, which was to teach the doctrine of the church in a way that could be applied to every situation, and not just to the peculiar circumstances of North Africa.

But by far the most serious and intractable of the heresies Augustine faced was Pelagianism. This was imported into North Africa and had a worldwide following so that the claim that it was not "catholic" could not be so easily used against it. It was also much more subtle than Donatism because it went beyond outward behavior and struck at the heart of the great questions of sin, grace, and salvation. Before Pelagianism arose, Christians had believed that Jesus saved them from the power of sin, but few had bothered to consider how great that evil power was. They instinctively believed that they had to cooperate with God in order to benefit from his mercy, without enquiring too deeply as to how that would work in practice. Pelagius probably thought that he was doing no more than stating clearly what most Christians subconsciously believed, and to a large extent he probably was. That made it much more difficult for Augustine to do battle with him and his followers, some of whom were as well educated and articulate as he was. In attacking Pelagius, Augustine was forcing his fellow Christians to think more deeply about their own sinfulness, their inability to do anything to put that right, and their total dependence on the grace of God for their salvation. What had always been known subconsciously now had to be expressed and confessed, which the church as a whole had never done before.

Augustine's anti-Pelagian writings can be divided into three distinct types. First of all, there are the treatises directed against the heresy in gen-

---

[27] *Post collationem contra Donatistas.*

eral. Most of them were composed between 412 and 418 and it was in them that Augustine developed his understanding of original sin. One of the first things he wrote was a three-volume work addressed to Marcellinus, dealing with the just deserts of sin, forgiveness, and the baptism of infants. This was followed by a commentary on some related New Testament texts sent to him from Carthage by his friend Honoratus. There then followed another book sent to Marcellinus, outlining Augustine's understanding of divine grace.

Around 415 Augustine wrote a lengthy response to a book by Pelagius on nature, in which he defined the difference between nature and grace and affirmed the necessity of holding them both together in the scheme of salvation. There soon followed another book, dealing this time with the notion of sinless perfection, which Augustine rejected. In 418 he wrote yet another book on original sin and the grace of Christ, affirming the absolute necessity of the latter as the only way of dealing adequately with the former. He demonstrated that neither Pelagius nor his followers believed in the existence of original sin, an error that fatally compromised their understanding of the gospel. Augustine also managed to write four books on the origin of the soul, which he was provoked to do because he had been criticized for not coming down on the side either of the creationists (who believed that each soul was created independently by God) or the traducianists (who thought that souls were inherited along with the flesh). Augustine took the opportunity to explain his position, but he never did decide in favor of one of these views over the other.

The second group of his anti-Pelagian writings was directed specifically against Julian of Eclanum, who had written against him at great length. Julian had accused Augustine of denying free will, relativizing the importance of the law, downgrading baptism, slandering the saints, and opposing matrimony, as well as trying to revive Manichaeism! Augustine responded with four books of his own, followed soon afterward by two others dealing with the specific question of matrimony. These were all written in 419–420, but Julian would not be deterred, and so in 421 Augustine wrote a further six books against him, refuting his arguments point by point. These works summarize the earlier ones and are the most important to have come out of the Pelagian controversy. Some years later, Augustine took up his pen against Julian once more, but had only managed to complete six out of a projected eight books when he was overtaken by death.

The last group of his anti-Pelagian writings were the two tracts written to the monks of Hadrametum and Marseilles, who had questioned his understanding of the relationship between grace and free will. The first tract dealt specifically with that problem and the second explained how spiritual discipline could be harmonized with the efficacy of divine grace. Augustine expounded salvation in terms of human freedom, making a clear distinction between the freedom of Adam at creation, our freedom now, and the freedom of the blessed saints in heaven. It is in our present condition that grace comes to aid our free will by giving it the strength and the motivation to do what it knows is right but cannot achieve on its own. In this way, he managed to harmonize what might at first sight appear to be the contradictory forces of grace and free will, though it must be said that his solution to the problem was not to be definitive. Controversy over this would rumble on for centuries, and it is not over yet.

Letters and Sermons

Augustine's letters and sermons extended throughout his career and touched on all the above subjects and more. They are invaluable as a guide to his state of mind at particular points in his life and shed considerable light on the nature of the controversies that took up so much of his time. They also show Augustine at his pastoral best, since in both his letters and his sermons he speaks directly to the needs of his addressees. Most of his letters have been known for centuries, but new ones are still being discovered, and there is a real possibility that more will turn up in the years to come. Much the same can be said for his sermons, though the authenticity of some of them has been questioned. Many of them cannot be dated with precision, so it is difficult to use them as source material for the details of Augustine's life, but they give us a good general picture of the state of the church in Hippo during the years of his ministry there.

Augustine has left us a corpus of material that is enormous, even by modern standards, and remarkably varied. It is no surprise that his work became the foundation of almost all serious theological writing in the Middle Ages and beyond, nor that his more important works are still in print and readily available today.

Augustine's Basic Beliefs

Augustine lived at a time of great turmoil in the church, but his own beliefs were clear in his mind, and he never deviated from the path of creedal orthodoxy, even though he played little or no part in framing it. At the time of his conversion in 386, the church had already condemned the doctrine of Arius, who denied the divinity of Christ, and of the many semi-Arians who tried to find a compromise between his position and that of the great Athanasius, who insisted that the man Jesus of Nazareth was the Son of God in human flesh. There had been two universal, or "ecumenical," church councils—one at Nicaea in 325 and another at Constantinople in 381—both of which had asserted that the Father and the Son were of the same divine substance, and Augustine fully concurred with them on that. At the same time, his own relationship to the councils and the Arian controversy was relatively distant. There are indications that he knew of the Creed of Nicaea but he probably did not use it.[28] Certainly, he never wrote a commentary on it as he did on the baptismal creed, which he also cited in different versions in his sermons.[29]

In his own lifetime, trouble was brewing in the East. On one side were those who stressed the Athanasian principle that in Christ, the Word of God had become flesh by adding a human nature to his preexistent divinity. On the other side were those who objected to this by claiming that the human nature of Jesus had its own integrity and he would have been a man even if the Holy Spirit had not introduced divinity into the womb of Mary. Controversy erupted in 429 when Nestorius, recently elevated to the patriarchate of Constantinople, challenged the Athanasian position and was denounced by Cyril of Alexandria, who appealed to Rome for support. That support was forthcoming, but by the time Nestorius was condemned (at Ephesus in 431), Augustine was dead, and there is no indication that he knew anything of this dispute. His own position, which is set out in the first book of *On the Trinity*, leaned toward a moderately Athanasian stance, and it was this that Pope Leo I drew on in his efforts to resolve the Nestorian conflict at the Council of Chalcedon in 451. Because of this connection, Augustine's

---

[28] He mentioned it in *Contra Maximinum Arianum* 2.14.3, but only in passing. It should be noted that this creed was not the one that we now call the Nicene Creed, which is thought to have been composed at or shortly after the first council of Constantinople in 381. Augustine never said anything about that one.
[29] Augustine cited the creed used at Milan in *Sermones* 212–14, and the one used at Hippo in *Sermones* 215. The form of it that he commented on was actually shorter than either of these. See *De symbolo ad catechumenos*. The text of all three can be found side by side in Allan D. Fitzgerald, ed., *Augustine through the Ages: An Encyclopedia* (Grand Rapids: Eerdmans, 1999), 255.

christology appears to be Chalcedonian ahead of its time, and later generations have often read him in that way, perhaps not realizing that the doctrine they have believed he was upholding was not formulated until more than twenty years after his death.

Augustine's christology was well received at Chalcedon, but it was a different matter with his doctrine of the Trinity, despite the fact that his christology was formulated within a Trinitarian context.[30] Augustine quickly realized that the Arian controversy was essentially about the nature of the divinity attributed to the Son and the Holy Spirit in contrast to that of the Father. There had already been considerable speculation about the Trinity in the Western church, and Augustine was happy to take over the work of his great North African predecessor Tertullian, who had done more than anyone to lay down the ground rules for talking about the doctrine. Augustine was also aware of the contributions made by the Cappadocian fathers in the Eastern church, having imbibed their ideas from Hilary of Poitiers, a Latin-speaking bishop who had visited Cappadocia during his exile in the late 350s and who had written his own book on the Trinity in order to explain their thinking.[31]

Augustine had problems with the standard formula of three persons in one divine substance and wished that better terms could be found, but he recognized the difficulty in doing this, and in the end he stuck with inherited tradition for lack of anything better. Modern commentators have sometimes interpreted his hesitation as a potential denial of Trinitarian doctrine, but that is not the case. That there were three in one and one in three was undoubted; the difficulty was in knowing what best to call them. It has also been claimed that he misunderstood the Cappadocians, but that assertion, which comes almost entirely from the Eastern church and its sympathizers, must also be treated with caution. It may be true that his Greek was not good enough to appreciate the Cappadocians' subtleties, but he read them through Hilary, who was well informed about them and did his best to convey them to a Latin-speaking public. It is also true that the Cappadocians did not have a clearly defined doctrine in the sense attributed to them by later generations; they were making it up as they went along, feeling their way toward a viable solution to the various dif-

---

30 It was adopted by at least half the Eastern church, but the rest split into Nestorians and "Monophysites," who both rejected what they saw as its compromise formula.

31 The main Cappadocian fathers were Basil of Caesarea (ca. 329–379), Gregory of Nazianzus (ca. 330–390), and Gregory of Nyssa (ca. 330–ca. 395).

ficulties they encountered on the way. Augustine was doing essentially the same thing, and neither he nor they should be judged by the criteria of a later time.

What is true is that he made his own distinctive contribution to the doctrine. Augustine believed that the key to understanding the Trinity is the fact that God is love. Love is not a thing, nor is it a quality belonging to a thing. It is a relationship, which means that if God is love, there must be someone (or something) for him to love. Furthermore, if God is perfect, his love must also be perfect, which implies that what he loves must be perfect too. Following that logic, God must love himself, because he is the only being that meets the criterion of perfection. But for God to love himself, he must have a conception of himself, and that conception is the Son, who is his exact image.[32] Love must also be reciprocal. If I love someone but am not loved back, that is not perfection. So the Son must love the Father with the same love by which the Father loves him. It is this love that is common to them both and that binds them together. Augustine debated for a long time as to whether this shared love could be equated with the Holy Spirit, but in the end he said that it could; the Spirit is the love that proceeds from both the Father and the Son and that unites them.

From there, Augustine went on to say that the image of God in man is an image of the Trinity. The three persons in God are like the memory, intellect, and will in the human mind—distinct but inseparable, and all equally necessary if the mind is to function properly. This "psychological" image of the Trinity is fundamental to his thought and must be understood if his teaching on other things is to be appreciated. For a man to become like God is to realize the potential that has been given to him in the divine image, a picture that determined everything he had to say about living the Christian life.

The other fundamental principle that guided Augustine was his devotion to the Bible. The Scriptures were given by God to his people as the inerrant source of all true wisdom. The man who wants to live according to God's will must obey their teaching, and it is the duty of the church and its ministers to provide the instruction necessary to understanding what that teaching is. Augustine knew all about corrupt manuscripts and bad translations, and he offered guidance to his readers as to how to detect

---

[32] Note that "conception" can be used both of mental and of physical reproduction, making the human analogy of Father and Son particularly appropriate in this case.

such errors and correct them. But he never wavered in his fundamental conviction that the Bible was a gift from God to the church, which was charged with the duty of recognizing the books that belonged to it and of interpreting them correctly.

Augustine put great faith in the collective wisdom of the church, which had preserved the Scriptures and their teaching. He did not claim that popes, bishops, or church councils had taken decisions about biblical authority and imposed them on everyone else, because they had not. What he meant was that all Christians everywhere recognized the divine inspiration of the text; they knew from their experience that in these books God was speaking to them. That was why he accepted the so-called Apocrypha—books that had been added to the Greek Old Testament but were not in the Hebrew original. He argued that the church had received them as God's Word and that they should be accepted for that reason, even though his contemporary Jerome, who knew Hebrew and was an unequalled biblical scholar, disagreed with him about this. In Jerome's opinion, the limits of the Old Testament had to be determined by the people of the Old Testament—the Jews. For that reason, only the Hebrew text was valid. Unfortunately, the church followed Augustine in this, and it was not until the Reformation that Jerome's more logical view resurfaced and was adopted by the Protestants. Today, almost everyone (including most Roman Catholic biblical scholars) sides with Jerome against Augustine on this point, but at least Augustine's intentions can be respected, even if we must disagree with his conclusions.

Another important aspect of his theology was the way in which he conceived of human salvation. Here Augustine really did sort out a doctrine that had never been clearly expounded before. First of all, he insisted that the sovereign goodness of God meant that everything that happens in the world is under divine control. This is the doctrine known as providence. When it is applied to the destiny of individuals, it becomes predestination. As Augustine saw it, every human being has been predestined from the beginning, either for salvation in Christ or for destruction. Those who have been set aside for salvation are the elect, or chosen ones. Their history began with Abraham and continued through the generations of his descendants, the Israelites. Israel was not an end in itself however, but a nation that had been constituted and chosen to be a witness of the greater salvation that was to come in Christ. The Son of God came to Israel and made atonement for the sins of the people according to the law of Moses given to the Israelites after their departure from Egypt, but the accomplishment of his work meant that the nature of Israel changed in the process.

What had previously been expressed as a nation with its own religious cult now gave way to a universal gospel of salvation that extended to every tribe and people. The criterion of election was no longer circumcision but baptism into the Christian church. To be baptized was to be born again, and it was the duty of the church and its ministers to make baptism available to anyone who wanted it. Furthermore, he believed, baptism did what circumcision could not do—it washed away the guilt of original sin. It was Augustine's conviction that when Adam and Eve fell, sin entered the human race and brought death and destruction in its wake. He drew this conclusion from his reading of Romans 5:12, which (in his version) read: "Sin came into the world through one man and death through sin, and so death spread to all men, because all had sinned *in him*."

Modern scholars know that Augustine misunderstood this verse, not because his Greek was poor but because he was relying on the translation made by an unknown man whom we call Ambrosiaster (because it was once thought that the translator was Ambrose). However, we must be careful not to reject Augustine's teaching merely because one of the verses he used to support it does not say what he thought it did. For one thing, it is hard to see why death would have spread to everyone if Adam's sin had been personal to him alone. Second, other verses, including those in the immediate context in Romans, justify Augustine's view, even if this particular one does not. Here is a good example of how Augustine understood the overall sense of Scripture even if particular words and phrases had been mishandled or mistranslated.

Augustine thought that the spread of sin meant that no human being can escape from the wrath of God against sinners. Contrary to what Pelagius taught, there is no residue of goodness in the human soul that is able to fight back against the power of sin. Only the grace of God can do that, so the Christian gospel is a message that the divine grace which we need has been poured out and made available to us. The Bible is not a self-help manual for our improvement to the point where we are worthy of heaven, but the proclamation of God's rescue plan, which he devised, carried out, and has now implemented in the mission of the church. The Christian life is therefore an appropriation of that grace, not a striving to achieve something beyond our grasp. It is a message of forgiveness for our sins, not of condemnation for having failed to make the grade.

Once this is understood, the nature of our relationship to God changes beyond recognition. No longer can the church be seen as a school of moral achievement in which some pupils take all the prizes. On the contrary, it is a hospital for sick sinners, who are cured not by their own inner resources but by the healthy medicine of divine grace. What Christians need to know is not how to become better people, which is impossible, but how to receive the grace offered to us and let it shape the image of God in our hearts and minds. Only when we understand that will we understand what the Bible teaches and what God has done for us in Jesus Christ.

CHAPTER 2

AUGUSTINE THE BELIEVER

Conversion

The central fact of Augustine's life was his conversion to Christ at the age of thirty-two. Everything that happened before then he came to see as divine preparation for his conversion, and the rest of his life was governed by it. Had he never become a Christian, we would probably know nothing about him now. He has left us no preconversion writings, and it is only from hindsight that his early life is accessible to us. How "accurate" his analysis of his own youth was is impossible to say. No doubt other contemporary observers would have told his story differently and in some respects more objectively, but they could not have captured his intimacy, nor could they have known what was to be important to him in adulthood. Augustine included details of his childhood that seem trivial in purely objective terms but played an important part in his own spiritual journey—or at least he recalled them as having been significant moments in his early life. Here we have no choice but to take his word for it since we have nothing else to go on.[1]

It is clear that in its early years the Christian church grew mainly by conversions from Judaism or paganism, but we know surprisingly little about most of the people who made a profession of faith. The apostle Paul's conversion is told in great detail in Acts 9 and 22, and he himself fills in

---

[1] We know very little about the childhood of Jesus, remember, and almost nothing about that of the apostle Paul, though he occasionally speaks about his background in his letters. Augustine was the first person in Western cultural history to understand clearly that "the child is father of the man" and to consider his early years as genuinely formative in psychological and spiritual terms, which makes his *Confessions* unique.

some of the details in his letters, but this is virtually unique. We cannot even say when the disciples of Jesus were "converted" or what that would have meant in their case. When did Peter become a Christian? What about John? They were certainly followers of Jesus, but were they converted before the day of Pentecost, when the Holy Spirit came down on them in tongues of fire? The New Testament does not tell us.

Later on, we read of numerous professions of faith, which were normally followed by baptism, but the events are described from the outside, as they were observed by others. Almost nobody left a personal testimony of his or her own experience—except Augustine. Indeed, the whole idea of "testimony" was connected to something else entirely—not conversion, but martyrdom, from the Greek word *martyria*, meaning "witness" or "testimony." By Augustine's time martyrdom had largely ceased, a fact that caused severe spiritual dislocation in North Africa, where it had been especially prized. One of the strongest selling-points of the Donatists was their devotion to the idea; and their claim that there were no longer any martyrs because the church had sold its birthright by compromising with the state appealed to many. This had happened in 313, a generation before Augustine was born. At that time, Christianity was made a legal religion in the Roman Empire, though it was not until 380, when Augustine was twenty-six and still not a Christian, that it became the official state religion. Over the following fifteen years, pagan rites were suppressed, many temples were turned into churches, and bishops became important state officials. Augustine's conversion and subsequent career took place when the church was still in the process of establishing itself as the spiritual foundation of society, though by the time he died the conversion of the ancient world was virtually complete. Even the barbarian tribes that were replacing the empire were Christian, or soon became so—there was no other way the church could have succeeded in supplanting it.

It is therefore all the more remarkable that although formal "conversion" on a massive scale was taking place during Augustine's lifetime, he himself experienced it in a much more personal light. Perhaps the most interesting thing about Augustine's autobiography is the way it documents the spiritual state of the Roman Empire in the mid to late fourth century, at the very time when the church was advancing from legality to social dominance. From our perspective, Christianity was the up-and-coming thing, but it did not necessarily look that way at the time. Augustine did not grow up in a world where everybody went to church but few people took its message seriously; that now-familiar scenario would only develop later. In his day, there were still plenty of people who were openly pagan, who never went near a church, and who dabbled in philosophies and esoteric cults that were allowed to flourish without hindrance. In the world of country gentry in which Augustine grew up, the contact with Christians that he had through his mother was common enough not to be regarded as bizarre, but it was not a matter of course either. His father lived and worked quite well without any profession of Christian faith, and most of the friends Augustine made in his student days did the same. If there were nominal Christians around, or people who had joined the church merely for social or political advantage, Augustine did not know any, and there was never any pressure put on him to convert for that reason.

Augustine could have gone on being a pagan all his life, as many of his contemporaries did. He could also have accepted Christianity for intellectual reasons, as philosophers like Marius Victorinus did. He could have transitioned from secular to ecclesiastical life without much difficulty, like Ambrose of Milan or the somewhat infamous Synesius of Cyrene (ca. 370–ca. 413), who was a classic example of the worldly bishop of later times.[2] The choice was his—or so it seemed. Yet the story he tells is quite different from that. Augustine did not drift into the church in a "go with the flow" kind of way. Nor did he cling to some form of intellectual paganism for traditional or philosophical reasons, like the emperor Julian "the Apostate" (r. 361–363). As a young man Augustine was looking for moral and spiritual certainty, and Christianity was one of the options available to him. Perhaps because of his mother's influence, he was never antichurch and was more aware than most outsiders were of what went on in Christian circles. He sometimes read parts of the Scriptures and pondered them, but without being persuaded of their truth. Like many people in a similar position today, he felt no special attraction to the church's faith and preferred to look elsewhere for satisfaction, but he remained within its wider orbit.

In his *Confessions* Augustine looked back on his youth as a time when God was preparing him to accept the gospel, but this was the view from hindsight. Like the apostle Paul, who did much the same thing (and whose example no doubt served as a precedent), Augustine could see that God had been at work in his life all along, though he was unaware of it at the time.

---

[2] See Bengt-Arne Roos, *Synesius of Cyrene: A Study in His Personality* (Lund: Lund University Press, 1991).

His conversion was less dramatic than Paul's because he never persecuted the church and had no Damascus Road experience, but in essentials it was much the same. Like Paul, Augustine was deeply conscious that it was not he who had found God but God who had found him. This is the hallmark of true conversion and it shaped his entire outlook. Augustine had done nothing to deserve this wonderful gift from God, and he knew it. What he was, he was by the grace of God and not by any merit or action on his part. The more he came to understand of God, the less he trusted in himself and his own resources.

Augustine's *Confessions* are unique in the annals of Christianity because they are the only important book addressed to God. Obviously this was a rhetorical device. God did not need Augustine to tell him about his life, and Augustine knew perfectly well that this book would be read not by God but by other people. Other great leaders, including Paul, have sought to explain themselves by expounding the ups and downs of their spiritual journeys to their human audiences. By contrast, Augustine told his story as part of an extended prayer for forgiveness. In baring his soul, he was not trying to impress other people but to make peace with the God who had already made peace with him by the cross of Christ. The importance of this theme is underlined in the opening paragraph of the *Confessions*, where we read the famous words, "You give us delight in praising you, because you have made us for yourself and our hearts are restless until they find their rest in you."[3] For Augustine, conversion was coming to terms with the great mystery of the divine purpose in human affairs, a purpose that did not just manifest itself in the great acts of world history but touched the heart and mind of each individual to whom God has spoken and in whom he dwells. How could such a thing be? Augustine did not know how to explain it. As he says: "What place is there inside me to which my God can come, the God who made heaven and earth? Is there anything in me, O Lord my God, that can contain you? Do heaven and earth, which you have made and in which you have made me, contain you?"[4]

Augustine knew that there was a great gulf fixed between the Creator and his creatures, but he also knew that the gulf had been bridged not by man finding his way up to God but by God condescending to become man and to enter into the being of those whom he had created in his image

---

[3] *Confessiones* 1.1.1.
[4] *Confessiones* 1.2.2.

and likeness. Nor was this just an objective attempt to squeeze the infinite being of God into the finite dimensions of humanity. It had a subjective element about it, which gave meaning to the concept of conversion. For the human heart was not merely too small to contain God—it was also rebellious and sinful.

> Cramped is the dwelling of my soul. Expand it, O Lord, so that you can come in. It lies in ruins; restore it. There is something about it that must offend your eyes. I confess it and I know it, but who will make it clean? Who can I cry to, apart from you? "Cleanse me from my secret sins," O Lord, and protect your servant from those of other people.[5]

Augustine went on to tell God that he was not going to argue with him or plead his case for salvation, because he knew that he did not deserve it. Instead, he was going to cast himself on God's mercy, relying on the promises of Scripture that God would have compassion on those who turned to him for forgiveness.[6] Augustine did not know why his soul was troubled by his sins, and could not say why God had brought him into the world for such a trial. Yet he knew that everything he had and was had come to him as a divine gift. He understood that he had been conceived in his mother's womb by an act of God's grace, without which he would never have been born. His early nurture was entirely dependent on his parents and nursemaids, whom God had prepared so that they could minister to his most fundamental needs. Slowly he had begun to act for himself, but at first he could do no more than laugh or cry, because to express his inmost desires was beyond his capacities. All of this happened before he had any awareness of it; like us, he knew of it only by observing other babies and assuming that he must have been the same in his infancy.

But Augustine also knew that there was no such thing as childhood innocence. His own observations told him that babies demand attention and fight for it if it is denied them, even though they have no entitlement to it and may desire things that would be harmful to them if granted. A child's sinfulness is excused only because the child lacks the ability to obtain what he wants. As Augustine observed, "A child is innocent only because of the weakness of his limbs, not because of his will."[7] Later on, he learns

---

[5] *Confessiones* 1.5.6. The quotation is from Ps. 19:12.
[6] *Confessiones* 1.6.7. He alludes to Jer. 12:15.
[7] *Confessiones* 1.7.11.

from his parents how to speak and act, but this root sinfulness is there already—it is inherited, not learned. For that reason, it cannot be unlearned or corrected in the way that bad grammar or antisocial behavior can be. Sin is more than a habit picked up from others, but it is less than our created being. It is impossible for us to get rid of it by our own efforts, but God can forgive it without destroying us in the process.

Augustine recounts the trials of childhood in which the child's natural desire to play and waste time is reproved by adults, even though they often do much the same things. As a result, children become critical of their parents and disobey them without being able to surpass them in goodness. Their disobedience is self-willed and has no object greater than a desire to be like the adults they criticize. Like many young boys Augustine had mixed feelings about school—parts of it he enjoyed and parts he detested. He absorbed the literature and myths of his native Latin but disliked their Greek equivalents, not because of their content, which was almost identical, but because he could not enter into the spirit of a foreign language. For Augustine, education was more than mere verbalization; it touched the heart and subconscious part of a man that only the mother tongue can reach. It is at that level, and not in the mind only, that a true turning to God must take place.[8]

Augustine affirmed the power of baptism to cleanse souls from sin, and he believed that had he been baptized as a child, he would have been made a Christian. But he also said that if he had been baptized without understanding what the rite was about, his ultimate fate would have been worse, because postbaptismal sins are by definition greater and more dangerous than ones committed beforehand. He therefore saw the postponement of his baptism as divine mercy—an opportunity to sin, no doubt, but to do so in a way that would have less serious long-term consequences.[9] Augustine knew that this was not an ideal situation. He recognized that it would have been better for him if he had been cleansed of his sins at a young age, but he also understood that he was not yet ready, and that if he had received baptism then, temptation would have got the better of him before he understood the new life in Christ that he had entered into.

To our modern minds, much of this sounds strange. Few people now believe that the outward rite of water baptism can save a person, and we

[8] *Confessiones* 1.13.20–1.14.23.
[9] *Confessiones* 1.11.17.

tend to think that if Augustine had been baptized and then gone on in a life of sinfulness, his baptism would have been meaningless. Augustine, however, like most people in the early church, believed that baptism would have cleansed him from sin but that the overall effect on him would have been disastrous because he was not ready for it. How important is this difference of perception? At one level it appears to be very serious, since if an external rite administered to a person without his consent or understanding could save him from sin, that rite would be a kind of vaccination against evil and ought to be administered to everyone for the sake of their health, if nothing else. But if baptism reflects a personal relationship with God that can be known only by faith, bestowing it on all and sundry would be nonsensical and perhaps even blasphemous. At the same time, modern readers who are skeptical of Augustine's view of baptism need to remember that he did not regard it as a passport to heaven regardless of other considerations. A sinner still needs to repent in order to be saved from his sins; and to declare him saved through water baptism, when there was no repentance, would only lead to further and deeper trouble later on.

Perhaps the fairest thing to say about this is that Augustine was caught between two different theological positions without realizing it. On the one hand, there was the tradition of the church, which thought of baptism almost as a kind of exorcism, and a guarantee of salvation for infants who died in childhood, as many did. But on the other hand, he also knew that there was an element of personal involvement in being a Christian. Salvation was certainly a work of God's grace and nobody could save himself by making an independent decision to follow Christ, but if the heart and will were not engaged and transformed by the power of the Holy Spirit, pouring water over someone was no substitute. Eventually the two points of view would come into sharper focus and clash, as they did at the time of the Reformation in the sixteenth century. Augustine however, lived with the inner tension that these different views created. He distinguished quite clearly between conversion and regeneration, attributing the former to his spiritual experience (as we would) and the latter to his baptism (as we would not).[10] What we can say, though, is that he placed much more emphasis on his conversion than on his subsequent baptism, which he saw as a necessary consequence of his turning to Christ, not as a substitute for it.

Returning to his thoughts on infancy, perhaps the most important as-

---

[10] On his baptism and "regeneration," see *Confessiones* 9.3.6, 9.6.14.

pect of Augustine's meditations is the way in which he applied what he saw in others to himself. It was by studying the behavior of unself-conscious children that he realized what he was like, and what makes human beings act the way they do. By seeing that human selfishness was something innate, he came to recognize the fundamental unity of the human race in sin. We are all creatures of God, made in his image and likeness, and we have all been subjected to sinfulness because of the fall of our first parents, Adam and Eve. The work of Christ, who had come to put right what had gone wrong at the beginning was therefore of universal validity. Nobody can claim that the gospel is not meant for him, because we have all sinned in Adam, and it is the legacy of that sin which Christ came to take away. The church must therefore preach the way of salvation to everybody without exception, knowing that the remedy it proclaims is sufficient to meet every person's need. But just as there are people who miss out on the blessings of baptism, even when it is offered to them, so there are those who do not receive the message of redemption when it is proclaimed to them. Augustine did not know why he resisted it for so long, but he learned later that all through the years of his rebellion God had something better in store for him. He did not blame God for the delay in making this known to him, however, because he recognized that God's purposes are holy, just, and right, however they are worked out and whether we understand them at the time or not.

Moving on from infancy, Augustine described how the lusts of the flesh conspired to dominate his youthful life. In the *Confessions*, he looked back on those days with a deep sense of regret at the opportunities he had wasted, the wisdom of his elders that he had spurned, and the sins that he had committed. One particular incident stuck in his mind, as much for its absurdity as anything else:

> There was a pear-tree close to our vineyard that was heavily laden with fruit, though it was not appealing either for its color or its taste. Some of us young men went one night after we had stayed out late to play games in the street, and carried off great quantities of that fruit, not to eat ourselves but to give to the pigs after having eaten only some of them. We enjoyed doing this all the more because it was forbidden.[11]

Our minds are taken back to the sin of Eve in the garden of Eden, when she was tempted to eat the forbidden fruit, but in Augustine's case it was

---

[11] *Confessiones* 2.4.9.

not the immorality of his act but the sheer meaninglessness of what he had done that struck him most forcefully. As he put it, "I loved my own sin, not because of what it gave me, but for the pleasure of sinning in itself."[12]

This awareness led him to analyze what it is that makes people want to sin. His conclusion was that seldom (if ever) do we really believe that we shall gain anything from it, and when we see people committing crimes like murder, we are quick to condemn them for their folly. But what appears obvious when we see it in others is much harder to detect in ourselves. The fact that wrongdoing makes no sense is easy to understand when we think about it objectively, but that does not stop us from doing it, because we are not motivated by carefully thought-out considerations of self-interest. Our minds have been turned toward evil by something deeper than pure reason, and if we do not understand that, we shall merely go on sinning and finding better excuses to justify it. This was the underlying trouble with the philosophers. Believing (as they did) that all problems were susceptible to rational analysis, they could not come to terms with the depths of human sinfulness and had no remedy for it. All they could do was find more sophisticated ways of fooling themselves into thinking that they could live a better life by their own efforts. Augustine realized that it was a natural response to a real problem, but he insisted that it was totally inadequate. Only when we come to see that, however, and accept that we must cast ourselves entirely on the mercy of God for forgiveness and restoration, is real change possible, because only then are we getting to the root of the trouble.

Augustine experienced the attractions of a sinful way of life at first hand when he went off to Carthage to study. The sights and sounds of the big city quickly drew him in and he wanted to feel that he could compete with the most sophisticated people in town. Because his heart was not right with God, the greater opportunities that university life gave him whetted his appetite for more egregious forms of licentiousness. Before long he was eagerly lapping up the delights of the theater, which was regarded as a hotbed of wicked behavior, and he soon took a concubine as did so many students like him. But even at this low point in his life, his mother's influence did not entirely disappear. He continued to go to church from time to time, though without experiencing the power of its message in his own life, and he remained faithful to the woman he loved, which was highly unusual in the circles in which he moved. What he was doing was wrong, as he later

---

12 *Confessiones* 2.4.9.

came to realize, but it was not entirely dishonorable or unprincipled, as his friends and colleagues must have noticed. Even in the depths of his rebellion against God, Augustine felt his Savior's protecting hand and realized, when he looked back on it in later years, how he had been preserved from the worst consequences of his folly in spite of himself.

Augustine realized, even as a student, that the pleasures of Carthage were not the most important thing in life. Not long after he got there he came across Cicero's *Hortensius*, a book in which the great Roman statesman advocated the pursuit of philosophy as the way to obtain a better life. As he later interpreted it, philosophy was a form of desire for God, but it was ambiguous. It offered understanding and the happiness that supposedly came with that, but as the apostle Paul had said, it could also lead people astray.[13] Unable to discern which way he should go, Augustine fell into the trap of pseudo-intellectual pride and was soon deriding the Bible as something far too simple for serious minds to engage with. Instead, he found what he was looking for in the obscure and somewhat bizarre religious philosophy that derived from the Persian prophet Mani.

Manichaeism was an eclectic mix of contradictory principles, but it gave its followers a sense of intellectual accomplishment and superiority toward the less enlightened. It demonstrated how easily people who wanted to appear clever could be led astray by utter foolishness, which they readily imbibed and repeated as unchallengeable dogma. Meanwhile, as often happens with similar cults today, the leaders lived a highly immoral lifestyle under the pretense that they were reconciling good and evil by rising to a higher level of consciousness. To their followers they preached lofty principles and an ascetic lifestyle, but behind the scenes they profited from their disciples' gullibility. After his conversion Augustine saw this clearly, but as long as he was deceived by the Manichees and others like them, he was blind to their faults and inconsistencies. Plenty of people tried to persuade him to change his mind, but he refused and instead preached his false gospel to others in the hope of winning them over to his cause.

One man Augustine managed to influence was an old friend from Thagaste, but it did not work out as he hoped. As long as things were going well, both of them were happy to mock Christianity and the church, but then his friend fell ill and was baptized, even though he was unconscious at the time. Augustine wanted to make a joke of this concession to religious

---

[13] *Confessiones* 3.4.8. Augustine quoted Col. 2:8–9 to prove his point.

superstition, but when his friend rallied briefly, Augustine reacted very differently. In his words, "He shuddered at me as if I were his enemy, and with a remarkable and unexpected freedom he admonished me, that if I wanted to go on being his friend, I should stop talking to him like that."[14] Augustine put this rebuke down to his friend's disturbed mental state and hoped that when he got better he would come to his senses (as Augustine understood it), but that was not to be. The fever returned, and in a few days his friend was dead. Far from winning his case, Augustine lost everything: his friend, his self-respect, and his sense of assurance that he was doing the right thing. The deeper lesson he learned from this experience was that spiritual matters are issues of life and death and not to be trifled with. What appears to be folly when judged by the wisdom of the world turns out to be a priceless comfort in times of despair. His friend died in the hope of resurrection to a new and eternal life. Even if (as Augustine then believed) that hope was misplaced, it was still better than anything the Manichees had to offer. As that lesson sank in, Augustine found that another escape route from Christ was closing, even if the way to heaven had not yet opened up for him.

The bitter experience of losing a close friend led Augustine to meditate on the meaning and importance of love. Love lies at the heart of Christianity and corresponds to the deepest yearnings of the human heart. Everyone wants to love and be loved, but in human life all relationships come to an end. Over time we lose those who are nearest and dearest to us—our parents, our siblings, our friends, and even (as in Augustine's own case) our children. The only love that is constant is the love of God, and it is in his love that all other loves acquire immortality. If we know that our family and friends have gone to be with the Lord, then we cannot grieve unrestrainedly, because we know that our loss is only for a time. One day soon we shall be reunited around the throne of glory and live together in God's eternal love.

Love is stronger than death, a fact that we recognize from the grieving process and experience in our communion with the great minds of the past. But if that is so, then it must transcend the material world of change and decay in which we presently live. The materialism of the Manichees could not do this, nor could any belief system that relies on human perception as the only source of truth. A spiritual dimension to reality is therefore

---

[14] *Confessiones* 4.4.8.

both essential and normative. We have it in us to some degree because all human beings possess a spirit that cannot be satisfied by the good things of this world. As he came to understand this, Augustine moved imperceptibly closer to receiving Christ as his Savior. He later realized that the awareness of the importance of spiritual things was a necessary preliminary to experiencing those things themselves. To men in their fallen state, spiritual awareness does not come easily and is bound to be corrupted by idolatry of various kinds.

Augustine's newfound awareness produced a disenchantment with the Manichees, and he eventually abandoned their sect, but he was not led into the truth that he craved. Christianity did not come to him as a new and improved form of Manichaeism, doing essentially the same thing but in a way that actually worked. Having been burned once, Augustine was extremely reluctant to risk disappointment a second time by embracing a doctrine that demanded an equally total commitment of heart and mind. He toyed with Christianity to some extent, but failed to make any headway with it because he wanted to make it conform to his predilections. At the heart of his concerns was the nature of evil, which the Manichees had taught him to believe was a kind of substance. This clashed with the Christian claim that God had made everything good, which Augustine wanted to affirm, but he could not accept that evil had no objective existence. It might be inferior to the good and less powerful, but it was still there and was a force to be reckoned with.[15]

To appreciate why Augustine had a problem with this, we have to understand that in the ancient world the idea that God was spiritual could easily come to mean that everything spiritual was good and that what was opposed to it—the material world—was correspondingly evil. This was the foundation of philosophical dualism, which both the Manichees and the ancient Greek philosophers took for granted. The problem was that this belief contradicted the basic teachings of Christianity, which not only affirmed the goodness of the material creation but also taught that the spiritual Son of God had become a man as Jesus Christ. How could that happen if matter was inherently evil? The only answer was to say that evil is not a substance in and of itself. Everything that exists is therefore good by definition. Evil is a corruption of what is good and thus deprives the creature of something that is naturally inherent in it.

---

[15] *Confessiones* 5.10.20.

Today we accept that evil is fundamentally disobedience to God, a broken relationship with him that is not caused by the material creation. Where we differ from Augustine and his contemporaries is in the way we understand goodness. For us, goodness is not a substance any more than evil is; it is obedience to the will of God. In other words, we have moved the discussion of morality away from the nature of creation and located it (as the Bible does) in the sphere of relationships, which are inherently spiritual. It was because Augustine and his contemporaries thought of goodness as an attribute of the divine substance that they had such difficulty with the concept of evil; but once we make appropriate allowance for that, we can see that fundamentally we are not as far apart from him as the way he expressed his ideas might suggest.

When he left Africa for Italy, Augustine was already moving away from classical dualism as the explanation for good and evil, though he was not yet converted. After a short stay in Rome, he made his way to Milan, where the great Ambrose was bishop. Ambrose was a leading figure in the Roman world whom a provincial nobody like Augustine could not ignore. Augustine went to hear him preach and was gradually persuaded by his arguments, even to the point that he enrolled in baptism classes, at least (as he tells us) until something better turned up![16]

At this point in his life the building blocks that would produce the Christian Augustine were gradually falling into place. His entire family had by this time become Christian, and his mother, who had sailed to Italy to be with him, was doing all she could to further his conversion. At the same time, alternative ways of salvation were losing their appeal. The intellectual arguments of Ambrose, if not watertight, were at least as good as anyone else's, and Augustine found them hard to resist, even if he did not get as much opportunity to discuss them with the bishop as he would have liked.[17] But although he was steadily moving in the right direction, he was still not converted. Something essential was missing, without which he would never be a real Christian. He could go through the external motions, as he was intending to do, but faith could never be a matter of mere ritual. How Augustine could get beyond the superficial aspects of Christianity and penetrate to its inner heart he did not know, but one thing at least was clear. Christianity claimed to be a revelation from God that was contained in a

---

[16] *Confessiones* 5.14.25.
[17] *Confessiones* 6.3.3–4.

series of writings. Somehow or other he had to come to terms with them, and it was this that now started to preoccupy his mind.

As he proceeded along the path toward formal church membership, Augustine was brought face-to-face with the teaching of the Holy Scriptures, on which the church was based. He did not have a Bible in the modern sense of the word, because no such thing existed. There were the Old Testament Scriptures, translated into Greek before the coming of Christ and widely available, and the various books of the New Testament circulated independently of each other. Few people could afford a complete text, and translations into Latin were uneven at best. Nevertheless, it was to the sacred writings that Augustine was forced to turn despite his own reservations about them.

> After hearing many of the things in Scripture, that had previously appeared to me to be incongruous and offensive, expounded in a reasonable manner [by Ambrose], I went back to the depth of the mysteries, and its authority seemed to me to be all the more venerable and worthy of religious belief.[18]

Acceptance of the Scriptures as the Word of God was fundamental to Augustine's spiritual journey, because it was only then that he was open to hearing the Lord speaking to him. Many people find the Bible disagreeable for one reason or another and dispute whether or not it contains the truth. Such people may be sincere—Augustine certainly was—but their minds are closed to hearing God speaking to them. God does not want people to argue with him but to submit to his will, however hard it may be for them to understand it. Augustine had to get to that point before he could become a Christian, and it was Ambrose who helped him to do it.

But although a willingness to hear and obey the Scriptures was a prerequisite to his salvation, it was not the thing itself. For that there had to come a spiritual crisis, what we call "conviction of sin." A person must reach the point where he realizes how helpless he is without the grace of God. Only by casting himself totally on God's mercy can he hear and receive the word of forgiveness. In Augustine's case this moment came like a thunderstorm when pent-up emotions started overflowing and he was reduced to floods of tears. It was when he was in this desperate state that he heard

---

[18] *Confessiones* 6.5.8.

a child's voice which seemed to be calling out, "Take up and read, take up and read." Augustine took this to mean that he must pick up the portion of Scripture nearest to hand and read whatever his eye fell upon. It turned out to be a passage from Paul's epistle to the Romans.

> I grasped, opened, and in silence read that paragraph on which my eyes first fell: "Not in orgies and drunkenness, not in sexual immorality and sensuality, not in quarreling and jealousy. But put on the Lord Jesus Christ, and make no provision for the flesh, to gratify its desires." No further would I read, nor did I need, for instantly, as the sentence ended, a light of assurance poured into my heart and all the darkness of doubt vanished away.[19]

In the end it was not intellectual argument that won Augustine for Christ but a direct challenge to his moral and spiritual condition. Like so many others before him and since, Augustine was ready to accept the truth of the gospel in his mind, but he lacked the deeper spiritual motivation that alone could spell true conversion. He had turned away from the Manichees and the philosophers and was seeking the truth through the ministry of Ambrose, but he was still living in ways that were inconsistent with God's will. For him, the real stumbling block was not theoretical, as his doubts about the truth of the Scriptures might suggest, but practical. Would he—could he—abandon the lifestyle to which he had grown accustomed and which his friends expected of him? In his own words: "I came to understand from my own experience what I had read, how 'the desires of the flesh are against the Spirit and the desires of the Spirit are against the flesh.' My own desires went in both directions, but more toward what I approved of in myself than toward what I disapproved of."[20]

It was when God put the finger on this and opened his eyes to see what the real problem was that Augustine finally responded. He could have turned away, like the rich young ruler who kept the law but could not part with his possessions, but he did not.[21] Augustine was prepared to surrender everything, and surrender it he did. He could not have known at the time what that would involve. Before long he would abandon all hope of marriage, which he had wanted for so long, and would eventually abandon his

---

[19] *Confessiones* 8.12.29. The text is Rom. 13:13–14.
[20] *Confessiones* 8.5.11. The quotation is from Gal. 5:17.
[21] See Matt. 19:16–22.

desire for a quiet life when elected bishop of Hippo. He would get embroiled in controversies that he would rather have stayed out of and take on a career of teaching and writing far more demanding than anything a professor of rhetoric would have to face. But that was still in the future. When he got up from his reading and wiped the tears from his eyes, he was a Christian. The long struggle for his soul had reached its end.

The depth and extent of the change that came over him should not be underestimated. In his own words:

> How evil have my deeds been, or if not my deeds, my words, and if not my words, my will! But you, O Lord, are good and merciful, and your right hand observed the depth of my death, and removed the abyss of corruption from the bottom of my heart. The result was that I no longer wanted to do what I willed, but what you willed. . . . You cast out the vanities of this life and in their place you entered into my heart.[22]

Conversion was a new life and brought with it an equally new relationship with God. What that meant for Augustine is the subject to which we must now turn.

Augustine's Devotional Life

As with most Christians, Augustine's devotional life can be viewed as having two related but distinct parts—the private and the public. What makes Augustine unusual, and in the ancient world virtually unique, is that we know a great deal about his private devotional life but relatively little about the public side. We know that he went to church even before his conversion and that he participated in worship, and that in later life he was accustomed to preaching and leading services on a weekly, if not on a daily, basis. What we are less certain about is whether he had strong feelings about how public worship should be conducted. Eastern contemporaries of his like Basil of Caesarea and John Chrysostom composed liturgies that are still in use, but Augustine did not. He was aware that the Eastern church was more advanced in this respect, because he tells us that it was only about a year before his baptism at Easter 387 that the church at Milan had introduced congregational singing in imitation of the Eastern custom. The immediate cause of this innovation was an Arian persecution instigated

---

[22] *Confessiones* 9.1.1.

by the empress-mother Justina, but other factors were at work as well, and the habit gradually caught on elsewhere.

> At this time it was instituted that, following the custom of the Eastern church, hymns and psalms should be sung, so that the people would not pine away in the boredom of their sorrow. This custom has carried on since then and has been imitated by many, in fact, by almost all of your congregations throughout the world.[23]

Augustine thus had personal experience of liturgical development, but we get the sense that he was more a detached observer of events, not an initiator of change. What we can say for certain is that he had an ear for music and was deeply moved by it: "When I call to mind the tears I shed at the songs of your church soon after I had recovered my faith, and how even now I am moved, not by the singing but by what is sung, when it is sung with a clear and skillfully controlled voice, I acknowledge the great usefulness of this custom."[24]

But Augustine was well aware of the problem that the beauty of the music has a way of taking over from the meaning of the words to which it is set. He understood just how susceptible he was to that temptation and came down very harshly against it: "When I am more moved by the singing than by what is sung, I confess that I have sinned criminally and wish that I had not heard the singing at all."[25] How many people today know how he felt!

Like Basil, Augustine drew up a monastic rule that he used in the community he established at Hippo. It was revived eight centuries later as part of the monastic reform movement in western Europe and gives us some idea of what his devotional priorities were. Like many people in late Roman times, Augustine associated devotion to God with withdrawal from the world. Regular church services were too crowded and too full of people whose personal commitment to Christianity was questionable. They could not provide much spiritual nourishment for the truly dedicated, and monasticism stepped in to fill the need. At the same time, Augustine had an intense private devotional life, which he shared with others in his writings but practiced on his own, away from the gaze of even his closest friends and associates.

One of the best sources for our knowledge of Augustine's devotional

---

[23] *Confessiones* 9.7.15.
[24] *Confessiones* 10.33.50.
[25] *Confessiones* 10.33.50.

life is his *Confessions*. Much more than just an account of his spiritual jour-ney from unbelief to faith, the *Confessions* are a devotional work in their own right. They are a recollection of the past whose primary intention was not to impart autobiographical information but to reveal the nature of Au-gustine's relationship with God. Remembrance of things past and regret for failures and missed opportunities were certainly a part of that, but his main concern was with the way those things impinged on the present and affected his daily walk with Christ.

This is clear from the very beginning, where the first thing Augustine does is praise God for his greatness. There can be no true devotion if the one who receives it is not properly recognized and honored. To pray to God without knowing who he is would be meaningless; how would we know whether he merits our prayers or not? Augustine therefore begins where we must all start, with a confession of who God is and what he is like: "Great are you, O Lord, and greatly to be praised; great is your power, and there is no end to your wisdom."[26] We cannot understand God in his infinity, but we can at least say that he is "great," meaning that he is above everything else that exists or that we can conceive in our minds. To know God is to put him first in our lives and to recognize that he is in control of everything that happens to us. He is not just the supreme being, an abstract concept that undergirds the universe, but our Lord, a person with whom we have a relationship and to whom we are subject. The devotion we offer to him must therefore correspond to who he is and what his connection with us is if it is to have any value.

Furthermore, God is not just an object of our admiration; he is a being who is active in our lives, and in a way that is beneficial to us. That is why Augustine mentions God's power and wisdom. His power is the principle on which he acts, and his wisdom governs the way it is applied. It is per-fectly possible for someone with power to use it unwisely; the history of the Roman Empire provides many examples of that. But God's actions, even when they are hard for us to understand or appreciate, are governed by his infinite wisdom. Even if he takes us through the valley of the shadow of death, he does so for our benefit and blessing. This principle is easy to agree with when it does not touch us personally, but for those being put through the severe trials that can afflict us in this life, it can be very hard to believe that the benign wisdom of God is in control of events.

---

[26] *Confessiones* 1.1.1.

Augustine's second principle, also enunciated at the beginning of his *Confessions*, is that those who seek God will find him. As Christians we are used to hearing this, and familiarity has blunted the wonder that Augustine felt when he first contemplated it. Why should God condescend to man in this way? How could the infinite ruler of the universe enter his finite creation without ceasing to be himself? Augustine grew up in a world where the gods were conceptualized as personifications of natural forces like thunder and lightning. Intellectual people had long understood that such perceptions were inadequate and had replaced them with abstract ideas of the divine, but they had no concept of a personal relationship with them. The reason for that is simple. You cannot talk to "goodness" or "mind," even if there is something in us that makes us able to conceive of them.

In sharp contrast to this, not only did Augustine deem it possible to have a personal relationship with God; he also knew that although we cannot go up to him, he can (and does) come down to us. The eternal, all-powerful, and omnipresent God has made his dwelling in the hearts of his faithful people, hard though that is to believe and impossible to define. But although God's presence passes human understanding, it cannot be denied by those who have heard his voice and felt his power at work in their lives. The Christian life is an experience to be lived, not an idea to be analyzed, and only when we realize that can we hope to make sense of it. Christians know a God who is beyond our understanding but is both the source of our being and the one who has saved us from the consequences of our own folly. As Augustine expressed it:

> I will love you, O Lord, and thank you, and confess to your holy name, because you have put away my wicked and nefarious acts. I attribute to your grace and to your mercy the fact that you have melted my sin as if it were ice. I also attribute to your grace whatever evil I have not committed.[27]

God's relationship to us is one of guidance and protection. What sins might we commit if he were not watching over us! How often are we prevented from doing what comes naturally to us by circumstances beyond our control! Augustine knew well how God would unexpectedly intervene in his life in order to forestall the evil intentions of his own will. His words

---

[27] *Confessiones* 2.7.15.

resonate still, because all Christians experience this feeling, even if we often do not recognize it until afterward. Our innate wickedness is not taken away, but it is subdued and prevented from fulfilling its purposes by the intervening grace and mercy of God. For this Augustine was supremely grateful, and his prayers were full of thanksgiving for this wonderful and undeserved gift from on high.

But although Augustine acknowledged God's blessing and thanked him for it, he was not content to let things lie there. He wanted something more—he wanted to be united with God in eternity. His devotion was not only an expression of thanksgiving but also a longing for something that was both more than what he already had and qualitatively different from it: "I long for you, O righteousness and innocence . . . with you there is perfect rest and life unchanging. The man who enters into you enters into the joy of his Lord and will have no fear."[28]

Later on in the same book, he expressed this in terms derived from the words of the apostle Paul: "Let me know you, O you who know me; let me know you even as I am known [by you]."[29] As a Christian Augustine was brought face-to-face with the reality of his unequal relationship with God. God knew him and everything about him, but Augustine did not—and in this life could not—know God in the way he was known by him. More seriously still, Augustine imagined that he could hide things from God just as God concealed things from him! It was for this reason that confession formed such a central part of his prayers. He knew in his heart that there was much that he did not understand and that because of his ignorance he was always liable to fall into sin. Confession was therefore the ultimate form of self-knowledge that a believer could obtain in this life. Moreover, true confession was not to be confined to the private relationship between the individual and God. The sins of the believer affect those with whom he is in fellowship. Confession therefore has a public dimension, one in which all Christians share.

> The fruit of my confessions, not of what I was but of what I am, is that I may confess not just to you, in a secret joy with trembling and a secret sorrow with hope, but in the ears of the believing children of men also, for they are partakers of my joy, sharers in my mortality, my fellow-citizens

---

28 *Confessiones* 2.10.18.
29 *Confessiones* 10.1.1. The allusion is to 1 Cor. 13:12.

and companions on my pilgrimage, those who have gone before, those who will come after and those who are comrades on my way.[30]

Whether Augustine ever stood up in church and confessed his sins to the congregation, we do not know, and it seems unlikely that he did. But he did not hesitate to record them for posterity, making it clear that he saw this as an essential part of his devotional life. If he was to be a model for others, as a bishop was called to be, then he had to be as honest with his readers as he was in the presence of God. If he had not been transparent in this way, his credibility would have suffered and his example would have been less compelling. Here there is a delicate balance that Augustine knew he had to maintain. Honesty was important, but he had to share his experiences with his people in a way that did not lose their respect. By addressing his confessions to God and not to them, he was able to achieve this, because the God whom he adored was a God of grace, mercy, and forgiveness. To confess to him was not simply to recount a tale of sin but to exalt the remedy for it at the same time. The reader is made aware of Augustine's imperfections, but he comes away even more aware of the power of God to heal and redeem the broken sinner. It is this that Augustine was anxious to get across, and by revealing his inner secrets in the way he did, he made a lasting contribution to the devotional literature of the church.

Augustine's Family Life and Personal Values

What mattered to Augustine as a human being? Here again, he gives us an insight into his life that is rare in antiquity and unprecedented in its depth and scope. In the New Testament we read relatively little about the background and social life of the apostles and know next to nothing about how they related to the wider world. We know that Paul was a Roman citizen, but we have no idea what that really meant to him. It was a useful way of escaping persecution from local officials, and it is largely in that context that it is mentioned in Acts. But apart from general exhortations to respect the authorities (which would apply to everyone), there is little sign that he had any sense of his civic duty or of anything that might be described as Roman patriotism.[31] His family remains almost completely hidden from our eyes, and apart from a reference to his "kinsmen" in Romans 16:7, we

---

[30] *Confessiones* 10.4.6.
[31] See Acts 16:21, 37–38; 25:8–11.

know nothing about it. We are better informed about Jesus and his mother, but even there we know very little, other than that Mary seems to have followed him around to some extent. He regarded his disciples as friends, but only if they did what he told them, and apart from the somewhat mysterious references to the "beloved disciple" in John's Gospel, we know almost nothing about his relationships with them. Mary, Martha, and Lazarus were close to him, but again, our insight into their friendship is limited.

It is very different with Augustine. He tells us quite a bit about his family, and especially about his mother, whose saintly behavior toward him he constantly extols. He says much less about his father, who did not become a Christian until shortly before he died. Although psychologists have made great play of this, we should not be too surprised. Boys often have fairly distant (and often hostile) relationships with their fathers, so Augustine's rather neutral attitude toward his father is perhaps more positive than we might think. Certainly his love for his own son, Adeodatus, was deep and unfeigned, and it seems to have been reciprocated, though we have to take Augustine's word for that. On the other hand, he says virtually nothing about his siblings, and we must conclude that they played a relatively small part in his life. As far as we know, they remained in Thagaste and probably had little idea of what their brother was doing, either in Carthage when he was a young man or in Hippo.

What does come across very strongly, though, is his close attachment to his friends. Some of these he retained from boyhood, some were fellow students he met in Carthage, and some were people whom he came across in Italy or in later life. They were not very numerous, but his links with them went deep and seem to have shaped him as a person more than anything else in this world. Toward women, his attitude was respectful but fairly distant, as would have been expected in ancient society. However, he was faithful to his concubine, which was unusual for someone of his background, and he loved her deeply. In a different social milieu he would have happily married her, but for reasons that we shall see, that was not to be.

Beyond the private world of his family and friends, we know relatively little about how he engaged with the wider society of his time. He was a professor of rhetoric, and as such he had to deal with students, but his contacts with them were more like the formal distance typical of German or American universities than the more familiar approach that is the norm in Britain and Commonwealth countries. As long as his students paid their fees, he was content to watch them come and go without getting too close to them! We have no idea how he behaved as a citizen or whether he had any real associations with the secular government and its officials. Until the fall of Rome in 410 his patriotism seems to have lain dormant, and even when he wept over the city's fate, he could quite easily distance himself (and the church) from it. He was certainly no court chaplain!

Augustine showed the customary filial respect due to his parents and teachers, but too much should not be read into this. It was expected of everyone in antiquity, and if he had not done so, it would have been held against him. Traditional Roman religion, like its Chinese equivalent, was an ancestor cult, and failure to show proper respect to one's elders was almost blasphemous. Christians could not escape the pull of this tradition, even if they rejected its values. What is really surprising is that Augustine was as negative toward his elders as he occasionally was, especially when he rebuked them for administering discipline to their young charges that they were not prepared to apply to themselves.[32] Thus we see that although he observed the conventions of his time, he was actually quite critical of the education he received and longed to see it reformed along Christian lines, not only in its content but in the way it was imparted. In this he was well ahead of his time, and it is fair to say that it is only recently that his approach has found a genuine echo in the progressive and child-friendly educational methods now widely adopted in schools.

When he was fifteen, Augustine was forced by straitened family circumstances to spend a year at home, and it is from that time of his adolescence that we get a glimpse of his family life. His father comes across as a typical male, proud of his son's growing masculinity and indifferent to any moral or religious considerations.[33] His mother, however, was afraid that he might start sleeping with married women, and warned him against that.[34] He himself hung out with boys his age, who competed with each other in boasting of their nefarious exploits. Augustine is honest enough to tell us that he bragged well beyond anything he actually did, and the probability is that the other boys did the same.

Where Augustine was different from his companions was in the ambitions his parents had for him. His father wanted him to get a good education, and so did his mother, though for different reasons. As Augustine saw

---

[32] *Confessiones* 1.9.15.
[33] *Confessiones* 2.3.6.
[34] *Confessiones* 2.3.7.

it, his father wanted him to have a successful career, whereas his mother hoped that a good education would bring him closer to God. There is no way of knowing how true this assessment was, but his father's motives strike us as more probable than his mother's, which seem to reflect the glow of hindsight to some extent.[35] Whatever the truth of the matter, they both agreed that he should not marry, as most of his friends were probably doing (or getting ready to do) at that time, but pursue his studies instead. That was the decisive break with youth and his home. Augustine occasionally went back to Thagaste in later life, but he was never again to be part of the community in the way he had been before.

Augustine's father died shortly after Augustine left home to pursue his studies, and after that his main contact with his family was through his mother, Monica. She had other children, but it seems from the way she behaved that Augustine was her favorite—or at least the one she felt she had to keep a particularly close eye on. She was desperate to see him converted, but wiser heads warned her to leave him alone. She consulted a certain bishop, who told her to be content to pray for his conversion and assured her that it was not possible that a son over whom such tears had been shed would perish in eternity.[36]

It was wise advice. Although Augustine held up his mother as a saint after she died, there is little doubt that while she was still alive she must have been more of a nuisance to him than anything else. This comes across clearly when he decided to go to Rome to seek his fortune. Monica did not want him to leave Carthage and went there in a vain effort to stop him. So insistent did she become, and so hard was it for Augustine to deal with her, that he lied to her and sneaked away in the night![37] But Monica was not to be so easily put off. She found a ship, sailed to Italy in pursuit of her son, and followed him all the way to Milan—an arduous journey for a woman in middle age.

Augustine must have been impressed by her determination; at least, from this time onward, his tone toward her changed quite remarkably. He tells us that on the sea voyage she comforted the sailors during a severe storm, so convinced was she that God would not let her die until she had seen her son turn to Christ.[38] There is a distinct note of pride in his voice

---

[35] *Confessiones* 2.3.8.
[36] *Confessiones* 3.12.21.
[37] *Confessiones* 5.8.14–15.
[38] *Confessiones* 6.1.1.

here, not that she was following him but that she showed herself capable of rising above her status and assuming the leadership role of a man when trouble struck. She was obviously not just a nagging mother but a powerful personality in her own right, and Augustine was both forced and pleased to acknowledge that.

Monica was also obedient to the church authorities, at least if Augustine's testimony is to be believed. When she got to Milan, she brought offerings to the shrines of the martyrs, as she had always done in Africa; but when she learned that Bishop Ambrose forbade the practice, she immediately abandoned it and never questioned his decision.[39] The incident shows that her own faith was syncretistic, at least to some extent, because she followed practices that had carried over from paganism. Still, nobody in North Africa seems to have objected to this, which tells us something about the state of the church in that province and helps to explain why Donatism had such an appeal there.

After Augustine's conversion Monica did her best to sort his life out. The concubine was dismissed, a reasonably suitable marriage partner was found, and his plan to form a commune with his friends was quickly scrapped.[40] But Monica's influence over her son extended only so far, and her designs for him never came to fruition. In the end, Augustine abandoned all thought of marriage and chose the celibate life, though the communal aspect that he so cherished had to be worked out in the context of his episcopal responsibilities at Hippo and did not become a monastic foundation in the usual sense. Much of the ninth book of the *Confessions* is a paean of praise to his mother and an account of her holy death at Ostia, as the family was planning to return to Carthage.[41] There is no doubt that Augustine felt his loss deeply, but his account of her virtues must be understood in the context of the time. Pious funeral orations were the order of the day, and for Augustine to have done anything else would have dishonored both his mother and himself. This does not mean that what he had to say was untrue, but neither can it be taken at face value, without any qualification. The evidence we have forces us to conclude that however much he praised his mother after her death, Augustine did not always

---

[39] *Confessiones* 6.2.2.
[40] *Confessiones* 6.13.23–6.14.24. Augustine's bride to be was socially acceptable, but still too young to marry.
[41] *Confessiones* 9.8.17–9.13.37. The family included Augustine's son, Adeodatus, who had accompanied his father to Italy.

follow her advice when she was alive—their relationship was more complicated than that.

It was a different matter with his friends, and it was with them that Augustine had his deepest and most satisfying relationships. The first one he writes about is that childhood companion from Thagaste whom he persuaded to join him in his rebellion against Christianity but who was baptized on his deathbed—an incident that virtually destroyed their friendship.[42] We are not told the man's name, perhaps because Augustine was ashamed of his own behavior. This might explain why we do not know the name of his concubine either, though they lived together for more than fifteen years and she was the mother of his son. It seems that Augustine named only those whose relationship to him was positive and acceptable to God, even if he was the one largely responsible for the problems that his relationships caused.

Although his friendship with this unnamed man ended in tears, it left a strong impression on Augustine, who used the man's death as an occasion to extol the consolation of friends who helped him through his grief, even though their influence kept him far away from God.

> There were other things [than the love of God] that took hold of my mind. To talk and joke with them, to exchange kindnesses, to read good books together, to fool around and to be serious together, to disagree at times without getting upset, as one would do with oneself . . . sometimes teaching, sometimes being taught, longing for them when they were away and rejoicing when they returned. These and other things like them, flowing from the hearts of those who loved and were loved in return . . . were so much fuel to melt our souls together, and out of many to make but one.[43]

This picture of love freely given and freely received speaks volumes about what made Augustine tick. When he wrote about the Trinity, he perceived it as a community of love, and love was for him the foundation, if not the very essence, of the Christian life. Indeed, as he went on to say in the very next paragraph, it is only in the love of God that we have a truly adequate expression of what love is. The love of friends is bound to come to grief because sooner or later friends must part, and their love does not extend beyond their chosen circle. The love of God, by contrast, is more inclusive and more enduring: "Blessed is the man who loves you, O God, and

---

[42] The man recovered, but only briefly. The fever returned and he died.
[43] *Confessiones* 4.8.13.

who loves his friend in you, and his enemy for your sake. It is only the one who loves everyone in him who can never be lost who never loses anyone."[44]

Nevertheless, there can be no doubt that Augustine rejoiced in particular friendships, which he describes at some length in his *Confessions*. Perhaps closest of all to him was Alypius, a young man from the nobility of Thagaste who had been one of Augustine's students in Carthage.[45] Alypius was a man who enjoyed raucous entertainment, of which there was no shortage in either Carthage or Rome. Augustine was credited with confronting him about this and even with rescuing him from some of his more extreme passions, though as he pointed out, this was more by accident than by design. Augustine deplored the lasciviousness of some of the games staged at Carthage, and Alypius took it as a rebuke to him personally, though that was not Augustine's intention.[46] It was Augustine's beneficial effect on Alypius that encouraged the latter's father to allow him to study with Augustine, and their friendship blossomed out of that. Alypius went to Rome to study law even before Augustine did, and the two men were reunited there. Augustine later followed Alypius to Milan, and the two men were converted together, so close had they grown to one another.[47]

That did not mean that they were entirely alike, however. Augustine was deeply attached to life with his concubine and could not imagine permanent celibacy. But Alypius was different. After a few youthful indiscretions, he embraced celibacy almost as if it came natural to him, much to Augustine's amazement. Augustine even tells us that it was Alypius who converted him to the ideal of celibacy, pointing out that the two men could not live together as friends if one or both of them were married.[48] The incompatibility between marriage and the communion of friends was clearly demonstrated when Augustine and others put forward a plan for sharing their lives together. Everything seemed to be arranged for it to happen, but, he wrote, "When we began to ask whether the wives that some of us had already (and that others hoped to have) would tolerate this, our beautifully formed plan fell apart in our hands and was completely destroyed and cast aside."[49]

It is dangerously easy for modern minds to read all kinds of things into a statement like this, but we must be very careful. There was never any

---

[44] *Confessiones* 4.9.14.
[45] *Confessiones* 6.7.11.
[46] *Confessiones* 6.7.12.
[47] *Confessiones* 8.8.19.
[48] *Confessiones* 6.12.21–22.
[49] *Confessiones* 6.14.24.

suggestion that either of them was homosexual—certainly not Augustine, given his obvious preference! But even Alypius, though he had no particular desire to marry, was intrigued by the idea because it was so important to his friend and he wanted to find out why! He seems to have thought that if he had a wife (or at least a concubine), he would understand Augustine better and feel closer to him. Augustine, on the other hand, saw in Alypius the realization of a heroic ideal that he came to want for himself. What we see here is the natural result of a friendship—each party wanting what is alien to himself but natural (or apparently natural) to the other. In this case, as we know, Alypius would gain the upper hand in the end, but the two men never lived together. The ideal of celibacy that they both embraced was an ideal of dedication to God, not to sensual pleasure, and it must be understood in that light.

Another friend of whom Augustine speaks highly was Nebridius, a native of the Carthage region who went to Milan in order to study under Augustine.[50] He did not convert to Christianity at the same time as Augustine and Alypius did, but he did not hold out for long. As Augustine tells it, Nebridius was more intellectual than Alypius and accepted the truth of the Christian faith some time before he was willing to be baptized.[51] But once he took the plunge, his dedication to Christ was complete and unflagging. He returned to Africa, where he won his entire family over to his new faith, but he died soon afterward. This did not disturb Augustine unduly, however, since the two men had bonded in this life, and that bond, sealed as it was in Christ, would never be broken.

> Nebridius, my sweet friend, dwells now in Abraham's bosom . . . for what other place could there be for such a soul? He lives in the place which he used to ask me a lot about—me, an inexperienced and weak man! He no longer puts his ear to my mouth, but his spiritual mouth to your fountain, where he drinks as much as he wants to. . . . Nor do I believe that he is so drunk with it as to have forgotten me.[52]

Another friend of Augustine's followed a different path. This was Verecundus, who owned a country house outside Milan at a place called Cassiciacum, where Augustine went to reflect on his new-found faith.[53]

---

[50] *Confessiones* 6.10.17.
[51] *Confessiones* 9.3.6.
[52] *Confessiones* 9.3.6.
[53] *Confessiones* 9.3.5.

Verecundus was married, which forced him to work out his salvation in a different context. It is noteworthy that Augustine could describe their friendship as so strong that his own conversion did not diminish it, even though Verecundus was not yet ready to follow. We are left to infer that eventually he did, but the fact that Augustine never mentions it directly shows that it was relatively unimportant for him. What mattered was their friendship, which, in Augustine's mind, was deep enough to ensure that in the end Verecundus would also be saved.

Augustine could even develop a kind of passion for people he had never met. This was the case with Hierius, an orator whose style he greatly admired and to whom he dedicated some of his early writings.[54] But by the time he came to write his *Confessions*, Augustine had long recognized the vanity of his affection for this man, a judgment confirmed by a posterity that has never heard of him. His attraction to Hierius was hardly personal; he tells us himself that it was largely influenced by the reputation that Hierius had and that Augustine coveted for himself. Yet the extravagance of Augustine's language should serve as a warning to us not to read too much into his rhetoric:

> I loved the man because of the fame of his learning, for which he was renowned. . . . He pleased me all the more in that he pleased others, who extolled him in that, being a native of Syria who had learned his oratorical skills in Greek, he later became a wonderful Latin speaker. . . . Such a man is loved when his commender is thought to be praising him with an unfeigned heart.[55]

The context makes it clear what Augustine meant. Modern people are usually less inclined to such flights of rhetoric, but we live in a more prosaic age. Augustine's readers would have recognized themselves in statements like these and thought nothing of them, and we must remember to be similarly restrained in our assessment.

Augustine's Choice of Lifestyle

Few things are more puzzling to the modern reader than Augustine's choice of a celibate lifestyle. We can understand how and why he lived the way he did before his conversion. Taking a concubine and living a relatively free

---

[54] *Confessiones* 4.14.21–23.
[55] *Confessiones* 4.14.21.

and easy life in a university setting is not in itself surprising, even if not many people now would start as young as he did—at only sixteen or so! Our problems in trying to understand him begin with what happened to that relationship after his conversion.

Today, if a man in Augustine's circumstances becomes a Christian, he will probably be advised to put matters right by marrying his mistress and legitimizing his son. If she decides to leave him voluntarily, that will be understood, though perhaps regretted. But to suggest that such a man should put away the woman with whom he has been living because the relationship was wrong from the start strikes us as un-Christian and cruel. Why should a household be deliberately broken up just because one member has become a believer? In particular, why should a boy be deprived of his mother because his father has come to faith? This not only sounds odd to us—it sounds hypocritical as well. Are we not supposed to love one another and not reject those with whom we have chosen to share our lives, even if they do not follow us down the pathway of conversion?

It is here more clearly than anywhere else that we feel the great gulf fixed between our world and that of Augustine. What to us seems wrong, to him seemed inevitable and therefore right. This does not mean that it did not cause him great pain. As he recounted it: "When my mistress was torn from my side as an impediment to my marriage, my heart, which clung to her, was torn, wounded and bleeding. She went back to Africa, vowing to you [O Lord] never to know another man and leaving me with my natural son by her."[56]

To hear Augustine tell it, we would think that he was forced to give up his mistress in order to prepare for marriage. But although this may have been formally true, it was not the whole story. Even before this happened, Augustine was contemplating a life of celibacy rooted in his desire to pursue wisdom. There was nothing particularly Christian about this. Plato and the philosophers had advocated celibacy because they thought it necessary to rise above the limitations of carnal desire to attain true knowledge and happiness. Jesus and Paul may have been celibate, but not for that reason, and there was no compulsion on Christians to follow their example. Augustine even argued to himself that "many men who are great and worthy of imitation have applied themselves to the study of wisdom in the married state."[57]

---

[56] *Confessiones* 6.15.25.
[57] *Confessiones* 6.11.19.

Yet by the time he came to write his *Confessions*, Augustine had convinced himself that celibacy was the will of God for him, and probably also for most who were serious about their faith. The drift of his thinking along these lines is unmistakable:

> While I talked about these things [i.e., marriage and celibacy] and these winds veered around and tossed my heart to and fro, the time went on, but I was slow to turn to the Lord. . . . I thought I would be too unhappy if I were deprived of the embrace of a woman, and I never thought of your merciful medicine as a cure for that weakness, since I had never tried it. As for continence, I imagined that I could control it (though I did not find it in me), because I was so foolish as not to know that nobody can be continent unless you give them that gift, and that you would give it if with sincere pleas I should knock on your ears and cast my care upon you in faith.[58]

Here again it seems that we are dealing with a vision from hindsight. Augustine was not yet a Christian when he debated about celibacy, and his references to God in the above account must be understood accordingly. It is true that he had joined catechetical classes in preparation for baptism, but that in itself was no bar to marriage. On the contrary, his mother was very clear where she thought her son's interests lay.

> Active efforts were made to get me a wife. I wooed, I was engaged. My mother took the greatest pains in this, so that once I was married the saving grace of baptism might cleanse me. She rejoiced that I was every day being prepared for this, and remarked that her desires and your promises were both being fulfilled in my faith.[59]

For the saintly Monica at least, Augustine's future path was clear, but his concubine stood in the way of her plans. Why did she not simply advise them to regularize their union in marriage?

Here we enter a world that is strange to people in the developed world today, but one that will sound familiar to many in and from developing countries. Marriage in ancient times, especially among Romans, was not a love affair but a business transaction. People married for social advantage but seldom for love, which was regarded as a dangerous and destabilizing

---

[58] *Confessiones* 6.11.20.
[59] *Confessiones* 6.13.23.

force. It was one thing to build a life on a dowry but quite another to substitute feelings in its place—emotions do not put bread on the table. Augustine's relationship with his concubine had been a love match, and a very successful one at that. But his concubine had no money and no social standing. This was not good enough for a son of the local gentry, who would be expected to play a major part in the social and political life of Thagaste. His father had been impoverished by the expectations put on him, and Augustine needed to refill the family coffers if he was going to take up his inheritance. Hence the need for a proper wife—and the dowry she would bring to the marriage.

It is only when we realize these things that we can begin to understand why Augustine reacted to marriage in the way he did. It really was a worldly entanglement as far as he was concerned. He had nothing against the prospective bride, who was still two years underage—which means that she was only ten at the time and more than twenty years younger than he was. For him to have married such a "woman" would surely have been deeply unfair to her. That is not to say that there were not many such marriages in the ancient world. It is even possible that Joseph and Mary were that far apart in age—certainly, it is likely that Joseph was several years older than Mary. But it is not difficult to see why Augustine was less than happy with the arrangement; when he says that "he wooed," it was not the girl whom he approached but her parents. Here again we must try to appreciate that he was saying and doing what was expected in the context of his own time, and not impose modern values (and alien social conditions) onto his mind.

There is also Augustine's belief that his strong sexual drive was a worldly distraction from the love of God. As he put it: "I did not like the fact that I was living a worldly life. My desires for honor and wealth had subsided . . . but I was still in the grip of love for women."[60]

It was not the love of a particular woman that bothered him, but a love for women in general. He knew that there was nothing wrong with marriage, but that was not his problem. The marriage on offer to him would almost certainly have been loveless, or at least not the companionly affair that a marriage between equals ought to be. He could hardly have talked seriously to a child-wife, and the social responsibilities that such a bond would create were not to his liking. He felt called to other things, and it was only his strong sexual drive that held him back. In those circumstances, his

---

[60] *Confessiones* 8.1.2.

struggle to achieve celibacy makes more sense; we can understand that for him it was necessary to renounce the married state without making that a rule for everyone. Like Paul, his circumstances were particular to him, but his calling from God was clear. Celibate he must become and celibate he must remain in order to do the work that God had prepared for him. The rest of his life and career would show just how wise a decision that would turn out to be.

But if Augustine wanted to remain single, he did not want to live alone. We have already seen that his desire was to create a spiritual community in which friends could live together in harmony. Today we know such communities as monasteries, but these were virtually nonexistent in his lifetime. Monks were men who lived alone in the desert—the people we would now call "hermits." The idea that they might band together and live in community was still very new. Experiments had been tried in the East, but it would be some time before Benedict of Nursia would introduce monasticism as we now think of it into the Western church. In this respect, Augustine was a pioneer.

As far as we know, he never thought of going off into the desert to live, though he placed a high value on the contemplative life. Once he became bishop of Hippo, that kind of life was no longer a practical option. A bishop at that time was really the equivalent of the head pastor of a megachurch today, and the calls on his time were innumerable. It was vitally important that he should have a good staff around him, but Augustine did not see this in terms of running a small business with employees and contracts. On the contrary, his staff was his community—a group of dedicated, like-minded men who shared his devotional life and set an example to others of how Christians should live.

This seems strange to us now, but only because we no longer experience it. If we look honestly at the average pastor and his church today, we see the pressure placed on one man who is expected to carry out any number of tasks, plus bring up a family. Balancing the demands of home and work are particularly hard when he has to work from home, as most pastors do. It is a twenty-four-hour, seven-days-a-week job in which his wife and children are involved, whether they want to be or not. The strains that this can place on families are well known, but how many people today have the radical honesty of Augustine, who saw the problems and was determined to avoid them for the sake of his ministry? Rightly or wrongly, we are more likely to criticize him for his decision and regard it as the wrong one. Perhaps it is for many people—Augustine would not have denied that. But for him, it was the right thing to do, and at great personal cost to himself (and, it must be admitted, to others as well) he made the sacrifice that he believed God was asking of him. Was it worth it? We cannot answer this question for him, but we can at least be fairly certain that we would not now be reading his works if he had chosen the path that his mother had determined for him.

The Life of Faith

For Augustine, as for the apostle Paul, to live was Christ and to die was to gain more of him.[61] This was the basic starting point from which everything else flowed logically and, as Augustine would have seen it, inevitably. As Paul said, "He who began a good work in you will carry it on to completion until the day of Christ Jesus."[62] Everything that Augustine had to say about the Christian life can be understood as an explanation of the deeper implications of this.

Did Augustine believe in justification by faith alone as Martin Luther proclaimed it? Was he a kind of Protestant more than a millennium before that form of Christianity came into being? The answer to such a question must be no. We cannot say that Augustine would have agreed with Luther without qualification, even if Luther believed that he was following in Augustine's footsteps. The reason for this is not that their spiritual experience was fundamentally different but that it was expressed in different ways. Augustine could not have known that Luther would one day come along and use his theology to proclaim the doctrine of justification by faith alone, but neither did he have any idea that Luther's doctrine would be rejected by his opponents. The whole framework of the Reformation discussion was unknown to him, and it is anachronistic to force his thoughts into a mold of which he had no knowledge.

But if it is anachronistic to call Augustine a Protestant, he did stress the importance of faith, he had a living relationship with God, and he did not trust in his own works for salvation. He was a sinner saved by grace and he knew it. Luther and his fellow Reformers recognized this in him and claimed him as their forebear, even if they went on to adapt his approach

---

61 Phil. 1:21.
62 Phil. 1:6.

to meet the controversies of a later time. To understand the nature of Augustine's later impact, let us begin at the beginning.

First of all, there is the question of what is meant by *faith*. For Augustine this certainly included belief in the sense of intellectual assent to an orthodox creed, and there was never any question of his allowing heretics to claim that they belonged to the church or had any place in it. But doctrinal orthodoxy for him was the *result* of faith, not its foundation. It was because he had met Christ and knew what he was like that Augustine's confession was that of the church, which existed to proclaim the good news of salvation in and through Christ. Augustine was not persuaded to become a Christian by intellectual arguments in favor of creation or the divine inspiration of Scripture, but neither was he shaken by challenges to such beliefs. He knew that they were true because they had been taught by the God whom he had met, and so he felt no need to defend them in the court of public opinion. To put it another way, Augustine did not engage in what we would call apologetics. Instead, he proclaimed the faith that he had received in Scripture and sought to explain how it could be understood in the context of human life. He did not try to defend it as true—he accepted that already—but showed how its truth should be applied to the circumstances in which we are called to live.

Faith for Augustine included intellectual belief but went beyond it. For him, it meant union with Christ in a new life that could be understood only in the power of the Holy Spirit. Union with Christ was union with him as both God and man, not because a believer could become God in some way, but because his relationship to Christ was personal, and the person of the Son was divine. But the divine Son had become a man, taking on our nature, precisely in order to make it possible for us to relate to him. In other words, we are united to the *person* of the Son of God in his human *nature*, which we share with him, but not in his divine nature, of which we have no direct knowledge or experience. Everything that is human about Christ he shares with us as the second person of the Trinity, but in the secret recesses of his divine nature he remains, along with the Father and the Holy Spirit, incomprehensible to mortal minds. As Augustine expressed it: "This is the way. Walk in humility so that you may come to eternity. Christ as God is the country to which we are going; Christ as man is the way by which we get there."[63]

---

[63] *Sermones* 123.3.

This led naturally to the idea of the imitation of Christ, with which modern people are familiar, thanks to the famous devotional book by Thomas à Kempis (d. 1471), and which is also a New Testament concept.[64] It therefore comes as a surprise to discover that Augustine did not empha- size a theme that seems to have fit his way of thinking perfectly. It is hard to say why this was so, but perhaps his pre-Christian life offers us a clue. When describing his preconversion attitude toward Jesus, Augustine had this to say:

> I saw in our Lord Jesus Christ nothing more than a man of excellent wis- dom, which nobody else could equal. I thought his wonderful virgin birth was an example of how he despised temporal things in order to gain im- mortality for us, and such divine care for us gave him great authority as a teacher. But the mystery of the Word made flesh I had not begun to guess. . . . I thought that he excelled others, not because he was the per- sonal embodiment of the Truth, but because of the great excellence of his human character and his more perfect participation in wisdom.[65]

In other words, the pre-Christian Augustine saw Jesus as an extraor- dinarily gifted man who had achieved a level of wisdom that nobody had managed to equal, but which remained theoretically attainable by anyone with the strength and determination to do so. This view chimed in very well with that of the Platonists, who believed that a more-than-human sta- tus could be reached by a philosopher who devoted enough of his time to contemplation. According to Augustine, the great Neoplatonist Porphyry, who was a dedicated opponent of Christianity, actually believed that about Jesus.[66] Certainly there are many intellectual non-Christians today who hold a similar view. They are prepared to accept what they regard as the great moral teachings of Jesus but regard any claim to divinity as a myth imposed on the facts by his disciples, whether they were consciously in- tending to deceive the public or not.

Seen in this light, promoting the "imitation of Christ" becomes prob- lematic for a Christian theologian because of the danger of suggesting that such imitation was theoretically possible. The apostle Paul's words on the subject may even have encouraged this when he said, "Be imitators of *me*,

---

64 1 Cor. 11:1. See also Eph. 5:1–2.
65 *Confessiones* 7.14.25.
66 *De civitate Dei* 10.27–29.

as I am of Christ."[67] Since Paul made no claim to be divine, imitating him was obviously a real possibility for any well-disposed human being. And since he claimed to offer a model of how to imitate Christ, it is easy to see how the philosophical idea of human self-improvement could enter in by the back door, as it were.

The likelihood that Christians would fall into this kind of misunderstanding was made more acute by the teaching of Pelagius, who (according to Augustine) said just that. We must obviously be careful about accepting Augustine's interpretation of Pelagius at face value since he so strongly opposed Pelagianism and may have distorted what Pelagius actually taught. But there seems to be no reason to doubt that for Pelagius, the gospel was the creed by which "we can learn how we ought to live in theory, but not that we must also be assisted by his grace in order to lead good lives in practice."[68]

Where Augustine differed from Pelagius—and where those in the Augustinian tradition have always dissented from different forms of Pelagianism that have appeared over the years—was in his understanding of the cross of Christ. For Pelagius, the death of Jesus was a sacrifice to be imitated—as his life was to be imitated—the natural culmination of an asceticism that renounces this world, takes up the cross, and follows him. But Augustine did not interpret the crucifixion of Christ in that way. What the Son of God did on the cross was something no ordinary human being could ever do. He took our sins upon himself, not in order to set us an example that we should imitate but in order to remove from us the burden of sin and death that prevents us from enjoying fellowship with him and eternal life. We must be crucified with Christ, not strengthened by his example, so that, born again by the power of his Holy Spirit, we can live in the way he wants us to. That is what the "imitation" of Christ amounts to. It is what Paul taught and what we must apply to ourselves with the help of God's grace at work in us.

Augustine did not arrive at this understanding of faith overnight. He inherited a tradition of thought that understood the Christian life as a renewal of something that had been lost, obscured, or corrupted by the fall of Adam. Adam had been created "in the image and likeness of God," but that had been subtly misunderstood by most of the early fathers of the church. In He-

---

[67] 1 Cor. 11:1.
[68] *De natura et gratia* 40.47.

brew, the word for "image" (*tselem*) and the word for "likeness" (*demuth*) are virtually synonymous and could be used interchangeably, as they are in the New Testament.[69] But to the Greek mind, if two words were used to describe something, it must have been because they were different, and the theory emerged that at the fall, Adam lost his likeness to God but not the image.

As a result, salvation came to be understood as the restoration of the image of God in man to the likeness it had before the fall. According to this way of thinking, the image of God was something fixed in man's nature that distinguished him from the lower creation and was never removed, even after Adam's fall into sin.

> There must be in the rational or intellectual soul of man that image of the Creator which is immortally inserted into its immortality. . . . It is therefore called "immortal" because it never ceases to live with some kind of life, even when it is most miserable. Thus, although reason or intellect may by turns be dormant, small, or highly active in the human soul, the soul itself is never anything other than rational or intellectual.[70]

The likeness of God, on the other hand, is properly reserved for the Word that became flesh in Jesus Christ, though by relating to him the rest of the created order can share to some degree in the divine likeness: "The Likeness of God, through whom all things were made, is properly called the Likeness, because he is not like God because of some participation in the divine likeness, but is himself the principle of Likeness, in which those things that God has made through him are also alike."[71]

This innate likeness to God is fundamental, because without it the universe would lack coherence. If God is ultimate Being and Truth, then the things he has made must share in that Being and Truth to some degree, because if they do not, they would be a lie and would not even exist. Augustine makes this point quite forcefully:

> [Created] things can be said to be like the [original] One insofar as they have being, for it is to that degree that they are also true. But only the One is Likeness and Truth in itself. . . . Therefore, things are true insofar as they have being, and have being insofar as they are like the source of

---

[69] See, for example, James 3:9 where the word "likeness" occurs instead of the more usual "image," but clearly means the same thing.
[70] *De Trinitate* 14.4.6.
[71] *De Genesi liber imperfectus* 16.57.

all unity, which is the Form of all things that have being, the supreme Likeness of the Principle, and also Truth, for it is without any element of unlikeness [to the One].[72]

Working with this paradigm, we can see why the corruption of the likeness in man after his fall into sin was so disastrous. In principle he retained all the elements of the image in which he had been created, but he ceased to participate in the life of God because he was no longer like him in the way that he was meant to be. Within the created order, this was an anomaly that had to be put right, and that is what the Son of God, the form of the One, came to do in the incarnation of Jesus Christ.

There was (and is) however a difficulty with this model that the early church never properly faced or resolved. If Christ's work of redemption is tied to creation in this way, must it not be the case that the whole creation is redeemed? Did not the apostle Paul himself say: "As in Adam all die, so also in Christ shall all be made alive"?[73] The mission of Christ must therefore have been to begin the recapitulation of all things in him, which in practice meant the renewal of the entire created order—and by implication at least, the universal salvation of mankind.[74]

This did not necessarily exclude the operation of divine grace, and here it seems that Augustine and the Pelagians misunderstood each other. For a Pelagian like Julian of Eclanum, for example, the grace of God meant the divine work that brought nature to perfection. That in turn presupposed that when God made man in his image, that image was deliberately imperfect in the sense of not being fully formed, making its subsequent growth into what it was meant to be a natural process. In other words, what the Pelagians called "grace" was a natural development already inherent in the nature of creation and needing only divine action to bring it to fruition. Augustine recognized this and disagreed:

> You [Julian] say that it is the good nature of man that merits such a magnificent outpouring of grace. I would agree with this if you meant that it is because man is a rational creature that he merits this grace, because the grace of God through our Lord Jesus Christ is not bestowed on stones, trees, or beasts, but only on man who is the image of God. But I do not agree that man possesses a good will that acts apart from grace and even

---

[72] *De vera religione* 36.66. The "Form" here is to be understood as the Son in relation to the One (the Father).
[73] 1 Cor. 15:22.
[74] It was claimed that Acts 3:21 referred to this as "the restoration of all things."

sacrifices itself before receiving it, so as to give the impression that it was owed something in return. If that were the case, grace would no longer be grace because it would not be given gratuitously, but instead rendered as something that was owed [to the recipient].[75]

What Augustine is saying here is that grace is comprehensible only in the context of a relationship, which in turn is possible only between the Creator and those who have been made in his image. What Augustine does *not* mean is that something in the nature of man predisposes him to receiving this top-up grace of God, so that what God does for him is only to be expected in the normal course of events.

It was as he worked through the implications of Pelagianism that Augustine came to see that the traditional understanding of the image and likeness of God in man, along with the "restorationist" view of salvation that had been so popular until then, was incorrect. Redemption was not a return to the garden of Eden, but something else altogether. Adam and Eve were not created "imperfect" in the sense of being less than fully formed; their created nature neither gained nor lost anything by the fall, and when the Word became a man, it was in the "likeness of sinful flesh" that he did so.[76] The gospel was not a recipe for human self-improvement, even with the help of God, but the message of death and resurrection to a new life, following the Master who showed us the way and who has made it possible for us to share in his experience, not by imitation but by participation. In other words, it is not by doing what Christ did that we are saved, but by being united with him in his death so that it can be applied to us by the outworking of his grace.

The difference between Adam and the Christian is in effect the difference between the man who is given the freedom to save himself by his works and the one who is set free from the consequences of that.

Free will was given first, with the ability not to sin, but the last gift was the inability to sin. The first freedom was designed for obtaining merit; the last was concerned with receiving a reward. Because human nature sinned when it was given the power to sin, it is set free by a more abundant gift of grace, so that it may be brought to that condition of freedom in which it can no longer sin. The first immortality, which Adam lost by sinning, was the ability to avoid death; the last immortality will be the inability to die.[77]

---

[75] *Contra Iulianum* 4.3.15.
[76] Rom. 8:3.
[77] *De civitate Dei* 22.30.

For God to have restored sinful people to the state of Adam would have been pointless, because they would still have had the ability to sin and would have done so at the first opportunity, just as Adam did. Why go through all that again? Raising those who are saved to the state where they can no longer sin may seem like a deprivation of their freedom, but that is true only if they are perceived as autonomous beings who have been given something that in effect becomes part of their nature. Perhaps this can happen only by an infusion of grace, but the believer's dependence on Christ is not like a sick man's dependence on medicine. The sick person takes his medicine in order to be cured, and when that happens, he stops taking it because he no longer needs it. The Christian never gets to that state. To be united to Christ is more like being attached to a life-support machine (if we are to use a medical analogy) than like being prescribed a medicine. Christ makes it possible for the believer to live at all. The Christian is not "improved" in the Pelagian way but is allowed to thrive forever because he is attached to the source of his life, who is Christ. Words like *grace* and *faith* are used to describe this attachment—grace from the side of God and faith from the side of man. This is why we say that we have been saved by grace through faith, which is not our own doing, but the gift of God.[78]

With this we come back to the beginning of this section, where I asked whether Augustine believed in justification by faith alone. We recognized then that he did not use that terminology, which did not appear until a thousand years after his death and which he probably would not have understood. But when we examine what he did say and how it departed in some fundamental respects from the way of thinking that had governed most of the Christian world up to his time, we can see that his beliefs were not only compatible with the later doctrine of justification, but also foundational to it. What Augustine did was to shift the discussion from the realm of *nature* to the realm of *relationship*, which we might describe as *person*, *grace*, or *faith* according to the context.

Thanks to his engagement with the Pelagians, Augustine came to see that he had to reject any idea that human nature was improved, transformed, or fulfilled by divine activity, whether that activity was called "grace" or not. The image of God in man was not part of his "nature" in this sense, because while it was affected by the fall of Adam, it did not suffer any objective diminution of its powers. Insofar as it could be identified

---

[78] Eph. 2:8–9.

with the rational soul or mind of man, it remained unchanged. Had that not been the case, neither the incarnation of the Son nor the redemption of those who are saved could have taken place, because men and women would no longer have been properly human.

What the image of God in man really bears witness to is the fact that we are personal beings, created with a relationship to God that cannot be taken away from us even if we fall into sin. The negative side of this is that we are held guilty for the sin of Adam, not because we have sinned in the way that he did, but because we have inherited his sinfulness. Those who think that that is unjust need only reflect that if it were not so, we would not have inherited Adam's rationality either and would not now have any chance of being saved. Salvation is putting right something that has gone wrong, not creating something that was never there or adding something to a preexisting "nature" that makes it essentially different. The believer in heaven is the same person he or she was on earth, with the same capacities and the same identity. The sins that believers commit on earth will no longer be held against them, but neither will they disappear from memory entirely. As Augustine pictured the state of the blessed in heaven:

> Such is the power of knowledge—and it will be very great in the saints— that it will prevent not only their own past misery but also the eternal misery of the damned from disappearing from memory. Otherwise, if the saints were to lose the knowledge of their past misery, how would they "sing the mercies of the Lord for all eternity" as the psalm says?[79] Nothing will give more joy to the City [of God] than this song to the glory of the grace of Christ by whose blood we have been set free.[80]

What will change between this world and the next is that then we shall have a new nature, not the flesh and blood in which we live now, but a spiritual body adapted to the conditions of the heavenly realm.[81] But even in that spiritual body, we shall still know where we have come from, how we have been saved, and why we shall be singing to the praise of God's glory for all eternity.

---

[79] Ps. 89:1.
[80] De civitate Dei 22.30.
[81] 1 Cor. 15:50.

CHAPTER 3

AUGUSTINE THE TEACHER

Augustine and the Bible

When Augustine was struggling to accept the claims of the Christian faith, it was the Bible to which he turned in order to examine more closely what those claims were. He was well aware that the Scriptures were the fundamental documents of the church, the textbook from which all Christian theology was drawn. As a Christian he would affirm their divine character and infallibility on several occasions.[1] But as a young man with no faith of his own, he soon discovered that they lacked the polish of classical Greek and Latin literature, and contained statements that seemed quite absurd to a mind reared on Platonic philosophy. Once Augustine's mind had been exposed to the elegant Latin of Cicero, he turned away from the Bible as if it were somehow beneath him.

> [The Scriptures] appeared to me to be unworthy to be compared to the dignity of Cicero. My inflated pride shunned their style, and my sharp wit could not pierce their inner meaning. They were indeed capable of instructing little ones, but I disdained to be a little one. Swollen with pride, I considered myself to be a great one instead.[2]

Like many self-styled intellectuals then and now, Augustine preferred almost any sort of fable to the Bible. The Manichees had nothing very positive or profound to offer, but they were vocal critics of the Christian

---

[1] *Contra Faustum* 33.6; *Enchiridion* 4: *De civitate Dei* 11.6, 15.23, 16.2, 18.38, 20.1; *De Trinitate* 15.17.27–15.19.23.
[2] *Confessiones* 3.5.9.

Scriptures, and that was enough for him. Only as time went on did he realize that their objections to the Bible were not as formidable as they imagined, and that even the more awkward passages of the Old Testament could be interpreted as God's Word without sacrificing moral or theological integrity. It is true that Augustine was not immediately persuaded by the attempts of other Christians to do this, but gradually he came to recognize the possibility of looking at the Bible in a more positive way than he had originally done. Once that happened, the door was open to further acceptance of its message.[3]

It was Ambrose, the bishop of Milan and one of the great minds of the age, who persuaded Augustine to take the Bible seriously.[4] Augustine heard him preach and was deeply impressed by his expositions.[5] The main outlines of Ambrose's teaching were clear enough, and Augustine found them compelling. Ambrose believed that the image and likeness of God in man makes it both possible and natural for us to have access to knowledge of the divine. Our capacity for reasoning is a reflection of the divine mind, a belief that greatly appealed to those trained in Platonism and looking for absolute and ultimate truth.

The second thing in Ambrose's teaching that appealed to Augustine was the way he went beyond the literal text of the Scriptures, which he believed was superficial, to their underlying spiritual sense. Like almost all intellectuals of his time, Augustine believed that truth was hidden behind appearances and might be quite different from what it seemed to be at first sight. So he had little trouble absorbing the allegorical approach to the Bible that Ambrose advocated. Augustine did not hesitate to use 2 Corinthians 3:6 ("The letter kills, but the Spirit gives life") as biblical justification for this approach, and even wrote an entire treatise to justify it (*De Spiritu et littera*).

Of course, Ambrose was not the inventor of allegory—far from it. It owed its origins to pagan scholars in Alexandria who, several centuries before the coming of Christ, found it embarrassing to have to teach the Homeric epics. They thought that literature should be morally uplifting, but the stories of the Olympian gods and goddesses were anything but that. So in order to get around that difficulty, they came up with the notion that Greek mythology consisted of stories that conveyed hidden spiritual truths. Simple minds could be content with the narratives as they stood,

---

[3] *Confessiones* 5.14.24.
[4] *Confessiones* 6.4.6.
[5] *Confessiones* 6.3.3–4.

but more sophisticated people could go behind them and work out what deeper mysteries they contained.[6]

This allegorical method of interpreting Greek literature was taken over by Philo—a Jewish scholar in Alexandria who lived at the time of Jesus—and applied to the Old Testament. Later on, Clement of Alexandria, a Christian theologian who lived around AD 200, adapted the method for Christian use, and his pupil Origen developed it into a full-blown system. Allowing for developments and modifications over time, Ambrose got his basic technique from this Origenistic tradition.

In modern times the use of allegory to interpret the Bible has been so thoroughly discredited that it is hard for us to take it seriously, and when we meet it in the exegesis of someone like Augustine, we tend to discount what he had to say. This is unfortunate because, although the allegorical method has weaknesses and may not be viable now in the way that it appeared to be back then, there are important lessons to be learned from it that still pose challenges to the church today.

Most people in the early church thought that what the Bible said was objectively true, but few of them were very interested in the historical facts it contained. What concerned them most were the spiritual lessons to be drawn from its teaching. Nobody bothered with archaeology, for example, and most of what the Bible said came from an alien world. Hardly anybody studied Hebrew, and the great empires of Assyria, Babylonia, and pharaonic Egypt were little known. People believed that at some time in the distant past Moses had led the children of Israel out of slavery in Egypt, but the historical event did not matter much to them. There was no objective way of proving that it had occurred, and people had to rely on the credibility of those who had been eyewitnesses. This was even true of the Gospels, of which Augustine famously wrote, "I would not believe the Gospel unless the authority of the universal church moved me to do so."[7] The Israelites had believed that the exodus was fundamental to their national identity as God's chosen people, but as most Christians saw it, that exodus was primarily a spiritual deliverance from the slavery of sin. The experience of inner liberation from sin was at the heart of the gospel and was open to any believer, including those who were forced to live in physical slavery.

The life, death, and resurrection of Jesus were admittedly somewhat

---

[6] *De natura boni contra Manichaeos* 24.
[7] *Contra epistulam Manichaei fundamentalem* 5.6. By "authority of the universal church" Augustine meant the acceptance of the eyewitness testimony of the apostles.

different from events recorded in the Old Testament; Jesus had lived in relatively recent times and in the Roman Empire. Justin Martyr (ca. 100– ca. 165) had claimed that Pontius Pilate had deposited a report of his death and resurrection in the Roman imperial archives.[8] Tertullian picked up on the story and said much the same thing.[9] But nobody seems to have gone in search of the official Roman records in order to prove the accuracy of the Gospel accounts. What modern people would do eagerly and as a matter of course never seems to have occurred to the ancients! Nowadays many scholars assume that Justin and Tertullian were simply indulging in rhetoric without substance, which explains why the relevant documentation was never produced, but we should not judge them too hastily. It was not that investigating the source material could not be done; it was rather that it did not matter.

Today we have gone to the opposite extreme and rely as much as we can on whatever evidence archaeology, epigraphy, and related disciplines can produce. But have these discoveries made us any wiser about the meaning of the Scriptures? Demonstrating the historical truthfulness of what they say is useful, but that kind of proof does not change lives. What most people want to know is how to live, and if they look to the Bible at all, it is more likely in order to find moral and spiritual guidance for today and not to learn about the historical details of long-dead civilizations.

Much of the Bible's spiritual message is relatively easy to figure out: love God and your neighbor, do good to those who hate you, and so on. Putting commands like those into practice may be hard, but at least it is clear what we are supposed to do. Problems arise, however, when the Bible talks about things that we find repugnant. For example, in Psalm 137:9, we find that the psalmist blesses those who take the little children of Babylon and dash their heads against the stones. We can understand that someone who had been taken captive by the Babylonians would not have a very favorable attitude toward them, but the Christian message is that we should love our enemies, not try to exterminate them! Origen solved this apparent contradiction as follows:

> The righteous destroy their enemies, which are their vices, and do not
> spare even the children, which are the early beginnings and prompt-

---

[8] Justin Martyr, *Apologia I*, 48.
[9] Tertullian, *Apologeticum* 5.2, 21.24. Augustine probably did not know Justin's writings, but he would certainly have read Tertullian.

ings of evil. This is how we understand Psalm 137. . . . The "little ones" of Babylon (a name that means "confusion") are those troublesome sinful thoughts that arise in the soul, and one who subdues them by striking their heads against the firm and solid strength of reason and truth is . . . truly blessed. God may therefore have commanded people to destroy all their vices, even at their birth, without commanding anything contrary to the teaching of Christ. [10]

Augustine followed the same principle, but with a characteristic twist of his own:

When we were born, the confusion of this world found us and choked us, while we were still infants, with the empty notions of various errors. The infant who is destined to be a citizen of Jerusalem, and who in God's predestination is already a citizen, though still a prisoner for the time being, learns only to love what his parents have whispered in his ears. They teach and train him in greed, theft, lying and idolatry. . . . Babylon thus persecutes us when we are little, but when we grow up, what should we do? Repay her! . . . Let her little ones be choked . . . dashed against the stones and die. What are the little ones of Babylon? Evil desires at their birth. [11]

Augustine makes his interpretation more personal and detailed than either Origen's or Ambrose's, but the basic message is the same. The little children of Babylon are to be understood in a spiritual sense, and once that is done, crushing them is both a moral duty and a spiritual imperative. Nevertheless, there is an important shift of emphasis in Augustine's interpretation that was to become increasingly obvious as time went on. Whereas Origen and Ambrose had talked in general terms of being tempted and of resisting before the urge to sin became too powerful, Augustine situated the verse in the context of the early life of one who was predestined for the kingdom of heaven. It was not so much a matter of dealing with temptations when they came along as of renouncing an entire lifestyle that stood in the way of a believer's enjoyment of God.

Although it may not be obvious at first sight, this enlarged perspective gradually led Augustine to put much greater emphasis on the literal sense of the biblical text than either his mentor Ambrose did or was customary in

---

10 Origen, *Contra Celsum* 7.22. Ambrose said the same thing in *De paenitentia* 2.11.106.
11 *Enarrationes in Psalmos* 136.12.

his time. The more he looked into the text of Scripture, the more Augustine came to see it as a handbook of the Christian life, which must be lived not on some ethereal heavenly level but in the hurly-burly of everyday life. This is what the Son of God did when he became a man, and the incarnation of the eternal Word formed the basis for Augustine's increasingly literal interpretation of the temporal Word of Scripture. The latter was the image of the former, adapted for our use and understanding, but no less "real" and incarnate for that.

Having said that, Augustine could not let weighty matters of good and evil be reduced to the level of a talking serpent and a piece of fruit. Surely the Genesis account of the fall had to be symbolic of something more profound than that. As Augustine put it:

> The serpent signifies the devil, who was certainly not simple. His cleverness is indicated by the fact that he is said to be wiser than all the beasts. . . . We must not be confused as to how the serpent could speak to the woman when she was in Paradise and he was not. The serpent entered Paradise spiritually and not bodily.[12]

Then too, there are the seemingly endless dietary and tribal laws that Moses gave to the people of Israel, many of which were specifically abolished by Jesus and his disciples. In what way can they still be regarded as the Word of God? Here the Old Testament was not so much unbelievable as inapplicable—unless of course, a spiritual meaning could be found that would make passages like these still relevant to the life of the church. Augustine explained:

> The whole Old Testament Scripture, for those who really want to understand it, has been handed down with a four-fold sense—historical, aetiological, analogical, and allegorical. . . . In Scripture, according to the historical sense, we are told what has been written or done. . . . According to the aetiological sense, we are told *why* something has been said or done. According to the analogical sense, we are shown that there is no conflict between the Old and New Testaments. According to the allegorical sense, we are taught that not everything in Scripture is to be taken literally, but must be understood figuratively.[13]

---

12 *De Genesi adversus Manichaeos libri duo* 2.14.20.
13 *De utilitate credendi* 7.17.

It was considerations like these that prompted the early Christians to move toward allegorical interpretation. When we look at it the way they did, it is hard not to agree that the spiritual issues raised by the biblical text are much the same today as they have always been. The early Christians believed that since all Scripture was written for their learning, every part of it must have some practical application to them.[14] In cases where the literal meaning was unacceptable as it stood, another meaning had to be found, and that is where allegory came in. In reading the Old Testament, Augustine was caught between two different aspects to its interpretation, each of which had its place. On the one hand, there was the great theme of prophecy and fulfillment, which made it clear that the gospel of Jesus Christ was the goal to which Israelite religion was headed. As Augustine put it, "There is a veil placed over the reading of the Old Testament until the coming of Christ, when the veil is removed, that is to say that grace has come and we understand that we are justified by him, and so we do what he commands."[15] On the other hand, the New Testament reveals something that was already present in the Old, though hidden from our view: "This grace lay veiled in the Old Testament but has been revealed in Christ in a manner suited to the dispensation of the times, for God knows how to order all things correctly."[16]

Augustine never resolved the tension between these two approaches, but appealed to whichever one of them best fit his argument and circumstances. What really impressed him about the Bible was not the way in which it concealed spiritual truths behind its human words, but the way in which it proclaimed the coming to earth of the Son of God—the Word was made flesh![17] The truth was not just an idea but a person with whom it was possible to identify because he had come to earth in order to identify with us.[18] As Augustine understood, that act transformed the nature of reality, making the deepest mysteries of the universe accessible to those who had faith. How this was possible he did not pretend to know, and for a while it remained a problem that he could neither solve nor allow to coexist with his rational mind. But even before his understanding of the incarnation fell into place, Augustine was quite clear that Christian teaching was superior to anything the Platonists had to offer.

---

[14] 2 Tim. 3:16.
[15] *De spiritu et littera* 17.30.
[16] *De spiritu et littera* 15.27.
[17] John 1:14. See for example, *Confessiones* 7.19.25.
[18] *Confessiones* 7.18.24.

I believe that it was your will [O Lord] that I should stumble across the writings [of the Platonists] before I studied your Scriptures . . . so that I might discern what a difference there is between presumption and confession, between those who saw where they ought to go but did not see the way and the way that leads us not only to see but also to dwell in the land of the blessed.[19]

For Augustine the difference between Platonism and Christianity was that the former was an idea of ultimate reality whereas the latter was an experience of it. The experience did not deny the idea but went beyond it and made it seem pale and inadequate by comparison.[20] As Augustine saw it, philosophy is ultimately reductionist because it tries to explain with the mind things that go beyond the mind's competence. Christian faith, on the other hand, embraces the mind but leads the believer to appreciate a truth that is higher.[21] Personal knowledge is more immediate and more flexible than rational deduction, because it can handle the paradox of knowing and not knowing at the same time. An idea is an end in itself—you either understand it or you do not. But a person is a mystery that you have to keep penetrating more deeply and that, like God, can ultimately be known only by love.[22] The beauty and the wonder of the Bible is that it is not a philosophical system but a personal revelation from God. It makes sense in the way that all personal relationships do. At one level it compels us to enter into the experience of which it speaks, but at another level it contains mysteries whose depths we can never hope to plumb. In other words, it is just like another person—real and yet impenetrable at the same time.

If Augustine differed from his contemporaries in the way he interpreted the Bible, it was because he saw the "other person" as himself—the Scriptures were a mirror of his own soul, given to him (and by extension to us) in order to teach the way of salvation through the knowledge and love of the self in the light of the knowledge and love of God.[23] In interpreting the Bible, it is faith, working in and through love, that attains the true vision of divine things by living a pure life, because it is the pure in heart who see God.[24]

---

19 *Confessiones* 7.20.26.
20 *Epistulae* 137.5.17.
21 For Augustine's thoughts on the relationship of philosophy to Christian faith, see *De civitate Dei* 7.29, 8.9–10, 11.2, 22.22, 26–28; *De doctrina Christiana* 2.40.60.
22 *Confessiones* 12.15.19.
23 *De Trinitate* 10.3.5.
24 *Enchiridion* 4–5. See Matt. 5:8.

That Augustine understood the Bible like this is clear from the way he wrote about it. Apart from the creation story in Genesis, which he commented on no fewer than four times and regarded as foundational to the Christian worldview, he concentrated mainly on the Pauline Epistles; the Johannine literature (especially the Fourth Gospel and 1 John), with its strong emphasis on love and the incarnation; and the Psalms, of which he wrote, "What prayers I used to send up to you in those psalms! How I was inflamed by them and burned to repeat them, if I could, throughout the whole world, against the pride of the human race. And yet they are sung everywhere on earth, and nobody can hide from their heat."[25]

The intensity of the psalmist's personal relationship with God had a particular appeal to Augustine, who wrote on the Psalter at greater length than on any other part of Scripture. He believed that the devotional spirit that the Psalms so clearly encouraged was the key to the right interpretation of the Bible.[26] We see the effects of this when he was dealing with the question of miracles. Critics contended that miracles no longer happen, so the ones recorded in the Bible probably had not happened either. Augustine answered this not by saying that miracles were a thing of the past; on the contrary, he argued that they still took place, but were not recorded for posterity in the way that the biblical ones had been.[27] At the same time, he also claimed that miracles no longer took place very often because they were not needed as proofs of the gospel's truth, and if they were still a regular occurrence, people would be attracted to them rather than to the message they were meant to support and illustrate.[28] The real miracle, as he saw it, was that so many people had come to believe the gospel even though they had no personal experience of the events described in the New Testament.[29] Anyone who saw God at work in the world and praised him for it would have no difficulty in accepting the historicity of the more unusual events recorded in the biblical revelation.

Compared with Origen or his own Latin contemporary Jerome, Augustine was not really a biblical scholar or commentator at all. He did not know any Hebrew, and his Greek was elementary. This might not have mattered very much, but there was no reliable Latin translation of the Bible available

---

[25] *Confessiones* 9.4.8.
[26] *De doctrina Christiana* 2.41.62.
[27] *De civitate Dei* 22.8.
[28] *De civitate Dei* 22.8–9.
[29] *De civitate Dei* 22.5.

until Jerome produced one, which put Augustine at a distinct disadvantage.[30] But as the correspondence between him and Jerome reveals, Augustine did not appreciate this and did not see that he ought to defer to Jerome as the better interpreter. The two men were not on the same wavelength. Jerome was a genuine scholar, concerned with the meaning of the text, anxious to avoid allegory wherever possible, and determined to learn the original languages and translate them into acceptable Latin. He also wanted to restrict the Old Testament canon to books that were extant in Hebrew, rather than include the Greek additions that we now know collectively as the Apocrypha.

Augustine, on the other hand, had no desire to emulate Jerome's scholarly activity to any appreciable degree. He was open to allegory because of his views about the hidden truths of Scripture and saw no need to stick to the Hebrew text of the Old Testament when the apostles did not. This was particularly important in the Psalter, where the Greek is often different from the Hebrew. Jerome was alive to textual problems like these in a way that Augustine was not, so perhaps it is just as well that Augustine did not try his hand at commentary writing, or at least not very much.

But if Augustine disappoints us on purely textual matters, it is a different story when it comes to the science of interpretation, or "hermeneutics." Augustine excelled in this domain, and his writings on the subject remain of great interest to theologians and literary theorists alike. It is telling that his main treatise on the subject is called *De doctrina Christiana* (*On Christian Doctrine*, or *Teaching*). Augustine did not have a systematic theology in the modern sense, and even the creeds of the early church were not a major part of his thinking. Yet for him the Bible was a coherent body of theology that was authoritative for the life and teaching of the church. He did not despise traditions merely because they could not be found in the Bible, but he never elevated them to the level of the written Word of God. He allowed an appeal to extrabiblical witnesses in order to clarify ambiguities in Scripture, and in particular to the baptismal creed.[31] But the Bible remained paramount, and if nonbiblical traditions were advanced as a means of sanctioning unorthodox opinions, he fell back on the principle that Scripture alone was the source of Christian teaching.[32]

For Augustine, the true meaning of the Scriptures was revealed in their

---

[30] It appeared around 400, but Augustine apparently did not use it.
[31] *De doctrina Christiana* 3.2.2.
[32] *De baptismo* 2.3–4; *De natura et gratia* 37.44; *Epistulae* 93.10. See also *De doctrina Christiana* 2.42.60.

sacred character as divine oracles that could be read outside their historical context; indeed, they had to be, since otherwise they would have been of no use to the church. If the original context had been the dominating principle of his hermeneutic, the Bible would have been a historical chronicle of the development of God's people, not a handbook of Christian life and practice, which is a very different thing. It would have been a record of the past, not a guide for the present, and still less a promise of what was yet to come in the future.

The significance of this can be seen most clearly in the distinction Augustine made between the letter of the biblical text and the spirit that animated it. This was a Pauline doctrine of course, developed in the context of the struggle in the New Testament church over whether it was necessary to keep the Jewish law or not. Paul taught that the letter "killed" those who kept it in the wrong spirit.[33] Augustine agreed with that and used the same argument in refuting the Pelagians.[34] But as his hermeneutical understanding developed, he made increasing use of the Pauline distinction as a paradigm for understanding the Bible—in particular, the Old Testament. Behind the severity of the law, which on the surface might appear to be quite un-Christian, there lay the hidden message of divine grace, which was fully revealed in the gospel. Because of that, Augustine taught that the Old Testament should be read as a shadow and type of things to come, which allowed him to do justice to its literal sense without losing sight of its spiritual meaning.[35] In effect, he was turning allegory into what we now call typology, the difference between them being that allegory ignores the literal sense of the text, whereas typology takes it seriously but sees it as a prototype of something else.[36] Here more than anywhere else, Augustine came close to what the Protestant Reformers would call covenant theology, interpreting the Old Testament literally, but as the promise and harbinger of better things to come.

Augustine was writing for a church that wanted to find God in the Scriptures and grow in his grace. The information contained in the Bible was meant to lead to experience, and if it did not, it was of no value. He knew that plenty of people thought that learning how to read the sacred texts was a waste of time. As far as they were concerned, there were no

---

[33] 2 Cor. 3:6.
[34] *De spiritu et littera* 5.8.
[35] *De spiritu et littera* 15.27; *Epistulae* 102.17.
[36] This distinction is a modern one. Augustine himself would consider typology to be a variant of allegory. The apostle Paul did the same. See Gal. 4:21–27.

rules to guide (or restrain) the reader, and to impose them was a form of quenching the Spirit.

There are still many people today who think much the same thing—they believe that all you have to do is open the Bible and God will illuminate its meaning without further comment. To this idea, Augustine replied that it was the duty of a teacher to instruct his pupils in the art of reading. In this respect, the Bible is no different from any other book. Children learn their mother tongue from their parents and go to school in order to master their letters. It is not the job of their tutors to brainwash them into thinking along certain lines, but to equip them so that they can read and think for themselves. This is how Augustine saw his task as an expositor—not to tell others what the Bible means, as a commentator might do, but to give them the tools for reading and understanding the text themselves.

> The man who lays down rules for interpretation is like one who teaches reading, that is, who shows others how to read for themselves. The re-sult is that just as someone who knows how to read does not depend on someone else to tell him what is in the book that he is reading, so the man who has the rules that I am trying to lay down here, will not need an interpreter to explain an obscure passage that he may come across.[37]

In other words, if a man learns how to read the Bible, he probably will not need commentaries at all, except perhaps to explain obscure names and events! Whatever we think of this approach, at least it helps us to under-stand why Augustine did not write commentaries himself—he was trying to help people understand the Bible at an altogether more fundamental level.

Things and Signs

Augustine started his teaching about how to read the Bible by making a fundamental distinction between what he calls *things* and *signs*. A *thing* is an objectively existing object that does not point to anything beyond itself—wood, stone, cattle, and so on. A *sign*, on the other hand, points to something beyond itself. Words are necessarily signs because they have no objective existence in themselves; their meaning is entirely dependent on what they refer to. But things can also be signs, as is often the case in Scripture: "The wood that Moses cast into the bitter waters in order to

---

[37] *De doctrina Christiana*, preface, 9.

make them sweet,[38] the stone that Jacob used as a pillow,[39] and the ram that Abraham sacrificed instead of his son[40] may all be things in themselves, but they are also signs of other things."[41]

Furthermore, there is a sense in which signs, like words, are also things—not material objects to be sure, but intellectual concepts that can be defined. Words may have a range of meanings, but they are not unlimited or arbitrary; there is always a connection, even if it is largely imaginary, between one meaning and another. To take a modern example, a word like *mouse* refers in the first instance to a rodent, but its shape has given rise to the imaginary inference that such things may be found under the human skin—hence "muscles," or "little mice." In modern times, of course, the word has been extended to refer to a computer accessory, largely because of the latter's suggestive shape. In both these cases, the mind has made a link that is not there in objective fact but that helps us understand and define our conceptual universe.

This flexibility in the way we can use words to mean different things without losing sight of the underlying concept that unites them is important for understanding Augustine's interpretation of the Bible. On the one hand, he was a champion of what we now call the "literal sense" of the text and was wary of anyone who tried to overrule it: "When we read the inspired books in the light of the wide variety of true meanings which are drawn out of a few words and founded on the firm basis of universal Christian belief, let us choose the meaning that was doubtless the one originally intended by the author."[42]

Augustine was especially concerned that some people would reject the literal meaning of the biblical text because it did not correspond with what they wanted to find there. The Word of God is not tailored to meet our desires and expectations, but is designed to challenge us, often in very concrete ways. Therefore, the literal sense must be respected and not dismissed as impossible or inappropriate without good reason.[43]

The context in which Augustine said this was the question of the "right" interpretation of Genesis, a problem that plagued him for most of his life and that was one of the great debates of the early church. When

---

[38] Ex. 15:25.
[39] Gen. 28:11.
[40] Gen. 22:13.
[41] *De doctrina Christiana* 1.2.2.
[42] *De Genesi ad litteram* 1.21.41.
[43] *De doctrina Christiana* 3.10.14–15.

Moses wrote the text as we now have it, did he understand the many meanings that later generations would read into it?[44] Moses wrote, "In the beginning God created heaven and earth."[45] What did he mean by this? Augustine
was not sure. In speaking to God he said:

> I say with complete confidence that in your immutable Word you made all
> things invisible and visible. I cannot say with equal assurance that this
> was exactly what Moses had in mind when he wrote, "In the beginning
> God made heaven and earth." Though in your truth I see the proposi-
> tion to be certain, yet I cannot see in Moses' mind that this is what he
> was thinking when he wrote this. When he wrote, "In the beginning,"
> he could have been thinking of the start of the making process. In the
> words about heaven and earth in this text, he could also have meant not a
> nature endowed with form and perfection (whether spiritual or physical)
> but one that was inchoate and still formless. I see of course that all these
> propositions can be equally true, but which of them Moses had in mind
> when he was writing, I am not so sure. But whether he meant all this or
> even more, I do not doubt that what the great man saw was true and that
> he expressed it in appropriate words.[46]

It was in resolving questions like these that the distinction between
things and signs was particularly useful to Augustine. Moses described the
things, and there is no reason to doubt the truth of what he said. He may
also have understood that the things he wrote about were signs pointing to
a deeper truth, but of this we cannot be sure, nor can we say what deeper
truth he might have had in mind. Yet since God created the world for a
purpose, the things he made were also signs, and it is legitimate for us to
infer from them their meaning. We should read the text not in an "either–
or" spirit but in a "both–and" spirit; which is to say that we do not have to
choose between the material and intellectual interpretations, but accept
that both can be true and that Moses might well have understood that his
words were capable of different levels of meaning. Comparing himself to
the patriarch, Augustine wrote:

> If I were writing something at this level of authority, I would choose to
> write so that my words would convey whatever diverse truth each reader

---

44 Augustine accepted the then universal belief that Moses was the author of Genesis.
45 Gen. 1:1.
46 *Confessiones* 12.24.33.

could grasp, rather than state explicitly a single view of the matter that would exclude all others—provided that there was no false doctrine to offend me. . . . When Moses wrote this passage, he perfectly perceived and had in mind all the truth that we have been able to find here, as well as all the truth that we have not been able to find and that still remains to be discovered in it.[47]

So when push came to shove, Augustine came down on the side of those who believed that Moses was aware of the plurality of meanings that his words might convey, even to the point where he understood more about them than we do! Augustine was sticking his neck out here, and we might suggest that he was taking his argument beyond the bounds that he himself had recognized at an earlier stage. But if we recoil from his conclusion, we must not lose sight of the main point that he was trying to make: words can legitimately convey different but not incompatible meanings because they can both refer to things in themselves and be signs pointing to something deeper.

Augustine did not find this problematic. He believed that God had placed obscurities in Scripture in order to test us and make us think for ourselves. We are meant to wrestle with difficulties because they are challenges that help us grow in faith and love as we resolve them. This is how we educate children, and we should not be surprised to find that God uses the same method when teaching his spiritual offspring.[48] But the obscure texts must always be interpreted in accordance with the ones that are clear, and should never be used to overturn what God has plainly stated elsewhere.[49] The Bible is a message for simple minds as well as for intellectuals, and the latter must be humble enough to appreciate that.[50]

Once Augustine made the basic distinction between things and signs, he proceeded to analyze the concept of "things," which he subdivided into those meant to be used, those meant to be enjoyed, and those intended for both use and enjoyment. A thing that is meant to be enjoyed is one that gives us satisfaction for its own sake, whereas one that is to be used is a means to an end. The third category is a combination of the other two. In the big picture, human beings find themselves on a life journey that contains all three types of things. At the end of our pilgrimage is

---

[47] *Confessiones* 12.32.43.
[48] *De doctrina Christiana* 2.6.7.
[49] *De doctrina Christiana* 2.9.14.
[50] *Enarrationes in Psalmos* 146.10.12.

our heavenly home, the place where we really belong, which Augustine says is a "thing" meant entirely for our enjoyment. Here on earth, though, the means of survival and progress are things that are meant to be used in order to reach that desired goal. Unfortunately, we tend to admire the beauty of this world in such a way as to make us delay our onward journey and even forget our ultimate destination. This is a deception that has resulted from our fallen condition, and we must do all in our power to avoid and overcome it.

> We have wandered far from God, and if we want to return to our Father's home, this world must be used and not enjoyed. The invisible things of God must be seen in the things that have been made, so that by means of material and temporary objects we may lay hold on what is spiritual and eternal.[51]

At this point Augustine paused to clarify what the nature of our heavenly home is. Far from being a kind of eternal garden of Eden, full of delights of all kinds, heaven is the abode of God the Holy Trinity—Father, Son, and Holy Spirit—whom he describes as the true "objects of enjoyment," while at the same time specifying that they are not really "objects" at all, but the source of our being and perception. Here we come face-to-face with Augustine's deepest convictions. Ultimate reality is not a "thing" but a personal being in whom the perfection of truly balanced relationships exists and manifests itself: "In the Father is unity, in the Son equality, in the Holy Spirit the harmony of unity and equality. These three attributes are all one because of the Father, all equal because of the Son, and all harmonious because of the Holy Spirit."[52]

There is no way that the Trinity can be used to further some ulterior end; it is both the source and the end of all things. God can only be enjoyed for himself, and it is to that enjoyment that his people have been called for eternity.[53] In his inner being, God is beyond anything that can be expressed in human words, but he loves us so much that he has graciously made it possible for us to speak to him in our own inadequate way, and has promised to receive our praise and worship, even though it falls far short

---

[51] *De doctrina Christiana* 1.4.4.
[52] *De doctrina Christiana* 1.5.5.
[53] This idea is well known to Presbyterians, thanks to the first question of the Westminster Shorter Catechism: "What is the chief end of man?" The catechism's answer could have come straight out of Augustine: "Man's chief end is to glorify God and to enjoy him forever."

of what is his due. The word *God* itself points to this paradox because it is only a sound that cannot be adequately defined. Yet when we hear it, it points us to that ultimately inexpressible reality that we must be thinking about.[54]

The God who has made himself known to us is the supreme mind, and therefore he is also supreme wisdom, because wisdom is nothing but the application of the ideas of the mind to the business of life. God is invisible but he is not an abstraction, and everything we see with our physical senses points ultimately to him. It is obvious that if we are to enjoy God in the right way, we must be fit and able to do so. Unfortunately we are hindered in this, not by the limitations of our created finitude, which was given to us by God and is therefore very good, but by the corruption of sin, which has marred his image in us and made it impossible for us to connect with him as we were originally meant to. God has demonstrated this by sending his Son into the world in order to live a pure life within the constraints of our humanity.[55] At the same time, he also sent his Son to cure us of the disease of sinfulness. Because of the way that worked out in practice, we sometimes find that he did the opposite of what we have done. For example, whereas we sinned through our pride, he abandoned all pride and redeemed us in his humility. At other times though, we find that he did the same thing we have done. Like us, he was born of a woman, and he died a human death in order to redeem us who were spiritually dead. Having accomplished this work on earth, he returned to heaven but gave his church the keys to his kingdom.

> Whoever in the church does not believe that his sins have been forgiven will not receive forgiveness, but whoever believes, repents, and turns away from his sins will be saved by that faith and repentance, on the basis of which he is received into the bosom of the church. Someone who does not believe that his sins can be forgiven falls into despair and becomes worse, as if the greatest good for him is to do evil.[56]

This then is the wider context in which the pilgrimage of the individual believer makes sense and takes place. God is to be enjoyed above everything else, and the sacrifice of Christ has made that enjoyment a real

---

[54] *De doctrina Christiana* 1.6.6.
[55] *De doctrina Christiana* 1.11.11–1.12–12.
[56] *De doctrina Christiana* 1.18.17.

possibility for us. Everything else in the world is meant for our use, so that we may reach the full and unhindered enjoyment of God. This, however, raises an important question, which Augustine frames as follows:

> We who enjoy and use other things are things ourselves. Man is really a great thing, made in the image and likeness of God, not according to his mortal body but according to his rational soul which raises him high above the animals. It thus becomes an important question to know whether men ought to enjoy themselves, use themselves, or both.[57]

Augustine recognizes that we are commanded to love one another, but is this because we are meant to enjoy each other as we are, or for the sake of something else? In answer to this question, he says that our love for one another is ultimately directed toward a higher goal, which is the love of God. He says this because we are told to love other people as we love ourselves, not to love ourselves for our own sake. From this, Augustine concludes: "Whoever loves his neighbor rightly ought to urge him to love God with all his heart, soul, and mind. By loving his neighbor as himself in this way, a man channels the whole current of his love for both himself and his neighbor into the love of God."[58]

Having established that, Augustine goes on to point out that love can be manifested in four different ways. First, we can love things that are greater than ourselves. Second, we can love ourselves. Third, we can love things that are equal to ourselves, and last, we can love things that are inferior to us. He then adds that the human soul has no trouble with the second and fourth of these. We all love ourselves, and we love our bodies, which are less than ourselves. It is the other two kinds of love that require instruction, and this is why they summarize the law and the prophets, as Jesus said. We are commanded to love God, who is higher than we are, and our neighbors, who are equal to us, precisely because neither of these things is automatic. These truths do not impress themselves on us naturally, which is why God had to reveal them to us.

A modern observer may think that the above argument has taken us a long way from reading the Bible, but Augustine would be shocked at such a suggestion. To his mind, everything in the Bible pointed to Christ and spoke of our relationship with and in him. That was the framework within

---

57 De doctrina Christiana 1.22.20.
58 De doctrina Christiana 1.22.21.

which the Bible made sense because it was for that purpose that it was originally given. As Augustine said,

> To summarize our discussion so far, we should clearly understand that the purpose of the law and of all Holy Scripture is the love of an object which is to be enjoyed [i.e., God the Holy Trinity] and the love of an object that can enjoy the same thing in fellowship with us [i.e., our neighbor].[59]

This was how Jesus summed up the law and the prophets, and so it was the starting point for Augustine's interpretation of them as well. Jesus told the Jews of his time that the Scriptures they so eagerly searched spoke about him.[60] This became the chief theme of Augustine's hermeneutic too, and he used it to explain the many difficult passages he had to deal with in the Old Testament, as well as the New.[61]

Christ in All the Scriptures

When Augustine read the Scriptures, his most telling reaction was this realization: "Christ meets and refreshes me everywhere in those books."[62] It is no accident that this remark is found in a treatise arguing against the theology of a prominent Manichee, Faustus. Augustine had been deeply affected by the Manichaean dualism he had embraced before his conversion, when he could not see how a divine being could enter the world of sinful matter. In his words:

> Our Savior himself, your only Son, I imagined emerging from the mass of your dazzling body of light for our salvation. . . . I thought a nature like his could not be born of the Virgin Mary without being mingled with flesh. That he could be mixed with us and not polluted I did not see, because my mental picture was what it was. I was afraid to believe that he was incarnate for fear that I would have to believe that he had been defiled by the flesh.[63]

Somewhat surprisingly, perhaps, Augustine was rescued from this extreme position by reading the works of the Neoplatonic philosopher

---

59 *De doctrina Christiana* 1.35.39.
60 John 5:39–40.
61 *Enarrationes in Psalmos* 16.51, 45.1, 98.1.
62 *Contra Faustum* 12.27.
63 *Confessiones* 5.10.20.

Plotinus, who persuaded him not to despise matter but to use it as the first stage on the path of eventual enlightenment. As Augustine understood Plotinus, the body was the starting point for the philosopher to turn inward to the soul, which dwells within it. The belief that the spiritual soul can inhabit a material body and use it as a means of drawing seekers after truth to a higher awareness of themselves allowed Augustine to overcome his inability to accept the possibility of a divine incarnation. What the soul does in the individual, the Son of God has done for those who believe in him.

> Your Word, eternal truth, higher than the highest parts of your creation, lifts up those who submit to him [and draws them] to himself. In the lower regions [i.e., on earth] he built himself a humble house of human clay. By this means, he detaches those who are willing to be made subject to him from themselves and transfers them to himself, healing their diseases and nourishing their love. No longer must they have confidence in themselves. They must become weak, because they see at their feet how divinity has become weak by sharing our "coat of skin."[64]

This was a major step for Augustine, but he himself recognized that there was still some way for him to go. Initially, he thought that Jesus was a man of surpassing wisdom, and interpreted his virgin birth as a sign of his great authority as a teacher. When reading the Gospels, Augustine was struck above all by the way they portrayed Jesus as fully human, but he failed to see the deeper implications of this.

> Because the Scriptures are true, I accepted that there was a complete man in Christ, not only the body, or the soul and body without a mind, but a fully human being. I thought that he excelled everyone else, not because he was the embodiment of the Truth, but because of the surpassing excellence of his human character and his more perfect participation in wisdom.[65]

Modern readers have no difficulty in accepting the complete humanity of Jesus, so it is important to realize that not only did this go completely against the teaching of the Manichees, but many otherwise orthodox Christians rejected it too. Augustine's close friend Alypius, for example, did

---

[64] *Confessiones* 7.18.24. The quotation is from Gen. 3:21 and refers to Adam's clothing after he fell from grace.
[65] *Confessiones* 7.19.25.

not believe that Christ had a human soul or mind, but thought that he was a pure spirit clothed only in human flesh.[66] This was the heresy attributed to Apollinarius, which had been condemned at the first council of Constantinople in 381 but was evidently still alive and well among many ordinary believers, a reminder to us that the doctrinal decisions of church councils could take time to impress themselves on the mind of the church at large.[67]

Augustine stood out from many of his Christian contemporaries because of the way he confessed the complete humanity of Jesus, but he later came to see that this apparent orthodoxy was just an intellectual achievement and not the result of a spiritual transformation. He had resolved the philosophical problem of how spirit could enter flesh, but still had no idea of why the Son of God had become incarnate. He rejected Platonism more because it was inadequate than because it was false. To him, the difference between Platonists and Christians was, he wrote, "between those who see the goal but not how to get there and those who have found the way home to happiness, not merely as a target to be perceived but as a place to dwell in."[68] While he denounced Manichaeism as a false trail and regretted the years he had wasted among its followers, he continued to be grateful for having embraced Platonism before his conversion, recognizing that it had laid the foundation for his submission to Christ and admitting that had he come across it later, its similarity to Christian teaching might have deceived him and led him away from the truth. The extent of his debt to the Platonic tradition can be measured from the following:

> By the Platonic books I was admonished to return into myself.[69] With you [O God] as my guide I entered into my inner citadel and could do so because you had become my helper. I entered, and with my soul's eye, such as it was, saw ... the immutable light that was higher than my mind. ... It was superior because it made me, and I was inferior because I was made by it. The person who knows the truth knows it, and he who knows it knows eternity. Love knows it. Eternal truth and true love and beloved eternity—you are my God.[70]

---

[66] *Confessiones* 7.19.25.

[67] Apollinarius was a disciple of Athanasius, bishop of Alexandria from 328 to 373 and honored as the chief defender of Nicene orthodoxy in the fourth century. Athanasius's christology tended to minimize the importance of the human soul in Jesus, and Apollinarius took this to its logical conclusion. From then on, the Alexandrian church was suspected of Apollinarianism by its rivals in Antioch.

[68] *Confessiones* 7.20.26.

[69] Plotinus, *Enneades* 5.1.1.

[70] *Confessiones* 7.10.16.

It was thanks to Platonism that Augustine came to see how it was possible to have the incarnate God that the Christian gospel claimed was necessary to human salvation. If God had not entered human life, then he would not have been involved in it, and it could not have been transformed into something that was pleasing to him. The incarnation of Christ was the fulfillment of promises made to Abraham and worked out in the history of Israel. Divine involvement in human affairs was fundamental to the teaching of Scripture, and in the incarnation of Christ it reached its perfect and logical conclusion.

So far, so good. But even though Augustine came to accept all this, as he said later, he was still only applying Platonic principles to the biblical story, claiming that in the Christian Scriptures what the Platonists had dreamed of had actually come to pass. It would take further reading of the Scriptures—particularly the apostle Paul's writings—to make him see what the true uniqueness of the Christian gospel was. Before he had come to accept the logical necessity and the actual possibility of a divine incarnation, Augustine had found Paul's writings confused and confusing. His failure to share the apostle's fundamental principle meant that the rest of his teaching made little sense—a particular problem with Paul, who tended to assume that his readers were on the same wavelength as he was, even if they had misunderstood or misapplied his teaching. Only when Augustine embraced the incarnation of the Son of God in Jesus Christ did the rest fall into place.

What Paul taught Augustine was that the Son of God had come into the world not to manifest his divine ability to take on a human nature, as if that were an end in itself, but because of his love for the fallen human race. His incarnation was an embrace not just of finitude but of sin; the one who knew no sin became sin for us, so that by dying in our place on the cross he could open the gate of eternal life for those who believed in him. This realization changed everything for Augustine. Christ was no longer merely the supreme manifestation of the truth; he was the Truth itself. Moreover, he was (and had to be) the incarnation of the divine wisdom, because if he were not, he would have had no power to act as he did. In other words, Christ was a revelation of God not in a passive sense, but in an active one; he was the Word who had chosen to become flesh and as such could both reveal what God was like and act as God himself would act.

Augustine's turn toward the teaching of Paul was not entirely free of

Platonic and even Manichaean influences however. In the very first book that he wrote after his conversion, he mentioned that Christians offer prayers to "the power and wisdom of God"; for, as he put it, "What else is the one whom the mysteries present to us as the Son of God?"[71] This phrase, "the power and wisdom of God," was well known in the early church, and the Manichees made special use of it. Faustus even included it in his confession of faith, as Augustine tells us.[72] But it is important to notice how Augustine cited the verse, particularly when arguing against Manichees: "Let Paul tell us who Christ Jesus our Lord might be: 'To those who have been called,' he says, 'we preach Christ, God's power [*virtus*] and God's wisdom.'[73] Why does he say this? Does not Christ himself say, 'I am the truth'"?[74]

Even allowing for the fact that Augustine was quoting selectively (and probably from memory), certain things stand out and may be regarded as typical of his thought in his early years as a Christian. The first is his translation of the Greek word *dynamis* as *virtus*, when *potentia* would have been more exact. This matters because *virtus*, which is the standard Latin translation of the Greek word *aretē* and has given us our word *virtue*, is something rather different from what Paul had in mind. It is a moral quality, the kind of inner strength that produces noble behavior and that in pagan eyes merited a reward. By *virtus* a man could save himself—the very opposite of Christian teaching! There is also the intriguing fact that Augustine left out what is perhaps the most significant part of the verses he quoted. What Paul actually wrote was "We preach Christ *crucified, a stumbling block to Jews and folly to Gentiles*, but to those who are called, *both Jews and Greeks*, Christ the power of God and the wisdom of God."

We can perhaps pass over the omission of any reference to the Jews, who were not Augustine's target audience, but his failure to mention the Greeks is surprising, considering that (like Paul) he was attacking an overly philosophized version of the Christian faith. Even more significantly, he omitted the key word "crucified," which makes all the difference. The Manichees did not really know (or care) whether Christ was crucified. They did not believe he possessed genuine human flesh, so if he was not a real man, what did it matter if he appeared to die on a cross? Though the Manichees did not deny that Jesus of Nazareth underwent a "mystical crucifixion,"

---

[71] *Contra academicos* 2.1.1. The Academy was the school of Plato in Athens. The quotation is from 1 Cor. 1:24.
[72] *Contra Faustum* 20.2.
[73] 1 Cor. 1:23–24.
[74] John 14:6. Quoted in *De moribus ecclesiae* 1.13.22.

this had to be interpreted symbolically as a reference to universal suffering. In that context, Jesus's crucifixion was a sign of God's mercy, not of his vulnerability to human pain.[75]

This was essentially what the young Augustine believed in his Manichaean days, and in later years he came to realize that it was an inadequate perception that made his true spiritual condition even worse. Describing the near-fatal illness that he contracted on his arrival in Rome shortly before his conversion, Augustine later wrote:

> I was on the way to hell, bearing all the wrongdoing that I had committed against you, against myself and against others, . . . You had not yet forgiven me in Christ for any of my sins, nor had he as yet delivered me by his cross from the enmity toward you that my sins had caused. How could he deliver me from them, if, as I then believed, his cross was a phantom? To the extent that I thought the death of his flesh was unreal, the death of my soul was real. Conversely, the degree to which the death of his flesh was real, the life of my soul, which did not believe that, was a fiction.[76]

This of course was a view from hindsight, when the issues had become much clearer in Augustine's mind. At the time, and for a number of years following his conversion, he struggled with the meaning of Christ's crucifixion, and it was only as he penetrated more deeply into the thought of Paul on the subject that its true significance became clear to him. Through his reading of Romans, Augustine understood that there were four ages into which the history of God's saving work could be divided. The first of these was the time from Adam to Moses, when sin lay hidden in the human race, making its presence felt by the universal reign of death but without being exposed for what it was.[77] Next came the era of the Mosaic law, when sin "sprang to life," as Paul put it, and its true nature and significance were revealed.[78] That lasted until the coming of Christ, whose example of a sinless life showed that such a thing is possible, and whose grace, given to those who believe in him, allows them to live in a way that is pleasing to God, even if not wholly free from sin. The fourth and final stage has not yet arrived. It will not come until Christ returns, when what

---

[75] Contra Faustum 33.1.
[76] Confessiones 5.9.16.
[77] Rom. 5:13–14.
[78] Rom. 7:9 NIV.

is now revealed only in part will be fully known and experienced by all who put their faith in him.[79]

In this scheme of things, the transition from the law of Moses to the grace of Christ is critical because it marks the shift from a concept of salvation based on works to one rooted in dependence on the grace of God. The pre-Mosaic age was not one of innocence but one of blindness; in that sense, the giving of the law was indeed a revelation and a blessing to those who received it because it taught them what their true spiritual condition was. But just as sin was a temporal phenomenon that had been introduced into the creation and was not an integral part of it, so the law was a temporal remedy, valid for a time and to a limited degree but incapable of getting to the root of the separation of man from God. Only the grace given in Christ, which opened up the vista of eternity and gave believers an experience of a divine reality above and beyond the merely temporal, could truly overcome the power of sin. But the way in which Christ did this was the way of the cross, which believers had to take up for themselves.[80]

At this point, Augustine came to understand that at the heart of the gospel was the message that Christians have been crucified with Christ; the historical fact has become a spiritual experience that transcends time and space. This common Pauline theme became central to Augustine's understanding of the Christian life: "The crucifixion of the old man is signified in the cross of the Lord, just as the rebirth of the new man is signified by the resurrection."[81]

Here we come back to the now familiar distinction that Augustine made between things and signs. The signs of the cross and resurrection are the same, but the things they signify are different. They may refer to Christ's historical death on the cross and his physical resurrection, but they may also refer to our spiritual death and regeneration. The first of these things was a fulfillment of the temporal law of Moses; the second is the eternal result which that fulfillment made possible by bringing the law to an end. This did not invalidate the historicity of the events recorded in the Old Testament. On the contrary, it made sense of them by showing that what happened in the past, under the old dispensation of the Mosaic law, has a direct application to the present. What allegory tried to do by making an imaginary link between the worlds of time and eternity, the

---

[79] *Expositio quarundam propositionum ex epistula ad Romanos* 13–18.
[80] See Matt. 16:24.
[81] *Expositio quarundam propositionum* 32–34.3.

cross of Christ did in reality. The God whom we worship now is not a deity whose true nature was hidden behind the appearances of human history and has now been made known, but one who actually lived a human life and who has taken that history into his eternal self. In other words, we do not transcend the material world in order to experience something above and beyond it, but we discover in our material existence the transforming power of the Holy Spirit who translates the historical work of Christ into our earthly lives.

Augustine believed that this work of "translation," so to speak, opens up the meaning of the Old Testament and allows us to see how it is the Word of God for all time, and not just for the Jews before the coming of the Messiah. It also helped him to interpret what Moses and the prophets had written. A good example of this can be found in Deuteronomy 21:23, which says: "A hanged man is cursed by God." This was universally held by Christians to apply to Christ on the cross, following Paul's statement to that effect in Galatians 3:13, "Cursed is everyone who is hanged on a tree." But did this mean that Moses had cursed Christ? Or were Moses's words uttered unknowingly, reducing his credibility as a prophet and exposing Paul to the charge that he was misusing Scripture? The Manichees were quick to level such accusations, but in an aside on Romans 6:6, Augustine used this verse to penetrate to the theological heart of the crucifixion.[82] As he saw it, Moses wrote what he did not because he wanted to attack Christ, but because he understood that the Messiah would bear the sins of the people on himself. In Paul's description in Galatians 3:13, he would become a curse on our behalf because he would take upon himself the burden of our sins.

To appreciate what was going on here, we have to understand that Augustine was using a Latin translation of Paul's epistles that occasionally misrepresented what Paul was saying. The most famous example of this is in Romans 5:12, where Paul wrote, "Sin entered the world through one man, and death through sin, and in this way death came to all people, because all sinned"; but the Old Latin version that Augustine was using read, "Sin entered the world through one man, and death through sin, and in this way death came to all people, because they sinned *in him*." In other words, not just death, but also the sin of Adam spread to the entire human race. When Christ came as the new Adam, he could undo what the first man had done and set the human race free from his original sin. Much has been

---

[82] *Expositio quarundam propositionum* 32–34.

made of this misreading in modern times, especially by people who want to say that Augustine's doctrine of original sin is unbiblical. But although he unintentionally misinterpreted this particular verse, his overall theological sense was sound enough. The universal fact of human death was all the evidence that Augustine needed to show (1) that sin was equally universal—otherwise universal death would have been unjust—and (2) that only through the death and resurrection of the new Adam could the fall of the old Adam be put right.

Another verse that Augustine unintentionally misread was Romans 8:3. Paul wrote: "[God sent] his own Son in the likeness of sinful flesh to be a sin offering. And so he condemned sin in the flesh" (NIV); but the Old Latin text read, "God sent his Son in the likeness of sinful flesh, and in relation to sin, he condemned sin in the flesh." Augustine understood Paul's point that Christ came in the *likeness* of sinful flesh and not as a sinner himself— a reminder that the material body is not evil and that it is possible to lead a sinless human life, even if nobody who is descended from fallen Adam can now do so. Unfortunately, the Latin text that Augustine was working with changed sin from being the problem to being the means by which the Son eradicated the problem. According to that misreading, the sinless Son became sin in his human flesh, making it seem that human sin had been overcome by a kind of divine sin!

The Latin version made little sense as it stood, but Augustine was able to get around it by appealing to his theological principles. Jesus Christ became our substitute on the cross, taking our place by offering himself for our sins. The precise means by which he did so were secondary. By using his distinction between signs and things, Augustine was able to reconcile the idea that Christ became sin for us (as a sign) without committing actual sin (a thing). In other words, his interpretative method led him to the right conclusion, even though the translation he had in front of him was faulty.

A third verse that Augustine misread was 2 Corinthians 5:21. Here Paul wrote, "God made him who had no sin to be sin for us" (NIV), but some Latin manuscripts omitted the "him," making the sentence read, "God who knew no sin committed sin for us."[83] Here again, Augustine got around the difficulty by appealing to the figurative language of signs, thereby arriving at an orthodox reading of the text despite the mistranslation.

Modern readers, who are used to a high standard of textual accuracy,

---

[83] The Latin verb *make* can also mean "commit" when used of sin.

find it hard to understand this. We have to remember that until the invention of printing, more than a thousand years after Augustine's death, everyone had to rely on handwritten texts that invariably contained errors. What we do not always appreciate is that this problem was well known, and readers developed a skill for discerning what the text ought to say, even when what they had in front of them did not match their expectations.[84] Occasionally, of course, they miscorrected what they read, thinking that it ought to say something different than it did, but that problem was relatively infrequent. Far more serious was the kind of difficulty we find here. A scribe could easily let his eye skip over something he was supposed to be copying, and once the mistake was made, it would spread like a virus to all the manuscripts subsequently copied from it. In such cases Augustine's sixth sense of what the text ought to say came to the rescue. Because he understood the general tenor of the Scriptures, he could make awkward verses like this fit into it, and so he did. Today we cannot accept his methods, but we must remember the problems of transmission that he had to deal with and recognize that on some occasions at least, his hermeneutical principles saved him from falling into errors that would otherwise have arisen from faulty manuscripts.

Having said all this, it remains true that Augustine still had not completely liberated himself from the influence of Manichaeism. The Pauline verses that spoke about Christ being in the *likeness* of sinful flesh were ambiguous. On the one hand, they could be read in a perfectly orthodox way, which was that Christ was a real human being just as we are, although without sin. But on the other hand, they could also be read to imply that although Christ looked like a human being, he was not really one—much as angels could appear as men without being human. The verse that forced him to move more firmly into the orthodox camp was Galatians 3:13, where, as we have already seen, Paul says that Christ became a curse for us.

In his interpretation of this verse there was no way that Augustine could take refuge in the figurative language of signs. Either Christ was a curse or he was not, and Paul clearly said that he was. Of course, a curse is not an objective thing in the way that a sin is. The word itself implies a value judgment on something that in itself might be quite neutral. But neither could the word "curse" be described as a figure or allegory. In Michael Cameron's words: "Paul's phrase . . . referred not to the soul's spiritual self-

---

[84] *De doctrina Christiana* 2.12.18, 3.1.1–3.4.8.

crucifixion but to Christ's unique and unilateral self-surrender to death in love for sinners."[85] What Augustine had previously thought of as a figurative picture of a spiritual experience he now came to see as a material fact containing and transmitting spiritual power. In the former view, Christ's sacrifice was primarily intended to be a model for others to follow, but in the latter it was something quite different. By becoming a man and dying for us on the cross, the Son of God accomplished something that no mere human being could ever do on his own.

But Augustine went further than this in his understanding of how Christ became a curse for us. It was not only that he suffered and died on the cross, but that from the moment he began his public ministry, he taught his disciples the true meaning of the Mosaic law. As Augustine understood it, when Jesus permitted his disciples to eat grain they had plucked on the Sabbath and when he himself healed people on that day of rest, the die was cast. Pious Jews could not accept such behavior because they insisted on keeping the law to the letter, regardless of any other considerations. If doing what was right entailed suffering, then so much the better; such sacrifice by a righteous man would be pleasing in the sight of God. But by claiming that the Sabbath was made for man and not the other way round, Jesus undercut their whole approach to God and his Word.[86]

The supreme irony of the Gospels is that the man who knew no sin was regarded by his Jewish contemporaries as one of the greatest sinners who ever lived. He was prepared to disregard the letter of the law in cases where doing so would have denied its spirit. Interpreted too literally, the law had become a curse, and it was in that sense that Jesus felt its condemnation falling on him.[87] He surrendered to the claims of worldly justice in order to point his followers to the spiritual righteousness that overturned it. Only a true man could pay the penalty inflicted by the law, which was designed for human beings, but only a man who was God could rise above it and bring new life out of it. By his act of self-sacrifice in the flesh, the Son of God made it possible to live, not by following the letter of the law but by the grace of his saving presence. The crucifixion was not a model for others to follow but death to that way of thinking and rebirth to an entirely new kind of life.

As a man Jesus took on sin as the essential part of his sacrifice on our

---

[85] Michael Cameron, *Christ Meets Me Everywhere: Augustine's Early Figurative Exegesis* (Oxford: Oxford University Press, 2012), 149.
[86] Mark 2:27.
[87] *Expositio epistulae ad Galatas* 22.1.

behalf. Even though he was God in human flesh, it was as a man that he suffered and died, and as a man that he submitted to his Father's will in this respect. It was not his will but the will of the Father that was to be done, as sure a sign of his human submission as there could be.[88] It was by that act and the events that followed from it that we have been saved and that our own crucifixion with him becomes both conceivable and necessary. We cannot stand in the place of God, but we can participate in the sufferings of a man who is like us, and it is by doing so that we have been redeemed. By dying on the cross for us, Christ destroyed the body of sin, making it possible for us to mortify our flesh as well. This is how Augustine interpreted Galatians 5:24, which he read as follows: "Those who have been crucified with Christ have crucified their passions and desires." It can be argued that this is not exactly what Paul wrote, but the original text is sufficiently vague that Augustine's interpretation is plausible, if not certain. Paul simply wrote, "Those of Christ," which is usually translated today as "Those who belong to Christ." But, of course, those who belong to him are those who have been crucified with him, as Paul had already said in the same letter, so Augustine's interpolation can be justified in this case.[89]

This is important for his argument, because the crucifixion is central to the believer's experience of divine grace. By his cross, Christ demonstrated the reality of his love, and his love unleashed the power needed to change lives. The grace of our Lord Jesus Christ was not just an empty formula but a real spiritual energy that made a difference to those who experienced it, and it gave them not just a set of new ideas but the firstfruits of eternal life in their everyday experience.[90]

It was when he realized this that Augustine finally understood the importance of Christ's role as "mediator between God and man." The expression is Pauline, occurring as it does in 1 Timothy 2:5, where the apostle stresses that it is as a man (and not as God) that Christ fulfills his mediatorial role. He could not have done so as the Word of God, because the complete identity of the Father and the Son precluded it. A mediator could not represent one side only; he had to be fully God and fully man in order to accomplish this all-important task: "The one and only Son of God became a mediator who was both God and man when the Word of God, who was

---

[88] Matt. 26:42.
[89] See Gal. 2:20.
[90] Augustine developed this in his commentary on Galatians, the only complete commentary of his on a New Testament book, but also in a treatise against Adimantus, which he wrote at roughly the same time. See especially *Contra Adimantum* 21.

God with God, laid aside his majesty to the point of becoming human, and raised up human humility to the level of the divine, in order to become the mediator between God and man."[91]

Once Augustine understood this principle, it became one of the main hallmarks of his writing.[92] The death of Christ's human body not only underscored the reality of the curse, but also guaranteed the genuineness of redemption. His suffering was not a picture lesson in humility and endurance, a kind of Jewish Stoicism. On the contrary, it was the end of one life and the beginning of another (and higher) one. In fact, it was the event that made the Christian life possible. Not only that—the mediatory role of Christ was the link that joined the Old and the New Testaments, the key that unlocked the meaning of the former in light of the revelation of the latter.

Augustine arrived at this remarkable synthesis through his reading of Galatians 3:19–20. Once again, we are faced with a misreading due to mistakes made by the Old Latin translators. Paul wrote, "The law was given through angels and entrusted to a mediator" (v. 19 NIV), by which he meant Moses. But Augustine read this as "the seed was given through angels in the hand of the mediator," interpreting both the seed (correctly) and the mediator (incorrectly) as Christ himself. The effect of this was to make the law of Moses a revelation of the promised seed of Abraham (who was Jesus), which functioned in a mediatorial capacity, but only because it was a foreshadowing of Christ. In other words, the man who read the law correctly saw Christ in it and interpreted its meaning accordingly. In practice, this meant that Christ was already incarnated in and as Israel, the nation that was watched over by angels until such time as the Word would become flesh and fulfill in his body what had up to then only been promised and foreshadowed in the words of the Old Testament. But although the Old Testament was no more than the shadow of what was still to come, there should be no mistake about it—the words of the Hebrew Bible were the words of Christ himself.

> Just as the Word of God is in the prophet, and it is right to say that "The Lord spoke," because the Word of God (that is, Christ) speaks the truth in the prophet, so he also speaks in the angel when the angel proclaims the truth, so it is correct to say that "God spoke" and that "God appeared."[93]

---

[91] *Expositio epistulae ad Galatas* 24.8. This is Paul's point in Gal. 3:20.
[92] See Gérard Remy, *Le Christ médiateur dans l'oeuvre de Saint Augustin* (Lille: Presses de l'Université de Lille, 1979).
[93] *Contra Adimantum* 9.1.

This, of course, is why the messengers of the Old Testament frequently prefaced their remarks with "Thus says the Lord." In their day there was, or at least there appeared to be, a distinction between the messenger and the message, but this distinction, such as it was, was revealed to be no distinction at all once Christ had come. Even in the Old Testament, the message and the messenger were both Christ—the former being the content of his Word and the latter the human instruments he used to convey it.

Once again, we have to admit that Augustine's method of arriving at this conclusion was based on a faulty text, but as in the other cases we have looked at, he managed to come to reasonable and even correct conclusions in spite of that fact. In this case, what we find is that his understanding of how Christ was revealed in the Old Testament led him away from certain types of allegorical interpretation that were common in and before his time. The most important of these was the assertion that in the Old Testament, God appeared to the patriarchs and prophets of Israel in the person of the Son, even though he was disguised as an angel.

Such at least was the way most ancient biblical commentators argued. For example, in the case of the appearance of the three angels to Abraham at the oak trees of Mamre in Genesis 18, the only argument was whether this was a manifestation of the Son, accompanied by two angels, or of all three persons of the Godhead. Augustine rejected all such interpretations, however, because of the way he understood the relationship between Christ and angels. To his mind, the persons of the Trinity revealed themselves as such only in the New Testament. In the Old Testament God remained hidden from the eyes of the people, although he occasionally communicated with them by means of angels. In other words, the three angelic figures who appeared to Abraham at Mamre were just that—not God, but three of his messengers. The same principle applied equally to all such angelic manifestations.

> It has been established by all rational probability . . . and by firm authority as far as the divine words of Scripture have declared it, that whenever it is said that God appeared to our ancestors before the incarnation of our Savior, that the voices heard and the physical manifestations seen were the work of angels. Either they spoke and did things themselves, as representatives of God, just as we have shown the prophets used to do, or they took created materials that were distinct from themselves and used them to give us symbolic representations of God.[94]

---

94 *De Trinitate* 3.27.

This view is closer to what most biblical scholars today are prepared to accept than anything Augustine's contemporaries or predecessors would have said. That is not enough to make him a "modern" interpreter of Scripture, but it does at least show (once again!) that his hermeneutical conclusions were not as adversely affected by the inadequacy of his textual sources as we might at first imagine. As before, we can see that his underlying theological principles preserved him from error, even if they were somewhat dubious themselves.

Much of the time, it must be said, Augustine's hermeneutical presuppositions had little practical effect because he did not often quote the Old Testament. Apart from the creation story in Genesis, the only part of it that retained his attention for long was the book of Psalms. Augustine was attracted to the Psalter at least partly because of his love for music. Hearing Christians sing drew him to the church even before his conversion, and the Psalms were central to Christian worship and devotion. There are of course the usual textual problems that tend to diminish the value of what he has to say—the inadequacy of the Old Latin translation and the unusually large distance between the Hebrew and the Greek texts.[95] But what stands out in his commentary is the way he understood the voice of the psalmist. Today we know that the Psalms were written by a number of different authors over many centuries. The traditional ascription to King David may be genuine in some cases, but there can be no doubt that many psalms are considerably later in date. Psalms 126 and 137, for example, speak of the exile in Babylon, so they must have been written at least four centuries after David's time!

Augustine, it may be said at once, had little interest in whether David was the author of the Psalms. As far as he was concerned, the voice of the psalmist was the voice of Christ speaking through the human writer, whoever he may have been. The principle that he applied was the same one that governed his interpretation of the rest of the Old Testament: Christ speaks to his people through the intermediaries of angels and prophets. But in the case of the Psalter, the voice of Christ takes us much deeper into the mystery of God, because so many of the psalms reveal the inner heart of the man who wrote them. Every aspect of human emotion is covered, something that Augustine interpreted as a sign of the extent to which the Son of

---

[95] The Old Latin was based on the Greek, but not long after Augustine wrote his commentary, Jerome retranslated the psalter from the Hebrew.

God identified with our humanity. This was especially true of psalms like Psalm 51, where the writer confesses the depth of his own sinfulness. Here, Augustine believed, we see just how far Christ went in taking our sins upon himself and dying for them! As he said:

> No matter how great our crimes, forgiveness of them should never be discounted in the holy church for those who truly repent, each according to the measure of his sin. In the act of repentance, where a crime of such seriousness has been committed that it has cut the sinner off from the body of Christ, we should not consider the amount of time [he spends repenting] as much as the degree of sorrow [he demonstrates]. For "a contrite and humble heart God will not despise."[96]

Given this perspective, it is hardly surprising that for him, the most important of the psalms was Psalm 22, whose opening verse Jesus uttered on the cross: "My God, my God, why have you forsaken me?"[97] That famous quotation naturally lent credence to Augustine's hypothesis; Jesus had indeed uttered these words, and so the psalm must be interpreted with reference to him! Moreover, it was the perfect psalm to use as an illustration of Paul's emphasis on being crucified with Christ, since it was on the cross that Jesus experienced the fullness of the emotions it describes.

> Through the voice of the psalmist, which our Lord appropriated to himself, in the form of our weakness, he spoke these words: "My God, my God, why have you forsaken me?" He was undoubtedly forsaken in the sense that his plea was not directly granted. . . . The benefits of the old covenant [in this life] had to be rejected so that we might learn to pray and to hope for the benefits of the new covenant [in the life to come]. . . . In his humanity and through his servant form we can learn what it means to be despised in this life and what is to be hoped for in eternity.[98]

Psalm 22 would form the centerpiece of Augustine's interpretation of Scripture and the basis for its application to the Christian life. The suffering of Christ on the cross and his triumph over death were together a promise to Christians that the sufferings of this world would find their fulfillment and justification in the resurrected life of heaven.

---

96 *Enchiridion* 17.65. The reference is to Ps. 51:17.
97 Matt. 27:46; Mark 15:34.
98 *Epistulae* 140.

The passion of our Lord signifies our time on earth, the time in which we weep. . . . What do all his sufferings mean for us, except to signify the time through which we are now passing, the time of sorrow, the time of mortality, the time of trial? It is a foul period, but let that foulness be dung in the field and not dirt in the house. Let grief arise because of our sins, not because our desires have been frustrated. A foul period, if used to advantage, is a fertile period. . . . A field covered with dung has been reduced to that state in order that it might be more fruitful.[99]

Where Christ went before, his people follow after. But to understand the full implications of this it is necessary to go one step further. Christ's sacrifice was not an event in itself, divorced from any purpose or context in the overall plan of God. On the contrary, it was the supreme manifestation of God's love for fallen man, and only when we understand that can we read the Scriptures and apply them in the right way. Augustine made this very clear when he wrote:

The fulfillment and the end of the law and of all the Holy Scriptures is love; love of the thing that is to be enjoyed, and of the thing that can enjoy it with us, because there is no need for a commandment to tell us that we should love ourselves. . . . If you think that you have understood the Holy Scriptures, or any part of them without understanding that you must build up this double love, of God and neighbor, then you have not yet understood them.[100]

Love is the fulfilling of the law, and there is no greater love than the love that Christ showed by laying down his life for those whom he had chosen for salvation.

The Destiny of the Human Race

The Gospels state clearly that the Son of God came into the world in order to die, and the life and ministry of Jesus are presented in that light. That obviously presupposes that his sacrifice was necessary and intended by God, not because he needed it but because the parlous state of the human condition required it. The Christian message was that God had created the world good, but sin had entered in and corrupted what he had made.

---

99 *Sermones* 254.5. Augustine was preaching on Ps. 22.
100 *De doctrina Christiana* 1.35.39–1.36.40.

This was a difficult idea for the ancient world to grasp. Most people who thought about the problem of evil assumed that it was something objective, like matter, as opposed to "spirit," which was good. Human beings sinned because their souls had been corrupted by their flesh, and there is much in the New Testament that can be read in support of that view. The apostle Paul often spoke of the "flesh" as the evil principle in man, and it was easy for people accustomed to pagan ways of thinking to interpret that in dualistic terms.[101] The idea that God was above and beyond the material world, and therefore immune to its pain and suffering, was also very strong.

The Arians, for example, insisted that Christ could not be fully God because he suffered and died, which God cannot do. The theologians of Augustine's time had to combat that heresy, and in the process they found themselves restructuring their picture of what the world was like. They had to construct a picture of humanity that could be compatible with divinity, at least in moral and spiritual terms, since otherwise the incarnation of the Son of God would have been impossible. That in turn meant rethinking the whole problem of sin and evil, which Christians had to understand as something aberrant, and not inherent in the created order.

What brought sin into the world was not some imperfection in creation but the disobedience of creatures who had been given the free will to choose whether they would do God's will or not. That choice was originally made by Satan, the great fallen angel whom we know as the prince of this world, along with his retinue of angels (or demons as we now call them). The fall of Satan and his angels was a cosmic mystery that was not fully revealed in the Bible. But we know that when God made the material universe, Satan had already fallen, because he appears in the creation story as the Tempter of the first human beings. Like the rest of the created order, Adam and Eve were originally good, but unlike the other creatures, they enjoyed a special relationship with their Creator because they were made in his image and likeness. That relationship was destroyed not because of the inherent limitations of their material nature, but by their disobedience to the clear commands of God. Satan had tempted them to do something that God had forbidden, and when they listened to him, they were fully aware of what they were doing. Their sin was not an accident, but a deliberate choice, and so the punishments they suffered were fully deserved. Adam

---

101 Rom. 7:25; 8:8; 2 Cor. 10:3; Gal. 5:13, 17.

and Eve were expelled from the garden, the protection against death that they had enjoyed there was removed, and they were sentenced to eternal damnation. After that, their descendants, who still retained the image and likeness of God given to them by virtue of their creation, inherited their broken relationship with God, otherwise known as their sinfulness, as a matter of course.[102] Together they constituted a condemned mass (*massa damnata*) of humanity, from which no one can now escape. This was one of Augustine's most frequent refrains, and it is the basic premise on which everything else that he taught on the subject was built.[103]

In saying this, Augustine was not teaching anything that had not been said many times before, not least in the Bible itself, but he went beyond it, because he had his own original take on the standard narrative. Whereas everyone else in the early church assumed that "the image and likeness" in which Adam and Eve were made referred to God in the oneness of his being, Augustine interpreted it as a reference to God as a Trinity.

This was more logical than it might sound, especially if we consider how the Trinity was being debated in his time. Although the precise terminology had not yet been adequately defined, it was becoming clear that all discussion about God had to view him as having two different "levels" or dimensions of being. In what we now call his "nature" God was one, but human beings were definitely not created in the image of that. Even if we agree that the image must be interpreted in spiritual terms and applied to something like the rational soul, we are still light-years away from the being of God. The modern mind might think that the "spiritual" nature of the soul would provide a link with the divine being, but Augustine would have seen that as a form of Platonism or some other ancient Greek philosophy.[104] For him, as for all orthodox Christians, even the rational soul of man was a creature, which meant that in terms of its being, it was diametrically opposed to the Creator who had made it.

The Trinity, on the other hand, was the side of God that was relational and therefore open to contact with human beings. We can pray to the Father, the Son, and the Holy Spirit as persons, and join in fellowship with them at that level, but we cannot link up with their divine being. It therefore makes sense to say that we are created in the likeness of the Trinity,

---

102 *De libero arbitrio* 3.18.52, 3.19.53; *De peccatorum meritis et remissione* 1.9.9–10.
103 *Ad Simplicianum* 1.2.16; *Enchiridion* 27; *De civitate Dei* 21.12; *De dono perseverantiae* 21.53.
104 The idea was that the "soul" would be a portion of the divine spirit that had broken off from it, rather like a spark that has flown out of the fire.

even if we would now interpret this in a way that is different from what Augustine said about it.

Today we would probably say that the image of God is something that gives us a personal relationship with him and the ability to engage in personal relationships with others. For Augustine though, the image of God in man was Trinitarian in the sense that the rational soul manifests a three-fold character, which he described either as being, self-awareness, and self-love, or as memory, intellect, and will. Much of his *De Trinitate* was taken up with developing these themes, with the result that today Augustine is sometimes hailed as the founder of the science of psychology. That may be stretching things a bit, but he was undoubtedly the first thinker who probed the inner recesses of the mind and his analysis is key to understanding the way he approached the fall of man and its effects.

Augustine did not produce his doctrine of the image out of nothing, and when he first suggested that the mind had an innate threefold pattern, he was cautious in the way he applied it to the Trinity:

> I wish that people would think about three things that are present in themselves. These three are very different from the Trinity, but I mention them to challenge people's minds to examine just how different they really are. The three things I am talking about are being, knowing, and willing. . . . I am a being that knows and wills. I know that I am and that I will; I will to be and to know. In these three life, mind, and essence are inseparable, yet they are distinct.[105]

At this early stage, Augustine was careful not to say that the human mind is an image of the Trinity; it is only a possible illustration of it. But when he later returned to the subject, he was much more definite:

> God said, "Let us make man in our image and likeness." . . . The term "our" would not have been used correctly if man had been made in the image of a single person . . . but because he was made in the image of the Trinity, it was said, "in our image." But it is also said that man is made in the image of God, lest we should think that there were three gods in the Trinity.[106]

In making a conscious effort to develop this theme, Augustine naturally started with the principle that God is love. The divine Trinity consists

---

[105] *Confessiones* 13.11.12.
[106] *De Trinitate* 12.6.7.

of one who loves, one who is loved, and the love that flows between them.[107] The human image of this is the mind, which exists in itself, and when it is functioning normally, it knows itself and loves itself in equal measure.[108] But like God, the human mind is not consumed in and by itself. It has the capacity to reach out beyond its own being to know and love other things, and when it does so, it acts in the full realization of its own inner potential. In itself, the normal human mind is perfect because all three aspects of it share the same substance.[109] Of course, the difference between the human mind and God is the usual difference between the creature and the Creator; the human mind is subject to change and decay in a way that the divine Trinity is not.[110]

Here Augustine found a picture of the Trinity, but it did not fully satisfy him because it was self-contained and inherently inadequate, despite its relative perfection. No human mind can fully know itself, and it follows that no human mind can fully love itself either. We love what we know, but if what we know is imperfect, then what we love will be correspondingly imperfect.[111] For the mind to be an adequate image of God, it must be not only perfect within itself, but also capable of relating to its archetype, which is perfect in an altogether superior way. To explain how this can be, Augustine moved on to a second image of the Trinity, which he described as "memory, intellect, and will."[112] Once again, he insisted that all three of these are equal and interconnected:

> If they were not equal, not only to one another but also each individually to the whole, they could not contain each other. Not only is each of them absorbed by the others, but all of them are present in all. I remember that I have memory, understanding, and will; I understand that I understand and will and remember; and I will that I will and remember and understand.[113]

The beauty of this threefold scheme as an image of the Trinity is that while each of the three parts can be considered separately, none of them can be conceived apart from the others. Memory, for example, is clearly not

---

107 *De Trinitate* 8.10.14.
108 *De Trinitate* 9.4.4.
109 *De Trinitate* 9.4.7.
110 *De Trinitate* 9.6.9.
111 *De Trinitate* 10.4.6.
112 *De Trinitate* 10.11.18, 14.8.11.
113 *De Trinitate* 10.11.18.

the same thing as intellect or will, but it would be unimaginable without them, just as they would be inoperable without it. If there were no intellect, there would be no way of perceiving memory; and if there were no will, it would be impossible to do anything with it. Yet in fact, memory not only exists; it is constantly being employed by the intellect in order to shape human action in and through the will. Much the same can be said of each of the other elements that make up the mind. The intellect cannot function without data, and they are supplied by the memory. The will would be irrational without the input of the data of memory and the analysis of that data by the intellect. We may find this easier to understand today than previous generations did, because we know that our computers function in much the same way, with stored memory forming the raw material on which a software program operates according to the will of the person using it. The similarity of the computer to the human brain is obvious, but to Augustine the brain that would devise the computer is made in the image of God, whose three persons reflect the same distinctions and community of operation as our minds do.

For Augustine, the analogy of "memory, intellect, and will" is closer to the Trinity than the earlier one of "being, self-knowledge, and self-love" because it places greater emphasis on the activity involved in mutual relationship. In the earlier picture, the first element was simply there while the other two related to it in some way, but here we see an interaction involving all three parts functioning together in the same unity of mind: "We found the mind, in its memory, understanding, and willing of itself, to be such that it must be understood as always remembering, knowing, and loving itself at the same time, since it was perceived as always knowing and loving itself."[114]

Of course, as always there is a gap between the image and the prototype, which is God himself. In this case, Augustine noted that the mind is not always thinking of itself and frequently acts as if the three elements that make it up are in fact one and the same because they are almost impossible to distinguish in particular instances. As Augustine described this, "There is, in the hidden part of the mind, knowledge of some things which comes out into the open when they are thought of, for then the mind discovers that it remembers, understands, and loves itself, even when it was thinking about something else."[115]

---

[114] De Trinitate 10.12.19.
[115] De Trinitate 14.7.9.

For the human mind to know itself properly it must pause and reflect, something that is not necessary for God to know himself.

> The sight of itself is something that belongs to the nature of the mind, and it comes back to the mind when it thinks about itself . . . but when the mind is not thinking about itself it is not in its own sight, nor is its vision formed out of it, but it still knows itself as if it were a memory of self to itself.[116]

Augustine recognized the superiority of this analogy of the Trinity over the earlier one, because it spoke of a word that was formed by the thought of the mind and was then united to it by a common will.[117] In the first analogy the mental word was an end in itself, but now we find that it is active and creative, making it more like the Word of God, which it was meant to reflect.

It remained for Augustine only to bring his mental analogy to perfection by making the final leap from the self to the other. In the two pictures just given, the human mind is essentially absorbed in itself, but this was not good enough. As he said: "The trinity of the mind is not the image of God just because it remembers, understands, and loves itself, but because it is also able to remember, understand, and love the one by whom it was made. It is when it does this that it becomes wise."[118]

Here is where Augustine really started to engage with the personal relationship between man and God that was so essential to human well-being and salvation. Self-love is only natural and to be expected, but if it is divorced from the love of God, it really amounts to a form of self-hate because it cuts itself off from the source of its being and identity.[119] The man who fails to see himself as he truly is, made in God's image and beholden to him for everything that he is and has in this life, has forgotten who he really is and is bound to suffer as a result.

> [A man must know himself] in order to understand himself and live according to his nature. What that means is that he must try to order his life in accordance with his nature, in subjection to the one who merits [his obedience], and in preference to everything else. . . . The mind does many things through depraved desire, as if it has forgotten itself. It sees the

---

[116] *De Trinitate* 14.6.8.
[117] *De Trinitate* 14.10.13.
[118] *De Trinitate* 14.12.15.
[119] *De Trinitate* 14.14.18.

beauty of God's more excellent nature, but although it should concentrate on enjoying them, it turns away and attributes God's excellence to itself. It tries to be like him not by depending on him, but by imitating him in its own strength, and so while it thinks it is rising higher and higher, in fact it is slipping down lower and lower. It cannot exist on its own, nor can anything be adequate for it, if it turns away from the one who alone is sufficient.[120]

The practical importance of this for Augustine is that when man fell into sin, God was insulted because his image, the sign of his power and dominion over the creation, was taken captive by his enemy the Devil. What had been intended to be the crowning glory of creation now became an instrument for evil, which was all the more serious given the inherent ability of the image of God to exercise dominion over the creatures. Augustine did not believe that the image had been corrupted or destroyed in any objective sense. Adam was not mentally handicapped after his fall, and he retained the full use of his rational faculties, including the freedom of his will. But the uses of those faculties were altered dramatically. Instead of serving God, they became instruments of rebellion and disobedience, making it possible for man to harm himself and the rest of creation through the very means that were originally intended to help him govern it. Even the freedom of the human will did not mean that fallen man could escape from sinning. That freedom offered a choice of where and how he could act, but since he was cut off from God by his sinfulness, anything he might choose to do, even if good in itself, would still be inherently sinful.[121]

This captivity of the human mind to the power of sin was total. In particular, it was not possible to imagine a depraved will functioning alongside a memory and intellect that remained intact. When the apostle Paul said that he could not do the good that he wanted to do, this was not because his intellect understood what was good and his will was incapable of acting on it. His mind was able to appreciate the good and even to want to do it, but he could not achieve this desire because spiritually he was enslaved to a power that was opposed to God. That made him not merely helpless but guilty. Commenting on Romans 7:18 ("For I have the desire to do what is right, but not the ability to carry it out") Augustine had this to say:

---

120 *De Trinitate* 10.5.7.
121 *De libero arbitrio* 2.10.29; *De vera religione* 14.27; *De gratia et libero arbitrio* 2.3–6. This same principle is affirmed in article 13 of the Thirty-Nine Articles of the Church of England (1571) in the context of works done before justification, which "partake of the nature of sin" even if they are good in themselves.

To those who do not understand him correctly, it seems that Paul is here abolishing freedom of choice. But how can he be doing that when he says that he knows what is right and wants to do it? Wanting to do the right thing is within our power, but doing it is not, because of the consequences of original sin. Nothing now remains of the original nature of the human race apart from the punishment due to sin. Because of that, mortality has become a kind of second nature, and it is from this that the grace of the Creator frees those who have submitted to him in faith.[122]

The sinless man Jesus Christ was not afflicted with this burden of guilt however, because his spiritual union with the Father and the Holy Spirit in the Godhead made it possible for his rational human mind to function as it should. Jesus was neither a superman nor a freak; he was what Adam would have been had he not fallen into the clutches of the Devil.[123]

The fall has touched every aspect of the individual's life and has spread to the entire human race. We are all one in Adam, whether we have personally sinned or not. This is especially true of infants, who are sinful even though they have not committed any actual sin.

> A child does not know where it is, what it is, or by whom it was created. It is already guilty of sin, even though it is not yet capable of obeying a command. It is involved in so thick a fog of ignorance, and is so overwhelmed by it that it cannot be roused, as if from sleep, so that it might become aware of such things if they were to be pointed out. We have to wait until it has slept off this drunkenness of sorts . . . and that takes many months and years. Until that happens, we tolerate so many things in infants that we would punish in adults that we cannot count them all. But if infants only acquired this great evil of ignorance and weakness after they were born, where, when, and how did they suddenly become wrapped in such darkness by committing some great act of godlessness?[124]

Adam's alienation from God is what we have inherited. Because it is spiritual and not moral or intellectual, it can be put right only by a spiritual rebirth. The philosophers tried to achieve this by elaborate moral and intellectual schemes, but good as some of these were (and Platonism was especially impressive in this respect), they were unachievable because of

---

[122] *Ad Simplicianum* 1.1.11.
[123] *De peccatorum meritis et remissione* 2.24.38. See also the sections leading up to this one, in particular 2.22.36 and 2.23.37.
[124] *De peccatorum meritis et remissione* 1.36.67.

the spiritual deficit in human life that could not be met in that way. This was why the apostle Paul had such a negative view of philosophy. However good it was in theory, it was useless in practice, and Christians had to be particularly vigilant not to be seduced by a counterfeit of the real thing. Augustine knew that he could easily have fallen into that trap himself, which is why he was so determined to make sure that others were warned about its dangers.

God dealt with the problem of inescapable human sinfulness not by enlightening the human mind with knowledge that would enable it to escape sin, but by restoring those who believed in him to a new life in Christ. Fallen human beings were not given a set of goals to aim for, as if salvation could be compared to a physical fitness test, but were assisted by the indwelling presence of the Holy Spirit, who united them to Christ. In this way God applied to them the saving power of Christ's blood shed on the cross for their salvation and made up for their inevitable failures and deficiencies by forgiving them, relieving them of the burden of sin, and adopting them into his family and fellowship. All of this he did freely for the benefit of his chosen people, and for this reason his saving work is known collectively as *grace*, a word that simply means "favor."[125] Augustine was well aware that our adoption as children of God was in some respects still a work in progress. We have been taken into his family but have not yet been totally conformed to his likeness. Commenting on 2 Corinthians 4:16 ("Though our outer self is wasting away, our inner self is being renewed day by day") he had this to say:

> Obviously those who are still being renewed from day to day have not been fully renewed. And to the extent that they have not been fully renewed, they are still in their old condition. . . . Even though they have been baptized, they are still children of the world to that extent. . . . But to the extent that they are wise in the Spirit and lead lives corresponding to that, they are children of God.[126]

For Augustine, the creation, fall of man, and incarnation of the Son were all parts of a comprehensive divine plan. Nothing that happens in the world is an accident, whatever it looks like on the surface. We may think that particular incidents are good or bad, or that it is possible to go against

---

125 *De Trinitate* 14.16.22.
126 *De peccatorum meritis et remissione* 2.7.9.

God's will, but this impression is only superficial. At a deeper level, God is fully in control of events, and even the Devil must bow to his commands. Furthermore, what is true in cosmic terms is also true in the lives of each individual human being. Augustine did not believe, as many ancient people did, that we are governed by some unknown and impersonal fate. Neither did he think that we must suffer whatever destiny is reserved for our family, tribe, or nation. On the contrary, the message of the gospel is that God cares for each one of his human creatures individually and that he deals with us on that basis. Jews were specially privileged, but since the coming of Christ the way of salvation has been opened to people from every nation, though not everyone benefits from it.

The reason for this is that God has appointed some to eternal life but not others. Here we come to one of the deepest mysteries of the Christian faith, something so hard to grasp that even Augustine advised preachers to be careful about how they expounded it, so as not to upset those who are slower to understand or weaker in their faith.[127] The challenge he recognized is still very much with us today, and many who would call themselves "Christians" reject this key element of biblical teaching.

There can be no doubt that the doctrine of predestination, as this mystery is called, is clearly taught in the Scriptures, especially in the epistles of Paul. Admittedly, it was not much developed in the early church, which preferred to think in terms of divine foreknowledge rather than predestination. The difference is that in the former view, God knew what was going to happen but did not cause it, whereas in the latter case, God ordained what would come to pass. Typical of the early church's perspective was the statement attributed to the second-century writer Tatian in his *Address to the Greeks*: "The power of the Word is able to foresee future events, but those events are not fated to take place. They occur because free agents have chosen them."[128]

Similar statements can be found in the works of Tertullian and the great Greek historian of the church Eusebius of Caesarea, who lived two generations before Augustine.[129] His great Eastern contemporary, John Chrysostom, expressed what was then the common (and later became the standard) view of the Greek church:

---

[127] *De dono perseverantiae* 16.40, 22.57–59, 61.
[128] Tatian, *Oratio ad Graecos* 7.
[129] Tertullian, *Adversus Marcionem* 2.5; Eusebius of Caesarea, *Praeparatio Evangelii* 6.11.

God never compels anyone by necessity or by force, but rather desires everyone to be saved. He does not impose any necessity on anyone, as the Apostle Paul says: "He desires everyone to be saved and to come to a knowledge of the truth" (1 Tim. 2:4). So how is it that not everybody is saved when God wants them to be? The answer is that not everyone chooses to follow his will, and God does not force anyone to do so.[130]

Augustine inherited this tradition and never explicitly rejected it, since he recognized that even the New Testament sometimes described divine predestination in terms of foreknowledge.[131] Modern commentators have often stated that Augustine did not move from belief in divine foreknowledge to a more definite conception of predestination until after his encounter with Pelagianism in 411, but this is hard to substantiate. It is certainly true that he discussed the implications of predestination in much greater depth in his anti-Pelagian treatises than he had previously, but it is not clear whether he changed his understanding of the issues or merely developed ideas already present in his thinking. The probability is that he already had an unformed notion of predestination before he was forced by circumstances to expound it, and what he said about foreknowledge ought to be read with this in mind.[132] However, he certainly taught that predestination was based on foreknowledge in his unfinished commentary on Romans, a position that he explicitly retracted toward the end of his life.[133] In his early days, some of what he said sounded as if it could have come from Tertullian or Chrysostom, and yet it is cast in a way that only Augustine would have said it. Even when talking about the human mind, Augustine was really focusing on God and on his thought processes:

Just as your memory does not force you to make past events take place, so God's foreknowledge does not force him to bring about events in the future. And just as you remember some of the things you have done in the past but have not actually done all the things you remember, so God knows in advance everything that he will do but has not therefore already

---

[130] John Chrysostom, *Homiliae XXV in quaedam loca Novi Testamenti*, "De ferendis repraehensionibus et de mutatione nominum," 3.6, a sermon preached on Acts 9:4 (*Patrologiae cursus completus. Series Graeca*, ed. J.-P. Migne, 161 vols. [Paris, 1857–1886], 51:144). Jerome said much the same thing in his *Commentarius in Ieremiam* 5.26.3.
[131] *De dono perseverantiae* 17.41, 18.47.
[132] See for example, his remarks in *Ad Simplicianum* 1.2.8–9 and in his *Confessiones* 10.6.81, 10.29.40, 10.37.60, all of which predate his first encounter with Pelagianism.
[133] *Epistulae ad Romanos inchoata expositio* 60–61. For the retraction, see *Retractationes* 1.22.

done beforehand. He is not the wicked doer of evil things but the just avenger of them.[134]

Yet whatever Augustine may have suspected in his own thoughts, the evidence suggests that he taught the standard position of the church on the subject until he was challenged, at which point he reexamined it and recast it in the light of the controversies that the teaching of Pelagius and his followers had aroused. Whether this amounted to a change in his theology though, is hard to say because Augustine understood both divine foreknowledge and predestination in the context of the mind of God, which was beyond time and space and in which what we call foreknowledge and predestination amount to the same thing. In his words, "How can we, with our feeble mental capacity, comprehend how God's foresight is the same as his memory and understanding, and how he does not observe things by thinking of them one by one, but embraces everything that he knows in one eternal, unchangeable, and inexpressible vision?"[135]

The effect of this conjunction in the mind of God, of course, is to make foreknowledge irrelevant, since it is only compatible with a time-and-space framework, which does not apply to God. Predestination, on the other hand, though expressed in a time-and-space dimension (because otherwise we would not be able to comprehend it), is really an eternal phenomenon—as valid in the "past" as it is in the "future," since both are comprehended in the overarching and eternal present.

Let us pause to retrace the flow of Augustine's logic so that we can see what predestination meant to him and why he thought it such an important part of the gospel message. In his mind, the human race was condemned to eternal damnation because of the sin of Adam, from which it was impossible to escape. That in itself was a form of determinism—we are all going to hell whether we want to or not, and we have nobody to blame for it but ourselves. This is the situation that we have inherited. The wages of sin is death, and we shall all die, whether we like it or not. There is no choice here; we have to take what we have been given and make the best of it.

If we start with this self-evident fact, we can see that even before we do anything at all, our freedom of choice is severely limited. If we could

---

134 *De libero arbitrio* 3.4.11.
135 *De Trinitate* 15.7.13.

really choose to lead a sinless life, for example, we would be able to choose not to die, which is clearly impossible. In the end it is the universality of *death*, not of sin, that is the real clincher of Augustine's argument. Paul said that all die in Adam, and all shall be made alive in Christ, not that all have sinned in Adam and that all shall be made sinless in Christ.[136] The difference may seem trivial, but it is not, because those who are made alive in Christ are not also made sinless. On the contrary, they are sinners who are saved by grace—in other words, by what God has decided and not by what they have chosen. His judgments are beyond our understanding, but they are always right.

> All human beings are headed toward condemnation because they are born of Adam, unless they are reborn in Christ. Furthermore, God has provided that they should be born again before they die, and he is the most generous donor of grace to those whom he has predestined to eternal life, just as he is the most righteous avenger on those whom he has predestined to eternal death, not merely against those who have done something wrong but against infants who have not done anything at all, because of their original sin.[137]

This is important for several reasons. Heaven is God's home, and he is the one who decides whom he will let into it. We cannot choose to go there independently of him, nor have we any right to pick the seat that we want when we get there.[138] Those who have been saved do not deserve the gift they have received and do not have an entitlement to benefits. God does not operate a welfare state system! When seeking to explain why God created people whom he knew would be condemned to hell, Augustine did not cite their freedom to choose as the explanation, but relied on something much more fundamental:

> It would indeed be unjust if God had made vessels of wrath for destruction (Rom. 9:22), had they not belonged to the universal race of the condemned that descends from Adam. What is made a vessel of wrath by birth receives its deserved punishment, but what is made a vessel of mercy by rebirth receives undeserved grace.[139]

---

136 1 Cor. 15:22.
137 *De anima et eius origine* 4.11.16.
138 Matt. 20:20–28.
139 *Epistulae* 190.3.9.

This affirmation lies at the heart of Augustine's doctrine of predestination. Those who cry for justice are in fact crying for universal damnation, because that is what the human race deserves. The mystery and the miracle of the gospel is not that some people go to hell in spite of it, but that some people are saved from hell because of it! This is extremely hard for many people to accept, because we instinctively feel that people who work hard deserve a reward, while those who have done nothing do not. Yet in the kingdom of heaven we find that everything is turned on its head. The workers who have turned up at the eleventh hour get the same wages as those who have been there all day, whether anyone thinks this is fair or not.[140] It is not that the idle will be rewarded—there is clear evidence in the New Testament that those who do nothing will lose out on the day of judgment.[141] But although we are called to work hard, our work is meant to be service to the Lord in a spirit of love and thanksgiving for what we have received, not a struggle to earn something that can come to us only as a gift. Even if we perform miracles in Christ's name, we have no claim on his mercy and will be rejected in the end if our heart is not right with God.[142]

The idea that we can be saved only by the grace of God and not by any action (or lack of action) on our part is uncongenial to many people, but at least it can be understood. Far more difficult is the notion that God created Adam and Eve with the intention that they should fall away from their original goodness. Yet that is what Augustine taught:

> If God had wanted to preserve the first man in the good estate in which he had created him and to lead him on to better things at the right time, after he had had children and before the coming of death, so that not only would he not have committed sin but he would not even have wanted to sin, Adam would have desired to remain without sin, just as he had been created, and God would have known in advance that he would have the will to do so. But because God knew that Adam would misuse his free will and that he would sin, he prepared his own will for that eventuality, so that he might do something good even when Adam had done the opposite. Thus the good desire of the Almighty was not destroyed by the evil will of humanity, but fulfilled.[143]

---

[140] Matt. 20:1–16.
[141] Matt. 25:1–30.
[142] Matt. 7:21–23. See *De dono perseverantiae* 11.25.
[143] *Enchiridion* 104. See also *De Genesi ad litteram* 11.9.12, where Augustine says much the same thing.

Augustine knew that salvation was a work of God and that not everyone was saved, a combination of facts that led naturally to the conclusion that God has chosen some people for salvation but not others. But the basis for his choice remained a mystery that human logic cannot fathom.

> It is amazing how God regenerates some people in Christ and gives them the gifts of faith, hope, and love, yet does not add to these the gift of perseverance, when at the same time there are others whose wickedness he forgives and by bestowing his grace on them, makes them his children. Is this not amazing? . . . He alienates children from the kingdom into which he has brought their parents, yet brings others, who are children of his enemies, into his kingdom. He does this in spite of the fact that the children of believers may have done nothing bad and the children of unbelievers have deserved nothing good. The judgments of God are righteous and deep and can neither be blamed nor penetrated.[144]

Augustine, of course, was well aware of the biblical texts that appeared to contradict his doctrine, and he dealt with them clearly and frankly. When it was objected that in 1 Corinthians 15:22 Paul said that in Christ "all" would be made alive, which suggests a form of universal salvation, Augustine replied:

> This means that even though there are a great many people who will be punished with eternal death, all those who receive eternal life receive it in and through Christ, and in no other way. Likewise, the verse that says "God wants everyone to be saved" (1 Tim. 2:4) means that although there are a great many people whom he does not want to be saved, those who are saved are saved only because he wants them to be.[145]

The argument here is convoluted and not very satisfactory. In particular, his interpretation of 1 Timothy 2:4 inverts the text without explaining how it can be reconciled with a doctrine of predestination, and many people have rejected his explanation for that reason. But to be fair to him, elsewhere he returns to the same verse and gives a more plausible interpretation of it. By "everyone" God did not mean "every single individual" but "every type of person"—that is to say, not just Jews, the rich, the intelligent, or whomever. It is not possible for human minds to decide who will and

---

[144] *De correptione et gratia* 8 (18).
[145] *Epistulae* 217.6.19.

who will not be saved, and we must therefore preach the gospel to everyone without exception. Whether they respond or not is up to God, not us.[146] This is essentially the kind of explanation that would be given today, and it accords with our knowing that the gospel was preached to all kinds of people, in contrast to the law of Moses, which was given only to the Jews.

Augustine also insisted that the preaching of the Word was efficacious. We do not know why Christ came into the world when he did, or why God sent his messengers to some nations and not to others; but where his Word went, there people believed and were saved.

> When the Ephesians heard the word, they heard it not as the word of man but as the word of God. God therefore works in the hearts of men by calling them according to his purpose, that they should not hear the Gospel in vain but should be converted and believe, receiving it not as the words of men but as the word of God, which in truth it is.[147]

In other words, rather than sit around speculating about who is saved and who is not, Christians should fulfill their calling to preach the Word of God, and watch him use that to bring his sheep into the kingdom. Our calling is not meant to excuse us from working to spread the gospel, but the very opposite—we are the workers who have been sent to reap the harvest.[148] Our job is to gather in the wheat; the tares it contains will be separated out not by us but by God at the last judgment.[149]

Augustine did not boast of his spiritual calling from God or regard himself as superior to others on account of it. Nor did he claim to know who was (and more importantly, who was not) chosen and called in the way that he had been. But that there was such a calling and that it applied to all those who were saved, he had no doubt. It was not based on any human merit, whether that was determined by descent or by individual achievement. Nobody could say why God put his hand on some and not on others; that was the mystery of his sovereignty. But it was also the mystery of his love. A human being who had no claim on God's mercy could receive it and be transformed from being a sinner into being a servant of Christ. Nobody was so evil that he or she could not be changed in this way, so there was hope for even the most wretched human beings. At the same time, nobody

---

[146] *De correptione et gratia* 14 (44), 15 (47).
[147] *De praedestinatione sanctorum* 19.39.
[148] Matt. 9:37.
[149] Matt. 13:25–29.

was so blessed in this life that he or she could presume on the goodness of God. People who had a high opinion of themselves could (and often would) be brought low, because only those who were humble in spirit would enter into the kingdom of heaven. God's ways are not our ways, and whether we are "good" or "bad" in the world's eyes, we must all be transformed and made new by the grace of God.

Predestination is the foundation not only of our future life in eternity but also of our present experience of God. To know him is to love him, and to love him is to submit to his will, knowing that all things work together for good to those whom he has loved and called according to his purpose. This is the spirit that enables a believer to endure whatever may come his way and to remain triumphant in his spirit despite all the apparent setbacks of this life. In the end, this doctrine must be preached because the alternative is a form of works righteousness, which is a denial of the gospel.

> Either predestination must be preached in the way and degree in which Holy Scripture plainly declares it, so that the gifts and calling of God might be without repentance in those who are predestined, or it must be said that God's gifts are given according to our merits, which is the opinion of the Pelagians. . . . Grace precedes faith, because if it were the other way round, then the will would certainly precede faith, because there cannot be faith without will. But if grace precedes faith because it precedes will, it must certainly precede all obedience and love, by which alone God is truly obeyed. Grace brings about all these things in those to whom it is given, and therefore it must precede all these things.[150]

The Christian life is formed by the grace of God and can be lived only in response to it. That is what the doctrine of predestination teaches and why it is so important for believers. We are saved not by our works—either before or after our conversion—but by the love and mercy of God, who has chosen us in spite of ourselves and who will bring us home to the glory that he has prepared for us from before the foundation of the world.

---

[150] *De dono perseverantiae* 16.41.

CHAPTER 4

AUGUSTINE THE PASTOR

Augustine and the Church

From 396 until his death in 430, Augustine was bishop of Hippo, a medium-sized port city on the North African coast. In common with everyone who held that office, he was responsible for the preaching and teaching ministry of the church there. We have no way of knowing how many people would have heard him on any given occasion, but we can assume that one way or another, he would have reached most of the local population. It is very likely that a number of subsidiary churches or chapels dotted Hippo and its surroundings, for which Augustine would have had ultimate responsibility, but normally he would have delegated pastoral duties to one of the presbyters (elders) attached to him. Even so, he probably visited the outlying areas on occasion, and people could always go to hear him whenever they wished. Directly or indirectly, his influence would have been felt throughout the city and its environs. Occasionally he would also go to provincial synods as the representative of his church, and so he would have been able to minister in that context, and probably also in the churches of Carthage, the capital where the synods were held.

Beyond that however, he did not venture. He never attended an ecumenical council of the whole church, though he was invited to one to be held at Ephesus in 431. By then he was dead and North Africa had been overrun by the Arian Vandals, which would have made it virtually impossible for any of its bishops to attend. As a result, the greatest theologian of the Western church never went anywhere further than Carthage during his tenure as bishop, though he kept in touch with the wider world through his correspondence, much of which has survived.

The church to which Augustine belonged and which he knew most intimately was that of North Africa. It could trace its history back to the second century and was the first province of the Roman Empire in which Latin was used regularly in worship. The earliest Christian literature in Latin comes from Tertullian, who was writing in Carthage for about thirty years on either side of AD 200. He was soon followed by Cyprian, the energetic bishop of Carthage who was martyred for his faith in 258. By the time Christianity became a legal religion in 313, the church was well established, not only in the cities but also in parts of the countryside. Unfortunately, it was at the very moment that it came out of the shadows that the church split down the middle over a disciplinary matter that proved to be intractable.

North Africa seems to have had a special liking for martyrs, who were highly venerated from the time of Tertullian onward. Conversely, those who ran away to escape persecution were despised for their cowardice. In the early years of the fourth century there had been a severe and systematic attempt to eradicate Christianity throughout the empire, and many people compromised with the state in order to save their lives. They were required to hand over whatever portions of the Bible they might have, as well as offer worship to the emperor and the pagan gods. Some complied; others ran away. When the dust settled, however, many repented of their failure to resist and sought readmittance to the fellowship of the church. Whether (and on what conditions) that should be allowed was the most fundamental question at issue when the church was legalized.

Closely connected with this was the question of how much veneration should be given to martyrs. The problem was that much of this veneration bordered on superstition, as bones and other relics of those who had died for their faith were preserved and treated as semi-magical tokens. As we have seen, even Monica, Augustine's mother, did this, and had to be rebuked by Ambrose because of it. This is what happened in Carthage to a woman called Lucilla, who wanted her bishop to bless the bones of a martyr as she received communion. The bishop refused, whereupon Lucilla and her supporters accused him of collaborating with the enemies of the church who had so recently persecuted it. Lucilla seems to have been an inveterate troublemaker. When the bishop in question, a man called Caecilianus, was elected in 305, she and her friends rejected him on the ground that the man who consecrated him, Felix of Aptunga, had turned over the Scriptures to the authorities during the great persecution. They therefore proceeded to elect a rival bishop, a certain Majorinus, and did all they could to get him accepted in place of Caecilianus. They even wrote to the emperor Constantine, but failed to impress him with the justice of their case.

The result was that the protesters broke away from the mainline church, which they accused of compromise and impurity, and established congregations of true believers. They came to be known as Donatists, from a man named Donatus, who was one of their early leaders and by all accounts a bishop of exceptional quality and character. The Donatists were not heretics—they did not preach any unorthodox doctrine—but schismatics, because they broke away from the mainline church and refused to recognize its authority. The distinction was significant. It meant that while at one level, Augustine was able to mix with Donatists and use their writings—in particular, the biblical studies of Tyconius, a leading Donatist theologian, which Augustine incorporated into his own work on the subject—at another level, they were intolerable. Not only did they absent themselves from the mainline church; they attacked it as corrupt and subservient to a godless state. One of their bishops, Petilianus of Cirta, did not hesitate to criticize Augustine personally, using the *Confessions* as evidence of his dissolute character. In response to this, Augustine told his congregation: "[My critics] speak of many things which they know nothing about, and of other things that they know only too well. But these things belong to my past and I have dealt with them much more firmly than they have dealt with their past errors, because I have broken with them and put them behind me."[1]

He went on to add that he put no trust in himself, but only in the church, where he had learned to place his faith not in man but in the grace and mercy of God. None of this made much impression on the Donatists though. By the time Augustine came on the scene, they had developed the notion that a true church would necessarily be persecuted, so that in their eyes the legalization of Christianity from which the mainline church had benefitted was an abandonment of the gospel.

To Augustine's mind, the Donatists were a social and political nuisance. There was no doctrinal reason for their separation from the rest of the church, and Augustine put their schismatic tendencies down to

---

[1] *Enarrationes in Psalmos* 36.3.

obstinacy. As someone with an academic background, he might have been able to tolerate those who thought differently from him, but why people who shared his faith should refuse his fellowship was incomprehensible. As he saw it, the Donatists were spiritually ill, and he dealt with them accordingly. Speaking to his own flock and urging them to reach out to the Donatists and try to reconcile them, he had this to say:

> Harmony will come, light will come. Therefore, dearly beloved, I urge you in love to show these people [the Donatists] your Christian and catholic tenderness. Those you have to deal with are sick people. Their eyes are red and need long and gentle treatment. None of you should haggle with them as if you were after a bargain, nor should you get into an argument about religion, since that will only set the sparks flying. Perhaps you will be insulted—if so, be patient and pretend not to hear. Take my words literally. To nurse the sick means just that—it does not mean starting an argument. . . . Think things through and consider what is at stake here. Pray for your adversary.[2]

The extent of Donatism and its relative strength in relation to the mainline church are very difficult to determine with any accuracy. What we know is that it was strong enough to present a viable alternative to the mainline church, and in many rural areas it was dominant. Hippo was a largely Donatist city when Augustine went there, and he struggled against it for the first fifteen years of his episcopate. During that time, the Donatists were often tolerated by the state authorities, either because they secretly sympathized with them or because the Donatists were too numerous to be suppressed. Many attempts were made to heal the schism, including a very generous offer that would have seen the Donatist bishops and priests reintegrated into the mainline church without losing their episcopal status. At the church council held in 411 the Donatists knew that they were on the defensive, and they proved to be obdurate, but they lost the debate, which was adjudicated by an imperial envoy named Marcellinus.

Soon afterward, the emperor issued an edict that revoked their legal privileges and assigned their property to the mainline church. The Donatist clergy was instructed to submit in return for recognition of their status, and it seems that most of them did so, despite some opposition in

---

[2] *Sermones* 357.3.

the rural areas. Unfortunately, though, Augustine was so impressed by the success of the imperial edict that he began to soften his earlier opposition to the use of force against schismatics. He started to interpret Jesus's words "Compel people to come in" (Luke 14:23) as a justification for coercing the recalcitrant Donatists. When it was objected that the apostles never forced anybody to accept their faith, Augustine replied that they were fishermen, who were content with their catch. But after the fishermen, he went on to argue, God sent the hunters, as Jeremiah had prophesied he would.[3] In his eyes, "these hunters are ourselves, our duty being to beat up souls from the bushes at the base of those great heretical mountains named after Arius, Photinus, and Donatus."[4]

The continued obstinacy of a few when the majority were accepting the "truth" of the mainline church hardened Augustine's heart.[5] He continued to claim that tolerance was the normal principle on which a bishop should act, but that force had to be used from time to time, because although the most enlightened people were drawn to the truth by love, the majority responded only when under threat.[6] Perhaps his reaction was understandable in the circumstances, when he felt that he was dealing with a mop-up operation designed to weed out the kind of protesters who would never see reason, but it was to have disastrous long-term consequences. Like it or not, the persecution of heretics and religious dissidents that so disfigured later times derived much of its support and justification from this attitude of Augustine, leading to bitterness and accusations of hypocrisy that persist to this day.

Augustine ceased to worry about Donatism once force was used against it, but it did not disappear. In many places it went underground and survived every attempt to extinguish it until North Africa fell to the Muslims in the late seventh century. After that, it seems to have disappeared as the people were converted to Islam. Some members of the mainline church emigrated to Europe, but if any Donatists joined them, they must have left their schism behind as they went. Donatism died with Christianity in North Africa because it had never existed anywhere else—a limitation that was one of the arguments used by Augustine to show that it was not an authentic church.

---

[3] See Jer. 16:16.
[4] *De utilitate ieiunii* 12.
[5] *Epistulae* 86.2.
[6] *Epistulae* 185.21.

Augustine could not really criticize the Donatists for their devotion to martyrs and martyrdom, since that feeling was widely shared in North Africa and was regarded as one of their strongest points. From the standpoint of the mainline church that Augustine represented, Donatist weaknesses were two. First, their schism was purely local. There were no Donatists outside North Africa, and there was nothing like them elsewhere. How could they claim to be the true church if they had no adherents in the wider Christian world? What was it that allowed everybody else to come to terms with the new political situation, but not them? Could they really be right and everyone else wrong? The other weakness was their unwillingness to forgive repentant sinners. Like the Manichees, the Donatists were perfectionists, a stance that inevitably led to hypocrisy and double standards. But the church was not a body of perfect people. It was a hospital for sinners, who needed forgiveness and the grace of God in order to be saved and go to heaven. The greatness of the love of God was not that he made bad people good but that he extended his mercy to those who did not deserve it. This was the fundamental point, and it was here that Augustine's opposition to Donatism met his equally strong rejection of both Manichaeism and Pelagianism. In their different ways, all three movements denied the nature and power of God's grace.

But there was something more than this that motivated him. Like Cyprian before him, Augustine too believed that "outside the church there is no salvation."[7] The reason for this is that it was to the church that God had given the Scriptures and ensured that their message would be proclaimed in fullness and purity throughout the world. Schisms and heresies detracted from this mission, even if they preserved a substantial element of the apostolic teaching. Faith in Christ came by the hearing of the Word of God, and that was possible only in and through the ministry of the church.[8] This is why Augustine said that it was impossible for anyone "to regard God as a merciful Father unless he is prepared to honor the church as his mother."[9] On one occasion, when he was preaching in the city of Caesarea, he spotted a Donatist bishop in the congregation. Pointing to him, he told the people:

---

[7] Cyprian of Carthage, *Epistulae* 73.21.
[8] See Rom. 10:17.
[9] *Enarrationes in Psalmos* 88.2, 14; *Contra litteras Petiliani Donatistae*, 3.9, 10. This thought recurs often in his writings. See for example, *De sancta virginitate* 2; *De baptismo* 1.16–25; *De natura et gratia* 21.23, and a number of letters (392.4, 398.2, 402.1, 405.1, 408.3, 409).

It is quite true that this man can get whatever he wants outside the church. He can enjoy the dignity of office, he can receive the sacrament, he can sing Hallelujah and answer Amen, he can cling to the Gospel. In the name of the Father, the Son, and the Holy Spirit he can hold and preach the faith, *but he will not find salvation outside the universal church.* [10]

The importance of the church for Augustine was sealed by his conviction that there, and only there, a believer can find forgiveness of sins. [11] The purity of the church is to be sought not in the perfection of its members, who are all sinners saved by grace, but in the promises of God revealed in the preaching and sacraments by which men and women are united with it. The authenticity of these is guaranteed by the consensus of Christians across the world and by the presence in the church of a direct succession of authority from the apostles themselves. [12] Individuals might fail to do their duty, but the witness of the whole body remains unimpaired and can be used to counterbalance the misdeeds of the few who transgress. [13]

Ultimately such an objective view of the church and its status can be defended only by appealing to things that are equally objective—the Bible and the sacraments. In the Scriptures the gospel remains undiluted, and the sacraments speak of its promises. Those who preach the Word and administer baptism and holy communion might be corrupt or heretical, but the rites convey their own message and do not depend on them. [14] The Holy Spirit gives the church's ministers the grace they need to fulfill their tasks, and it is the duty of the church to examine ordination candidates to make sure that they are suitable, but their personal inadequacies do not of themselves invalidate their ministry. [15] On the other hand, Augustine pointed out that a minister who practices what he preaches is bound to have a greater effect than one who does not. As he explained:

Things that are right and true can be preached by a twisted and deceitful heart. This is how Jesus Christ is proclaimed by those who seek "their own interests and not those of Jesus Christ" (Phil. 2:21). But since good people who are believers listen obediently, not to any mere human being

---

10 *Sermo ad Caesareae ecclesiae plebem* 6.
11 *Enarrationes in Psalmos* 101.21.
12 *De utilitate credendi* 35.
13 *Contra Faustum* 13.5; *Epistulae* 400.2–3; *Contra epistulam Parmeniani Donatistae* 2.13.28.
14 Augustine was prepared to recognize Donatist baptisms, for example. See *De baptismo* 1.1–2.
15 *Confessiones* 4.12.19, 11.2.2. On the validity of the ministry of the unworthy, see *De baptismo* 3.10.15, 4.10.17, 6.2.4. Augustine's principle came to be official church teaching and is enshrined in article 26 of the Thirty-Nine Articles of the Church of England, among other places.

but to the Lord himself . . . even those who do not act in a useful way can be listened to with profit. They may be determined to seek what is their own but they dare not teach it from the pulpit, because it is founded on the ecclesiastical authority of sound doctrine. . . . Thus they benefit many people by saying things that they do not do, but they would benefit far more by doing what they say.[16]

Augustine was very conscious of belonging to the universal church, which he represented in Hippo, but his links with it were looser than they would have been in later times. He knew about the great councils of Nicaea (325) and Constantinople (381), where Arianism and Apollinarianism were condemned as heresies, and he too condemned them, though he never mentioned the creeds associated with those councils because they had not yet made their way into regular Christian worship. For him, the creed was the ancestor of what we now know as the Apostles' Creed, a text that originated in the rite of baptism, when prospective converts were asked to declare their faith. The basic content was the same as the conciliar creeds, of course, but its origin was different and ultimately more personal. This too sat well with Augustine's basic outlook. For him, the church was a society rooted and grounded in love. Those who loved God with all their heart would naturally seek to join it, while those who knew nothing of Christ would see his love revealed to them in the lives of believers as they gathered together for worship and witness. To his mind, the Christian faith gathers people into a fellowship where brotherly love can prevail. As he put it, "If this faith does not constitute a congregation and society of people in which brotherly love is at work, then it is less fruitful."[17]

The church is the body of Christ, to which his disciples are so attached that they become not merely Christians, but Christ himself.[18] At one point he even went so far as to state that whatever can be said of Christ can also be said of the church—and vice versa.[19] The love of Christ for his children is in effect the love of Christ for himself, just as the love of the members of his body for one another is the love of the body for itself.[20]

In later times, Augustine's remarks would be taken to apply to the vast international organization known as the universal church, but although

---

16 *De doctrina Christiana* 4.59–60.
17 *De fide et symbolo* 9.21.
18 *Tractatus in Evangelium Ioannis* 21.8.
19 *Sermones* 341.11–12.
20 *Homiliae decem in Iohannis Evangelium* 10.3.

he recognized the importance of the wider Christian world, it was not his primary focus. For him, the focus of Christian experience was the local congregation, where the love of God could be seen binding people together. A traveler who took that love with him to another place would find the same thing in any true church he might enter, but that was a secondary consideration. The love present in the universal church was the love that each Christian experienced in his own congregation, and it was that which gave him the standard he needed to be able to discern the spiritual state of believers and congregations otherwise unknown to him. At the same time, Augustine was alive to the danger of corruption inside the church and rejected the notion that belonging to it was enough to be saved, irrespective of other considerations.

> Those people who continue to the end of their lives in the fellowship of the universal church have no reason to feel secure, if their moral behavior is disreputable and deserving of condemnation. . . . Those who behave in that way will inevitably be in eternal punishment, seeing that they cannot possibly be in the Kingdom of God. . . . To eat Christ's body and to drink his blood is not just a matter of taking the outward sacrament. It is also the reality of living in Christ, so that Christ may live in him.[21]

As for the bishop of Rome, who would later claim jurisdiction over the universal church, Augustine never thought of him as his superior, although he recognized the primacy of Peter among the apostles.[22] He himself had been converted in Milan at a time when that city was the usual residence of the emperor in the West, so he was able to observe church-state relations firsthand, but the personality of Ambrose was not one to bend easily to secular pressure. On the contrary, Augustine witnessed a church that used its official position as the state religion in order to reprimand imperial officials, including the emperor himself, for failing to live up to Christian standards. Soon after Augustine's conversion, the emperor Theodosius massacred the population of Thessalonica, a crime for which Ambrose obliged him to do public penance. Ambrose's success in this demonstrated where the true balance of forces lay, and Augustine inherited this. When Rome fell to the barbarians in 410, he took it in his

---

[21] *De civitate Dei* 21.25.

[22] *Contra epistulam Manichaei fundamentalem* 4.5; *Epistulae* 397.3.7. Peter was generally regarded as having been the first bishop of Rome, though Augustine never made much of that tradition.

stride, using the occasion to demonstrate that earthly empires come and go, but that the kingdom of God, imperfectly represented by the church on earth, endures forever.

Just how imperfect the church could be was brought home to Augustine in the wake of the sack of Rome. Many wealthy people fled the city and took refuge in North Africa, where their presence, far from being resented, was regarded by many as an opportunity not to be missed. When a rich man called Pinianus, who had gone to stay with Bishop Alypius of Thagaste, turned up in Hippo, the congregation of Augustine's church demanded that he should be ordained then and there. Pinianus had no desire to become a presbyter and did his best to get out of this tricky situation as diplomatically as possible. He said that he would only serve in Hippo itself (which pleased his audience) but that he could not guarantee he would remain in the city. If it were to be attacked by barbarians, for instance, he would have to flee, as he had recently fled from Rome! Augustine was not particularly moved by such pleading, since he himself had been consecrated a bishop against his will, and it had not done him any harm. But Pinianus's wife, Melania, and her mother, Albina, who had stayed behind in Thagaste, were more direct. They realized that the Hipponese wanted Pinianus not for himself but for his money. If he were to become a clergyman in their church, they would expect him to use his wealth for their benefit. This shocked Augustine, who did not want to admit that it was true. In a reply to Albina's accusation, he wrote:

> Why do you accuse my people of the meanest kind of greed? They wanted something good—a decent presbyter. Is that greed? Why do you think that my people are so concerned about donations to the church? I was invited here when I had nothing. . . . Pinianus, by contrast, would be comparatively worse off if he were to come here than he is now, so you cannot say that my people were shouting for him because of his wealth—rather it was because he despised riches. Perhaps there were some beggars among those who clamored for him and they were expecting a hand-out, but a poor man who begs is not to be regarded as greedy![23]

Augustine tried his best to put a glossy shine on the situation, but it is not difficult to see that he was wrong and that Albina was right in her assessment of what was going on. It was Augustine, more than Pinianus,

---

23 *Epistulae* 126.1.

who was otherworldly and indifferent to material well-being. As he went on to say to Albina:

> Is the attack you make on my church meant for me instead? That would not be entirely unreasonable, because everyone here assumes that we live off church property, spending our money only on the cathedral and the monastery. Very little of the money goes to the poor and nobody can prove what happens to it, so your accusation would seem to be directed at me. . . . I call God as my witness and declare that I only engage in church administration against my will. It is a terrible burden. If I could get rid of it I would, and Alypius feels the same way.[24]

That at least has the ring of truth about it. Augustine was too busy with other things to have much time for worldly matters, including works of charity. As for Pinianus and Melania, they went back to Thagaste and eventually left for Palestine, where they met both Pelagius and Jerome. Augustine stayed in touch and even dedicated two of his anti-Pelagian works to them when he discovered what company they were keeping in Jerusalem.[25]

What we can glean from all this is that Augustine lived and worked in a church where people of wealth and status were more likely to rise to the top because they had the education and the contacts that would facilitate the tasks to which they were called. But at the same time, money was not everything. A genuine calling from God, a piously ascetic lifestyle, and—above all—an orthodox faith were essential qualifications for ministry that secular advantages could not buy. Those who led the church may have come disproportionately from the upper classes, but they were no less subject to its discipline for that.

The Trials of Parish Work

It is in the nature of things that bad news is more likely to be recorded than the opposite. If things are going well, they are usually passed over in silence, since there is no need to say anything about them. Only when there is trouble is it necessary to speak out. We see this quite clearly in the letters of the apostle Paul. It is easy to read what he wrote to the Corinthians, for example, and assume that their church was a disaster almost beyond redemption. It certainly had its problems, but these may well obscure many

---

[24] *Epistulae* 126.1, 6.
[25] *De gratia Christi* 1.1; *Retractationes* 2.50.

good things that were going on there, and the same is probably true of the other churches to which he wrote. After all, if the situation were really as bad as it seems, his letters would probably never have been read by or had any effect on the congregations to which they were sent. The very fact that Paul's letters were preserved and eventually canonized suggests that most people found them helpful in the immediate context and wanted to preserve them for future reference.

Augustine's letters and sermons are similarly one-sided in the picture they present. He wrote to different people for any number of reasons, and it is difficult to generalize about his correspondence. But we can assume that when he discoursed at length about some problem or other, it was because it needed to be cleared up, not because it had taken over the church to the exclusion of everything else. His sermons are different, in that they were preached regularly to the same congregation and therefore ought to give us a better picture of what was going on in the church at Hippo. But here too we must be careful. Ancient preachers did not think it their duty to flatter their hearers, who in any case would have been suspicious of such rhetoric. They knew that somebody who pandered to their egos probably had a hidden agenda; that was the way of heretics like Pelagius, who wanted people to think that they were good enough for God and not the miserable sinners that Augustine believed they were.

Augustine lived in a world where people expected to be reminded of the ideal, even though they knew full well that they did not measure up to it. They went to church because they knew that they needed to be challenged, both in their knowledge and in their lifestyle. A preacher who did not cater to this need was failing in his duty, and Augustine knew what was expected of him. It did not follow that every sin he warned against was rife in the congregation. As always, some listeners would have been guiltier than others, and many may have felt that they were not doing so badly after all. We have no way of judging this and are forced to rely on the cases that have come down to us in making our judgments. As long as we remember that by their nature, these cases were more likely to have been exceptional than the norm, we may perhaps avoid falling into an erroneous assessment of Augustine and his pastoral ministry.

In Augustine's time the Roman world was undergoing a profound social transformation. Traditional religions, which we lump together as "paganism," were out of favor and in terminal decline, though elements from them survived as superstitious practices, some of which are still common today.[26] In spiritual terms, they exerted their greatest hold on the lower classes of society, though some aristocrats still clung to the ancestral gods for traditionalist reasons. There was also a lively intellectual class that generally preferred philosophy over any kind of religion and regarded itself as completely free to pick and choose whatever beliefs it wished. Augustine belonged to that class before his conversion and so understood it particularly well, but it must not be forgotten that his father was a pagan (though he was baptized on his deathbed in 371). Most of the people in the church were new Christians, even if some of them were already second- or third-generation believers. For them, paganism was still within living memory in their own families, something of which Augustine was well aware. When confronted by a Donatist who defended his faith on the ground that he had inherited it from his deceased parents, whose memory he thought he had to keep alive, Augustine responded: "But you are not dead and buried yet. You are alive. Your parents were Christians, albeit Donatists. Their parents were perhaps Christians too, but their grandparents and great-grandparents were most certainly pagans—so why are you not a pagan too?"[27]

In Augustine's day, religious traditionalism was not really an option for Christians, because almost all of them were in the same position as this man. There was still a lingering sense that other options were available, that Christianity might not have come to stay, and that the church might even disappear—as the North African church eventually did after the Muslim conquest. In this situation, it is not surprising that many hedged their bets. They studied Christianity and became catechumens, but for one reason or another they held back from baptism. In this respect they were like the God-fearers in the synagogues whom the apostle Paul encountered on his missionary journeys, or perhaps like "adherents" in some churches today, who are associated with the church without being members of a congregation.

One of Augustine's priorities was to move people from this half-way house into full membership of the church. His concern was not primarily organizational; he was not trying to build a mega-congregation of which he could boast to his fellow bishops. It was much more serious than that. For a man who believed that there was no salvation outside the church and

---

26 Horoscopes, good luck charms, and the like are among the more widespread survivals.
27 *Sermones* 359.8.

that baptism was the essential requirement for church membership, the situation of the perpetual catechumens was tragic. They were on the edge of saving grace but not full participants in it. They ran the risk of spending their entire lives hearing the Word of God and even following it in their hearts and lives, only to lose their salvation when they died.[28]

This fear was very real in a world where few people lived beyond the age of fifty and where sudden death was an ever-present threat. We must not be surprised, therefore, to find that Augustine capitalized on it often. For example, when an earthquake hit the city of Sitifi, the capital of the neighboring province of Mauretania, the population was forced to spend five days in the countryside until things had calmed down enough for them to return to their homes. During that time, two thousand of the inhabitants were baptized.[29] When the barbarians were nearing Rome in 410, panic struck the inhabitants, and more than seven thousand of them sought baptism.[30] Augustine was even prepared to recount incidents where disaster was predicted but did not occur. Someone in Constantinople had had a vision that fire would come down from heaven and destroy the city, a prophecy that led to hundreds of baptisms even though it was not fulfilled.[31]

Sometimes catechumens had what they considered good reasons for not being baptized. One example was Caecilianus, the Roman governor of Carthage. As an important political figure, he had to perform a number of unpleasant tasks, including the execution of the tribune Marcellinus, a friend of Augustine's, who almost certainly perished unjustly. Caecilianus may have felt that in such circumstances baptism would have condemned him to hell because it would have led to unpardonable postbaptismal sin. Augustine sought to allay this fear by pointing out that as a baptized Christian, Caecilianus would be given the spiritual strength to do his job better, not worse:

> Cannot believing Christians serve the public good all the better if they are good and devout men themselves? What is the point of all your planning and worrying, if it is not to serve others well? If it were not so, you would be better off spending your nights and days sleeping soundly, instead of sitting up late over official business which never did anybody much good.[32]

---

[28] *Sermones* 27.6.
[29] *Sermones* 19.6.
[30] *Sermones* 19.6.
[31] *Epistulae* 228.8. The incident is supposed to have occurred in AD 398.
[32] *Epistulae* 151.14.

Of course, noble-minded men like Caecilianus were in the minority. Far more common were catechumens who did not want to be baptized because they preferred to carry on with their sinful ways, not least in the matter of adultery, which was common among the urban classes. They seemed to think that they could get away with this as long as they were active and healthy, and that later they could easily wash away their sins by a deathbed baptism. Augustine had no time for that sort of thing and condemned it in no uncertain terms.[33] An insincere last-minute baptism would not be taken seriously, he argued.[34] It may be true that Christ had once descended into hell and freed those whom he had chosen for salvation, but after that, hell became an eternal prison that would never again be opened. Some relief from its pains might be possible, but the punishment it provided was everlasting.[35]

Augustine deprecated a casual attitude toward baptism and salvation, but there was another problem that he had to deal with—overscrupulosity. Some who had been baptized were so afraid of contamination that they tied themselves in knots over minor questions that common sense should have sorted out. One of these was a senator named Valerius Publicola, who was the father of the Melania who had married the wealthy Pinianus. As a landowner Publicola had to deal with a wide range of people, by no means all of whom were Christians. He was particularly concerned with the lingering paganism of the peasant population, which was accustomed to swearing by the gods before planting their crops or before undertaking a long journey. Publicola believed that they were calling on demons for assistance, and he wanted to know whether he should tolerate such behavior. He was also concerned with a host of similar questions, some of which remind us of the New Testament church. For example, was it right to eat food that had been sacrificed in a pagan temple? What should Christians do if they found themselves having dinner with pagans who made ritual sacrifices to the gods in the course of their meal?[36]

Augustine's answers to such questions were sensible and reflected the teaching of the apostle Paul. He told Publicola not to worry about oaths sworn to pagan gods because they had no power, and the same applied to

---

[33] Denis, 20.6, in Germain Morin, ed., *Miscellanea Agostiniana*, 2 vols. (Rome: Tipografia Poliglotta Vaticana, 1930–1931), 1:116–17.
[34] *De civitate Dei* 21.17–25.
[35] *Epistulae* 164.14; *Enchiridion* 112.
[36] *Epistulae* 46.

eating meat that had been sacrificed to idols.[37] To our modern minds, all this seems so obvious that it is hard to understand why it caused such a problem, especially to a man as well educated as Publicola must have been. It is impossible for us to read his mind, but perhaps he was more concerned with public appearances than with any spiritual danger, real or perceived. Publicola must have known that his baptism protected him against the power of evil spirits, but the senatorial aristocracy in Rome was among the last to embrace Christianity, and what to him might have been no more than polite social concessions to his pagan colleagues may have seemed to them like hypocrisy. Had Publicola embraced Christianity for political reasons without really believing it himself? How much of the "old man," as Paul would have said, survived his conversion?

As long as society was not fully Christianized, these were real problems that had to be faced. In the modern world they are unlikely to recur in the same form, but many Christians today have to take a stand against the use of bad language and the presence of pornography in certain social environments, and they know how Publicola felt. The issues themselves may seem trivial, but the need to maintain a consistent and credible Christian witness remains as strong now as it has ever been.

Publicola was one of those who suffered from the sack of Rome by Alaric and his Gothic tribesmen in 410, and his scruples about paganism have to be seen in that light. Rome had not fallen to an enemy for eight centuries, and many believed that it could never be taken. From the perspective of hindsight, we can see that the city had lost its political importance, since the seat of government had been transferred to Constantinople and the north of Italy (first to Milan and then to Ravenna) long before Alaric got there. But it remained the spiritual center of the empire that continued to bear its name, and it was this aspect that caused the greatest turmoil. Had Rome fallen to the barbarians because the city had embraced Christianity and abandoned its ancestral gods, who had for so long protected it from harm?[38] Christians had similar feelings, although their spiritual agony was directed elsewhere. For them, Rome was the city where Peter and Paul had been martyred, but even their aura was not enough to protect it from the wrath of the Arian Goths.[39]

Augustine's first concern in all this was with the refugees who started

---

[37] *Epistulae* 47.
[38] *Sermones* 105.12–13.
[39] *Sermones* 296.6.

streaming into Africa and needed all the help they could get. The locals were not as welcoming as they could have been, and Augustine wrote to his own flock at Hippo, upbraiding them for their relative indifference.[40] Of course, many of those who got as far as Africa were wealthy, and there is always a certain *Schadenfreude* when people who have enjoyed a life of luxury are suddenly brought low. Why should the relatively poor provincials of Hippo put themselves out for aristocrats who, they thought, deserved what they were getting?

Augustine did not share that attitude. He had lived in Rome for a time and knew perfectly well that most of those who suffered in 410 were ordinary people, no different in social class or in morals from the majority in Hippo. He did not believe that Rome had been singled out for special condemnation because of its sins, and before long he was doing his best to put a positive spin on what had occurred. In a treatise he wrote about it, he argued that what Alaric had done to Rome was not nearly as bad as what had happened to Sodom, for example. Alaric and his troops had respected the churches, and everyone who had taken refuge in them was spared. Even the gold vessels from the cathedral, which had been discovered hidden in a private house, were returned to the church, which showed just how humane Alaric was.[41]

There was no doubt that Rome's capture was a punishment, but God had allowed it to happen not because he wanted to destroy the city but because he wanted to purify it. In a series of sermons that Augustine preached around this time, he emphasized that God's purpose was to purge the world of its sins so that the gold that it contained might shine with greater brightness. Rome was being chastised in preparation for its future greatness as a Christian metropolis, even if those who were presently suffering could not see that.[42] As for the Christians who wondered why the relics of Peter and Paul were unable to save the city, Augustine turned on them in no uncertain terms:

> It is true that the relics of the Apostles are in Rome. Yes, they are there, but you do not have them within yourself. If only they were inside you, these legacies of the Apostles, whoever you are—you who speak so foolishly and judge so foolishly, you who have been called by the Spirit yet

---

[40] *Epistulae* 122.2.
[41] *De urbis excidio* 2–9.
[42] *Sermones* 81.8–9, 105.12–13, 296.6–10.

continue to judge by the flesh! If only the relics of the Apostles were inside
you! If you only absorbed them in your mind, you would see whether it is
earthy happiness that you have been promised, or heavenly reward. If the
memory of the Apostles is really inside you, then listen to what Paul says:
"For our light and momentary troubles are achieving for us an eternal
glory that far outweighs them all . . . what is seen is temporary, but what
is unseen is eternal."[43] Peter's flesh was temporal, but you will not accept
that the stones of Rome are temporal too![44]

Augustine reminded his hearers that Rome had been built, according to
ancient legend, by survivors from the wreck of Troy, which its pagan sacrifices had been unable to save.[45] But Rome was far more deserving of punishment than Troy, because it had the gospel and knew that it needed to repent
of its evil ways.[46] Christians ought to have understood that their faith was
worth more than everything in heaven and earth put together, and that the
loss of a single city could do nothing to dim the promise of eternal life in
Christ.[47] What Augustine had to say was true enough, but it did not make
him popular. He was widely attacked for being unpatriotic and unwilling to
identify the cause of Rome with the will of God. To this he replied:

Vent your anger against me if you must. However much it affects us we
shall not curse you back, and if we are slandered by you, we shall simply
pray all the more for you. "Let him keep off the subject of Rome," that is
what they say. . . . But I do not accuse Rome. Rome is for me only a spur
to offer my prayers to God, and I use it as an example to warn you. Did we
not have brothers there, and are not some of them still in the city? Does
not a great part of Jerusalem, the city of pilgrims, have its dwelling there?[48]

Augustine could not imagine a world that was not centered on Rome,
and he believed that somehow or other the city would recover from its mis-
fortunes and rise again. He knew from bitter experience that much of the
problem lay in the empire's inadequate administrative structure, where it
was possible for a single general or governor to wreak havoc in pursuit of
his own selfish ends. The imperial throne was betrayed by those who were

---

[43] 2 Cor. 4:17–18.
[44] *Bibliotheca Casinensis* 1.133.6–7, in Morin, *Miscellanea Agostiniana*, 1:404–6.
[45] *Sermones* 296.7.
[46] *Bibliotheca Casinensis* 1.133.11, in Morin, *Miscellanea Agostiniana*, 1:408–9.
[47] *Sermones* 345.7.
[48] *Sermones* 105.12.

supposed to be serving it, and disaster was the inevitable result. From a distance of more than fifteen hundred years we can see that the empire was on its last legs and that the world Augustine knew would soon be gone for good. But we also know that the legacy of ancient Rome would survive in its language, its laws, and its aspiration toward universal peace and justice. As Augustine foresaw, it would be a Christianized Rome that would survive, one in which the follies and barbarities of paganism would be purged away and the ideals that had made the city great would be cloaked in terms taken from the gospel of Christ, which, unlike the stones of the ruined forum, is indeed eternal.

The apparent failure of God to respond to the intercessions of those who prayed for the safety of Rome raised the wider issue of spiritual power in acute form. The ancient world was familiar with temples, oracles, and healers who promised relief from pain and suffering. Whether they relied on folk medicine, psychology, or simple luck, there was no doubt that cures could be had from otherwise dubious spiritual sources. Just as today there are people in many parts of the world who are officially Christian but who in private rely more on voodoo and witch doctors, so in the ancient world the same phenomenon recurred with distressing frequency. Augustine had to face this, and as he so often did, he tackled the problem head-on:

> Someone says: "I have been baptized for years, but then I fell ill. I went to church every day, but nothing happened. Then I tried the secret remedy, and now I am well again. Remember too—for I have heard it myself—the witch doctor calls on the name of God and the angels." Perhaps, but these are angels of whom the Apostle Paul says that we shall judge them.[49]

It was a hard case to answer, and Augustine did not do it very well. His main recourse was to the trials of the apostle Paul, who prayed to the Lord three times for the removal of the thorn in his flesh but was told only that God wanted him to suffer because, as God told him, "My grace is sufficient for you, for my power is made perfect in weakness."[50] Here Augustine touched on something that has puzzled people from Old Testament times onward and has never received a satisfactory answer: Why do the wicked so often prosper and the good suffer?[51] Augustine had to admit that he did not know

---

[49] Morin, 8.3, in Morin, *Miscellanea Agostiniana*, 1:116–17. The Pauline statement is in 1 Cor. 6:3.
[50] 2 Cor. 12:9; *Sermones Wilmartiani* 12.3–5.
[51] See Ps. 73 for an early and classic formulation of this problem.

any more than anyone else, but in spite of the mystery of it all, some practical way forward had to be found.[52] Christians could not simply be left to despair of their salvation as they watched unbelievers make the most of the opportunities that this life afforded them. When asked about this, Augustine replied:

> You are wrong. Such a man is not happy, but like a sick man who is laughing in delirium. Soon the illusion of his so-called pleasures will disappear and he will be in real pain. . . . Did you become Christians in order to have a good time in this world? Are you bothered that the wicked should prosper for a time, when those same wicked will soon be bothered by the devil?[53]

The model for the Christian is not the prosperous sinner but Christ, who took our sins upon himself and suffered for them. To the objection that it was all right for him because he was God and could endure pain without difficulty, Augustine replied:

> Think what has been suffered for your sake, and by whom! Think how great that suffering was, and by whom—and for whom—it was endured. You grumble and say that he was God, so he could endure anything, but I am only human. Holy Apostle Paul, make us truly learn what you have said! You who complain, listen carefully, and do not close your ears! "Christ suffered for you, leaving you an example that you should follow in his steps."[54]

Augustine had no time for people who believed in God in the hope of getting something from him in return. He wrote: "If you ask your wife to love you for yourself alone, should you love God for some reason other than himself? Do you not, as a Christian, sing the psalm: 'I will freely sacrifice to you'?"[55]

Having said that, Augustine did not deny that it was legitimate for Christians to pray for benefits in this life; God is the Creator and Sustainer of all things and wants what is good for his people. What this meant in practice is explained in his letter to Faltonia Proba, a wealthy Roman woman who was so prominent that her husband and three of her sons were elected consuls, the highest honor that Rome could bestow and one that was often shared with the reigning emperor.[56]

---

[52] *Sermones* 311.13.
[53] *Sermones* 250.2.
[54] Morin, 8.5 in Morin, *Miscellanea Agostiniana*, 1:617–18. The quotation is from 1 Pet. 2:21, not Paul.
[55] *Enarrationes in Psalmos* 53.10. Augustine's text of Ps. 54:6 differs from the original Hebrew, which reads, "I will sacrifice a freewill offering to you."
[56] Her husband was consul in 371. Two of her sons were consuls together in 395, and the third was consul in 406. The letter is *Epistulae* 130.

Proba had been reading Romans 8:26, where Paul writes, 'We do not know what we ought to pray for" (NIV). Puzzled by this, she wrote to Augustine to ask for his advice, and he replied that she should pray for a happy life. Many things could come under that description, but Augustine rejected them all. Happiness is not pleasing oneself. Nor is it behaving uprightly or seeking the good of others, important and worthwhile though such desires may be. Ultimate happiness is described for us in the Psalms:

> One thing have I asked of the LORD,
> that will I seek after:
> that I may dwell in the house of the LORD
> all the days of my life.[57]

This is the best thing that can be given to anyone, and every other benefit flows from it. If we are in the presence of God, then whatever happens to us will be for our good, and we shall understand his purposes, even if the onlooking world cannot fathom what it is that we are happy about.

Augustine was aware that some people drew the conclusion that because everything was ordered and predestined by God, prayer was an unnecessary extra that could be dispensed with. To them he had this to say:

> There are some people who either do not pray at all or else pray half-heartedly, because they have learned from the Lord's own words that God knows what we need before we ask him (Matt. 6:8), and so why should they bother? Should we drop this belief and take it out of the Gospel merely because of these people? Of course not! It is clear that God has prepared some things, like conversion, to be given to those who have not prayed for them, but it is equally clear that other things will not be given to us unless we pray for them, notably the gift of perseverance to the end. Obviously someone who thinks he already has this gift in himself will have no need to pray for it. Therefore we must be careful not to stifle prayer and encourage arrogance because we are afraid that our exhortation to the former may grow lukewarm.[58]

Augustine did not lay down any hard-and-fast rules about the length or the precise content of our prayers. There are times when a short prayer is enough, and there are times when we are called to pray at great length.

---

[57] Ps. 27:4.
[58] *De dono perseverantiae* 16.39.

As he put it: "A multitude of words does not necessarily indicate a constant, good disposition. It is written that our Lord spent the night in prayer, and that when he was wrestling with death, he prayed even longer. What else was he doing other than setting us an example?"[59]

The earthly life and ministry of Jesus were fundamental for Augustine's teaching about prayer, because it was then that the Son of God was a petitioner like us. He attached particular importance to the Lord's Prayer, which he held up to Proba as the ultimate model for every Christian. The seven petitions contained in that prayer all point to the blessed life of the heavenly kingdom, and all the other prayers in Scripture, especially those in the Psalms and the Wisdom Literature of the Old Testament, ultimately go back to one of those petitions. Indeed, Augustine went further and said that a prayer that did *not* reflect some aspect of the Lord's Prayer was carnal and should be avoided by all true believers!

Prayer was a common feature of every believer's life, but Augustine seemed to think that it would spring naturally from the heart. He did not give detailed guidance as to how people should pray, nor did he have much to say about what we would now call meditative or reflective prayer. Even more astonishingly, he says almost nothing about public prayer in the church; the "common prayer" so typical of the Anglican tradition seems to have been almost nonexistent. That is not to say that people did not pray in public—they often did. Jesus warned against this in the run-up to his teaching the Lord's Prayer to his disciples, but that seems to have made little impression on Augustine. He thought it was quite normal, indeed commendable, for individuals to shout, sob, tear their clothes, and beat their breasts in public as they confessed their sins and prayed to God for forgiveness. In his words, "There is no respite from the thunder of people beating their breasts, and very properly so, for the cloud in which God dwells is always full of thunder."[60]

Of course, Augustine took it for granted that such behavior reflected a truly humble and contrite heart. At the same time, he was well aware that some might easily go through the motions without being sincere, and he did not hesitate to condemn such hypocrisy:

> You throw your bodies on the ground, you bend your necks, confess your
> sins and pray to God; I see where your body lies but I ask myself where

---

[59] *Epistulae* 130.
[60] *Enarrationes in Psalmos* 140.18. See also *Sermones* 19.2, 135.7, 332.4, 351.6.

your spirit is. I see your limbs stretched out, but show me whether your attention is standing upright or whether it has not been washed away by the flood of your thoughts. [61]

Augustine was well aware of the distractions that can afflict us when we are praying, and of the evil thoughts that can creep in and turn us away from the God to whom we are speaking. But he also knew that when trouble came, those distractions would disappear and the believer on his knees would have an open door to the throne of grace. We are weak in our faithfulness to God, but he is strong in his faithfulness toward us.

The realization that communal prayer was not a major component of public worship in ancient times makes us ask what was. In Augustine's case there can be little doubt that it was the preaching. Services were held on a daily basis, but it seems that most of the time only a few people attended them, except perhaps on Sundays. Large crowds could be expected on feast days, which were not as numerous then as they were later to become, but Augustine did not particularly like that. One reason was that the acoustics in the church buildings were generally poor and people at the back could hardly hear him unless everyone was quiet—a tall order! He also liked to speak for as long as it took him to cover the subject, which was often much longer than most people wanted to listen.

We know that he was preaching on one particular feast day in Carthage and was attempting to expound the spiritual meaning of the wedding feast at Cana in Galilee. He was just about to get into the meat of the exposition, which was the allegorical interpretation of it, when he suddenly stopped short because of the commotion:

> I would rather deal with this tomorrow . . . and not make things too difficult for my weakness or for yours. Maybe many people have come here today not to listen to a sermon but to join in the celebration of the feast. So I am inviting those who want to listen to the rest of what I have to say to come back tomorrow. That way I shall not shortchange those who are keen to listen, but I shall not bore the indifferent either. [62]

Feast days were social occasions when large crowds turned out for public worship, but they did not want the service to go on too long. They may

---

[61] *Enarrationes in Psalmos* 140.18.
[62] *Tractatus in Evangelium Ioannis* 8.13.

not have been there entirely for show—Christianity was the state religion, after all, and it was only right for the citizenry to support it on these occasions—but they did not come for spiritual edification either. To judge from Augustine's criticisms, it seems that most of the men were more interested in getting drunk afterward than in anything else.[63] But those who did return the following day were in for a treat. When the conditions were right, Augustine did not shrink from expounding the text to his heart's content. On another occasion in Carthage he was discoursing on Psalm 73 and realized only after two hours how carried away with it he was.

> I have forgotten how long I have been speaking. I have finally come to the end of the psalm, and to judge from the smell [of sweat] I gather that it has been a very long sermon. But what can I do in the face of your enthusiasm? Your very violence disarms me, and I hope that you will use it to conquer the Kingdom of Heaven.[64]

Augustine was a famous man and a brilliant orator, but even so, it is hard not to feel that he was embarrassed by the sudden realization that his apparently enthusiastic congregation had had enough! There was also the familiar problem that a lot of men thought that churchgoing was for women and children only. Augustine knew that many men were too ashamed to say they had been to church, and so they would not go at all and would even dissemble by saying that they had been doing something else.[65] Some things never change! The problem was compounded by the mockery they faced from their peers, even those who claimed to be Christians themselves. In Augustine's words: "The less these depraved individuals care about their own sins, the greater is their morbid curiosity with respect to others. They are not trying to make men better, but only want to find something they can get their teeth into."[66]

Most of those who stayed away from church were lazy and frivolous rather than atheistic or malicious; in fact, when Augustine announced that something important was going to happen, the church would suddenly be packed.[67] But it was hard work getting people to come even on feast days, especially if the feasts had little relevance to the congregation. Augustine

---

63 *Sermones* 225.4.
64 *Enarrationes in Psalmos* 72.34.
65 *Sermones* 306B.6.
66 *Sermones* 19.2.
67 *Sermones* 355.1.

thought it was important to commemorate Peter and Paul (on June 29), but his people evidently did not agree with him, because few ever turned up on that day.[68] If there was a rival attraction at the theater, hardly anyone would turn up at church.[69] One year he found himself preaching on St. Laurence's day (August 10), when it was extremely hot and a theatrical performance was also in full swing. Laurence had been martyred for his faith in 258 (the same year as Cyprian), and so his feast should have attracted a crowd. But it did not, as Augustine ruefully complained:

> The martyrdom of St. Laurence is famous—at least it is famous in Rome, though it does not seem to be so here, for I see that only a few of you have come. Yet we here can no more take away the victor's crown of St. Laurence than the people of Rome can. Why that crown has not appeared in this city I do not know.[70]

Augustine was so overcome by the heat on that occasion that he preached for only fifteen minutes, which was less than half the usual time he would give to a sermon. In defense of the congregation, they had to stand while Augustine sat to preach! Occasionally he would take pity on them and let them go home, telling them to come back the next day to hear the remainder of what he had to say.[71] On the other hand, there were times when the people asked him to go on, even though he had spoken for a long time.[72] Augustine appreciated this and did not hesitate to compliment his hearers on their dedication and endurance.

> I never become aware that you are getting tired, and yet God knows how I fear that I sometimes expect too much of you. . . . Yet I see the interest that so many of you display. . . . I am glad that your interest is greater than that of the fools in the amphitheater. If they had to stand as long as this, they would soon lose all interest in the spectacle.[73]

The occasional complaints about the length of the services and the failure of many people to turn up to some of them must be balanced by the knowledge that public worship was a daily occurrence and that many

---

[68] *Sermones* 298.1–2.
[69] *Sermones* 51.1–2.
[70] *Sermones* 303.1.
[71] *Enarrationes in Psalmos* 32.2.12, 90.1.12.
[72] *Enarrationes in Psalmos* 72.34, 147.21.
[73] *Enarrationes in Psalmos* 147.21.

people made the effort to attend whenever they could. Augustine often preached four times a week or more, and he always spoke every Saturday and Sunday. There was plenty of opportunity to hear him, and more people took advantage of it than his admonitions to the lazy might suggest. There was also a daily celebration of holy communion, which some people never missed and others attended once a week or so. As far as we can tell, nobody deliberately held back from participating in the sacrament, though not everybody made the obligatory confession of sins beforehand. When Augustine caught such people, he did not hesitate to turn them away, but of course he could not discipline everyone who came to church.[74]

In the nature of things, spiritual discipline had to be exercised mainly by encouraging people to practice self-discipline in their own lives. The early church introduced a number of fast days to be observed—a good practice in principle—but many failed to observe them. For Augustine the matter was complicated because of his experience of Manichaeism. The Manichees "fasted" by abstaining from meat but then gorged themselves on plates of highly seasoned vegetables.[75] Augustine understood the hypocrisy of this and did not want his own people to fall into it. He also knew that Manichaean practices were motivated, at least in part, by their dualistic view of the universe and that fasting was also common among heretics and Jews—it was no guarantee of spirituality! Nevertheless, he promoted it because it had been the practice of Moses, Elijah, and Jesus to fast and because of the benefits that accrued to those who did so in the right spirit. He has left us a full treatise on the subject, as well as six sermons, which shows that he took it seriously even though he counseled moderation and warned people of the dangers that hypocritical pseudo-fasting could bring.[76]

Closer to his heart and more serious in its social consequences was the whole subject of sexual continence. Once again, his own experience of having had two concubines—one for many years and another as a "stopgap" in preparation for marriage—made him particularly sensitive on this subject. It was complicated by the fact that Roman social custom was rather lax in certain areas and attempts to tighten things up were almost doomed to failure from the start. Women, and especially married women, were expected to be chaste, but it was quite different for men. In particular, there was no legal prohibition against a man having sexual relations with a female

---

[74] Sermones 392.5.
[75] De moribus ecclesiae 2.29–30.
[76] De utilitate ieiunii; Sermones 205–10.

slave, or of keeping her (or a free woman) as a concubine. The notion that this custom was a form of prostitution was deeply resented by many who practiced it, and Augustine was faced with complaints when he tried to point out the Bible's teaching. For example:

> My woman is no prostitute, she is my concubine. Holy bishop, you have called my concubine a prostitute! Do you really think that I would resort to a prostitute? I would never do that, nor would I touch a woman who belongs to someone else. The woman whom I keep is my own maid. Can I not do what I want in my own household?[77]

Promiscuity of this kind, as well as divorce, was easy in Roman law, and many practiced both, at least until they were baptized. It seems that those who submitted to baptism ceased from such behavior, or at least began to think it wrong. Some put away their concubines and remained married to their wives for fear of being publicly shamed by the bishop, something Augustine was only too ready to do if necessary.[78] But even so, the problem remained and we hear how Augustine dealt with it:

> You Christian people who hear me, if you have committed a sin of this kind, do not persist in it, but ask God for forgiveness. . . . If you have defiled yourself by an illicit union, then repent of it as the church has commanded, and let the church pray for you. Do not try to do it [repent] in private. . . . If the Emperor Theodosius could do it publicly without shame, so can you.[79]

Augustine did not stop there. He knew that it was hard for men to remain continent, so he appealed to their sense of honor and masculinity. The man was meant to be the head of the house, but what would happen to the family if its head were unreliable? Women remained chaste because their husbands forced them to, but men had to restrain themselves—a much more demanding task, yet a fitting challenge to their masculine pride.[80]

Women made up more than half of Augustine's regular congregation, and he addressed them as well. In his mind, they were too tolerant of their husband's failings and not sufficiently protective of their own honor.

---

[77] *Sermones* 224.3.
[78] *Enarrationes in Psalmos* 149.14–15.
[79] *Sermones* 161.10.
[80] *Sermones* 9.3, 12.

Let the women listen to me. Let them be jealous of their husbands. . . . I do not want a Christian wife to be too tolerant; on the contrary, I want her to be a jealous wife. I say this with all sincerity. I order it. I command it. Your bishop commands it. And Christ commands it through me. . . . Do not let your husbands make themselves guilty of unchastity. Appeal to the church against them. Be subject to them in everything else, but on this point defend your cause.[81]

Augustine's strictures were skillfully designed to confront the evil he saw around him in the way that would speak most eloquently to his contemporaries. He expected men to be responsible and women to claim equality with their husbands in sexual matters—not so that they could be as licentious as the men but so that they could use their rights to demand faithfulness from those who were more negligent of their duties. In this way, and perhaps without realizing it, Augustine was promoting the equality of men and women in a complementary marriage relationship. It was not so much the law that needed changing, although a certain tightening up would not have gone amiss, but the attitudes and expectations of those who lived under it. If they could be corrected, the problems would cease to exist, and laws against them would be redundant.

Augustine had a high view of marriage, which to him meant lifelong heterosexual monogamy, but he was also deeply affected by the appeal of celibacy, to which he had dedicated himself. Sexual intercourse within marriage was lawful, but its primary purpose was the procreation of children. This belief enabled him to defend the ancient Hebrew patriarchs, whom he imagined had taken concubines only because their wives were barren and they needed children for the covenant promises to be fulfilled.[82] Otherwise, his ideal was chastity within marriage, a state that he believed was not only attainable but also productive of true love and happiness because of its inherent unselfishness.[83]

In response to a man called Jovinian, who attacked him for his advocacy of continence within marriage and blamed it on his Manichaean past, Augustine wrote two books, one on marriage and the other on virginity.[84] In both of these, his message was the same. Marriage brought children, encouraged faithfulness, and united two people in a bond of sacramental

---

[81] *Sermones* 392.4–5.
[82] *De bono coniugali* 22.27, 26.34; *Sermones* 51.13.22–51.15.25.
[83] *De mendacio* 19.40.
[84] *De bono coniugali* and *De sancta virginitate*.

love. Virginity was a higher state, because it imitated the life of angels that we shall all live in heaven. But at the same time, it was meant only for those who had been specially called to it and was of spiritual benefit only to those who were humble and not proud of their "achievement." Virginity might be a higher state of life than matrimony, but it was far better, said Augustine, to be a humble married woman than a proud virgin! Once again we see that although we would reason differently nowadays, in the end we would come to a remarkably similar conclusion; like Augustine, we recognize that often God pays more attention to the spirit in which we act than to what we do, important though that is.

The family is the bedrock of society, and it is when we consider what Augustine had to say about it that we penetrate to the heart of the tension between the old pagan and the new Christian world that he had to live with. The Christian worldview was based on the belief that all have sinned and are equally in need of salvation, but that all likewise have been created in the image of God and therefore equally deserve respect. This antithesis shaped Augustine's approach to sexual relations between a husband and his wife. Each partner in the marriage had to respect the other, but also to recognize his or her own weakness and fallibility. Only by guarding against that would it be possible to show the love and attain the happiness that the married couple and their family were meant to enjoy. Happy families produced happy communities, but Augustine realized that there was still some way to go before this state of affairs would be achieved. On one occasion a hated official was lynched in Hippo, a tragedy that prompted Augustine to declare:

> One thing I know, as we all do. There are houses in this city where there is not a single pagan, and there is not a house that has no Christians in it. Indeed, if we look carefully, we shall find that there is not a single house in which Christians do not outnumber pagans. . . . It is therefore obvious that nothing evil could happen if Christians did not want it to happen. . . . Hidden evil can always occur, of course, but open evil cannot if Christians seek to prevent it. Every man can keep his son or his slave under control. . . . If that were done we should have far fewer occasions to make us upset.[85]

The Christian society of which he dreamed was still a work in progress, and Augustine knew that it would take a few more generations before the

---

[85] *Sermones* 302.21, 19.

implications of the gospel would really sink in. Perhaps he was fortunate to have lived at a time when such optimism was still possible; he did not have to deal with the legacy of centuries that would prove only that his perception of original sin and its effects was all too true and that the world he dreamed of would never be attained in this life. As it was, he lived in hope and placed his trust in the church, which he believed would be able to instruct the nations in the ways of godliness and peace.

> You, O mother church, instruct us children in a way that speaks to us. You teach the young with power and the old with patience, not according to the maturity of their years but according to the maturity of their understanding. You subject the wife to her husband in chaste obedience, not for the satisfaction of lust but for the propagation of children. . . . You make the husband the head of the wife, not to make the weaker sex fail but because this is the law of honest love. You subject children to their parents so that they may serve them willingly, and you give parents a loving control over their children. You unite brother to brother in bonds of faith that are stronger than those of blood. . . . You show who must be feared, who must be comforted, who must be admonished, who must be warned, who must be disciplined, who must be rebuked, and who must suffer. You tell us that not everything is owed to everyone, but that love is due to all and injustice to none.[86]

The purpose of the church was to teach people the love of God, and so the ministry of its pastors was to make that love a reality in the lives of all who called themselves Christians.

Preaching the Word

Most of Augustine's pastoral ministry was exercised through his preaching, which occupied him almost daily for nearly forty years. Just over five hundred of his sermons have survived, which represents only a fraction of the total that he would have preached, though if we count his discourses on the Psalms and the Johannine literature, we can increase that number to about 850. Apart from those obvious collections, we have no way of knowing why some sermons have survived but not others. We know that he devoted a considerable amount of his time and energy to sermon preparation, though what we now have was in most cases not written (or

---

86 *De moribus ecclesiae* 1.30.63.

edited) by him personally.[87] It seems that his church employed secretaries who took notes of what he said and then wrote them up afterward, though whether they deliberately selected only a few for publication is impossible to determine. It is certain that Augustine occasionally broke off what he was saying and continued the following day, but whether he preached the same sermon twice or more is unknown. Given that almost all of them were preached in Hippo or Carthage, that is unlikely, even if he often returned to the same themes.

The sermons vary enormously in length, ranging from about ten to fifteen minutes at the short end to more than two hours. Most of them seem to fall somewhere in the middle, and it would be fair to say that he normally spoke for about forty to sixty minutes. He must have done this at least three hundred times a year, and probably more often than that, which gives us some idea of the effort he put into them. His devoted following hung on his every word, but it cannot have been very large by modern standards. Often his church was half-empty, and he sometimes complained about the noise and inattention of his congregation, so it seems that he had to face the same problems that all preachers encounter one way or another.

One big difference between Augustine's day and ours is that back then, the ability to speak effectively in public was regarded as an essential ingredient of education. Today, the word *rhetoric* has a slightly pejorative connotation, but in ancient times it was regarded as a highly accomplished skill that anyone in Augustine's position would be expected to master. In a world where the written word was rare and expensive, oral communication was the norm, and the ability to move an audience was crucial to success. By contrast, the modern preacher is seldom trained in rhetoric, with the result that sermons nowadays are often eminently forgettable, and many people regard them as the low point of public worship. The content may be fine, but the delivery is poor, and in any case people are more accustomed to listening to sound bites than to extended expositions. There are exceptions, of course, but as a general rule, it is fair to say that ours is not a great age of preaching.

By contrast, Augustine was a master among giants of rhetorical skill. He had to measure up to high expectations and get his message across to a broad range of society. On the one hand, he had to be erudite enough to satisfy his learned clientele, who would not have appreciated it if he had

---

[87] The 124 sermons on John's Gospel are an exception here.

shown no knowledge of (or interest in) the classics; but on the other hand, he also had to persuade simple people of the truth of what he was saying, using language and illustrations that they would understand. How far the published versions of his sermons reflect this is impossible to say; it may be that a good deal has been left out, particularly if, as preachers often do, he repeated himself for the benefit of those who did not grasp what he was saying the first time around.

Of course Augustine was well aware that rhetoric was a means to an end, not the end in itself. In ancient times plenty of people taught (and mastered) the technique but were not always clear about what they were using it for. The classical expositors of the subject had concentrated on the art of persuasion; the aim of a good rhetorician was to convince people to accept what he was saying. By that standard, Adolf Hitler was a brilliant master of the spoken word, but nobody would want to take him as a model. That is not because we reject the technique of persuasion but because we believe that the content of what a speaker is trying to communicate ought to be true and (where appropriate) morally uplifting. A Christian preacher would go even further and insist that his message should be spiritually edifying as well. Rhetorical skill was justified, and even considered necessary, because it was seen as the best way of inculcating these virtues.

> Since by means of the art of rhetoric people can be persuaded to accept both truth and falsehood, who would suggest that truth should be defended by people who are unarmed against the power of the lie? Why should those who want to convince people to accept falsehoods know how to make their listeners receptive, attentive, or at least acquiescent in their presentation, while the defenders of the truth lack this skill?[88]

In teaching the art of rhetoric, Augustine started from the principle laid down by Aristotle, which is that an effective speaker must state at the beginning what he is going to say and why it is important for his hearers to listen to it.[89] This means pointing out why it is in their interest to pay attention to what he is going to say, and it helps us to understand why Augustine sometimes digressed from his main theme in order to apply a point to a particular situation that he knew was relevant to his congregation. We know of at least one occasion when a man was converted by this.

---

[88] *De doctrina Christiana* 4.2.3.
[89] Aristotle, *De rhetorica* 3.14.

Augustine had digressed onto Manichaeism, but unknown to him, one of those who heard him was a Manichee himself and was convicted of his error by what Augustine had said.[90]

Sometimes these digressions were almost certainly deliberate, since Augustine knew the rhetorical art well enough to be able to manipulate it when he chose to do so, but at this distance in time it is impossible to know exactly when he was doing this. What we can say for certain is that he strongly disapproved of digressing onto trivial matters of no real concern to the people, ramblings that served only to show how clever the preacher was.[91] We also know that he put effective communication before stylistic construction. He knew the rules of public speaking well enough to be able to improvise, which gave his sermons a spontaneous and personal quality that they still possess. His advice to other preachers was that

> in all their utterances they should, above all, try to speak so as to be understood, speaking as best they can with such clarity that either those who do not understand are very slow witted, or the difficulty and complexity lies in the nature of the subject that they are trying to explain, and not in the manner of delivery.[92]

Sometimes the need to speak clearly might involve finding words that are not in the biblical text but that can help to get its message across. It might even be necessary on occasion to make up words to describe something that could otherwise require a long and convoluted argument. (The word *Trinity* is a good example.) Techniques of this kind were permissible, but only to the extent that they clarified the subject under discussion and did not distort it.[93]

The best way for a young preacher to pick up the art was by listening to others who were more practiced and learning from them.[94] But the greatest examples of godly eloquence were to be found in the Scriptures. Augustine was aware, in a way that we today are not, of the essentially spoken quality of the written word. Most of the Old Testament had originally been given orally, and when it was finally written down, the qualities of that tradition of delivery were retained in the text. The same was true of the Gospels.

---

[90] Possidius, *Vita Augustini* 15.211–12.
[91] *De doctrina Christiana* 4.14.31.
[92] *De doctrina Christiana* 4.8.22.
[93] *De doctrina Christiana* 4.10.24.
[94] *De doctrina Christiana* 4.3.4.

Jesus was not a writer but a speaker, and we cannot read the records we now have without bearing that in mind. Even when the biblical text itself was written—as in the letters of Paul, for example—the rhythms of ancient rhetoric were likely never far away. To illustrate this, Augustine went through Romans 5:3–5 and 1 Corinthians 11:16–17, pointing out to what extent they echoed the sound and style of the pulpit, even though they were probably never preached.

Augustine was conscious of being a channel for conveying God's Word to the people. As he told them on one occasion, "I shall tell you whatever the Lord entrusts to me."[95] In other words, he did not have a prepared agenda and was open to the moving of the Spirit as the circumstances demanded. He understood that a preacher has to have a clear idea of what he wants to say, but he resisted the temptation to be mechanical in his presentation. Augustine did not believe in reading a prepared text as the "sermon," because that would distance him from his congregation and almost guarantee that they would not listen.[96] This was the secret of his success—he was engaged with his hearers, and they engaged with him in return, guided (as he believed) by the controlling power and presence of the Holy Spirit in their midst. This sense of engagement is something he himself insisted on:

> Why do I preach? Why do I sit here in the preacher's chair? What do I live for? For this one thing alone, that we may one day live with Christ. This is my desire, my honor, my fame. This is my joy and my treasure. If you have not heard me attentively, despite the fact that I have not remained silent, then at least I have saved my own soul—but I do not want to attain everlasting salvation without you.[97]

This judgment has remained constant down through the centuries. Augustine's colleague and biographer Possidius wrote that although people who read his theological works profited from them, "those who could hear him speak in church profited still more."[98] A modern scholar has compared Augustine with his contemporaries and judged that he stood out from them in his style and presentation. He lacked the satirical wit of Asterius and the incisive clarity of John Chrysostom, neither of whom he

---

[95] *Sermones* 111.1.
[96] *De doctrina Christiana* 4.11.26.
[97] *Sermones* 17.2. Augustine's words here echo Ezek. 33:1–20.
[98] Possidius, *Vita Augustini* 31.244.

could have heard personally, and he did not exhibit the majesty or solemnity of a Leo or an Ambrose (whom he certainly did hear on a number of occasions). But,

> through his genius for the right word he surpasses all the church fathers. Never once does he fail to make an idea unforgettable. Never once does he fail, when he desires to do so, to turn a simple statement into an aphorism. He never uses the sharpness of his mind to wound; on the contrary, every word he says carries its conviction by reason of an irresistible tenderness.[99]

There may be a touch of exaggeration here, but it is only a touch, as the surviving sermons bear witness. It is all the more remarkable in that Augustine did not see himself as a gifted preacher and would far rather have spent his days in quiet meditation. As he told his people: "Nothing is better or sweeter for me than to gaze upon the divine treasure without noise or bustle—that is what is sweet and good. To have to preach, to exhort, to admonish, to edify, to feel responsible for each one of you—this is a great burden, a heavy weight on me, a hard labor."[100]

Having said that, Augustine was well aware that he had been called to preach, whether he wanted to or not, and believed that it was essential for him to live up to the expectations of that calling. He was doing it not for himself, after all, but for the benefit of God's people whom he had been chosen to serve. They had come to be fed, and it was his duty to feed them.[101] Furthermore, he knew that they had come not to hear his words but to meet with Christ, who was using his words to speak to them.

> The sound of my words strikes your ears, but the Master is within. You must not think that anyone learns [spiritual things] from a man. The noise of my voice can be no more than a prompting; if there is no teacher within, it is useless. . . . Outward teachings are only aids and encouragements; the teacher of your hearts has his seat in heaven.[102]

Time and again Augustine returned to this theme, insisting that God only listens to his own voice and trusting that that is what God was hearing

---

[99] Frederik van der Meer, *Augustine the Bishop: The Life and Work of a Father of the Church*, trans. Brian Battershaw and G. R. Lamb (London: Sheed and Ward, 1961), 412.
[100] *Sermones* 339.4.
[101] *Sermones* 95.1. See also *Tractatus in Evangelium Ioannis* 9.9.
[102] *Tractatus in Evangelium Ioannis* 3.13.

through the human preacher.[103] Augustine was the means by which the people were fed, but he was not the food himself, just as the doctor is the dispenser of medicine but does not himself have its curative effects.[104] It was his conviction that he was doing the will of God, and not simply pleasing himself, that gave Augustine the confidence he needed to preach and that continues to strike modern readers, even when we know that his biblical translation was sometimes faulty and his applications seem strange or irrelevant to us.

Augustine's firm conviction of his calling helped him deal with the sorts of embarrassment that afflict all preachers from time to time. On one occasion, for example, he had decided to preach on a particular psalm (we do not know which one) but the lector mistakenly read Psalm 139 instead. Rather than give any indication that something had gone wrong, Augustine rose to the challenge and preached on what had been read, without notes or preparation of any kind. He believed that it was God's will that he should speak on Psalm 139 and trusted God for the strength and presence of mind to do so in a way that would edify the congregation.[105]

Augustine was a child of his age and spoke to it as he was called to do, but time and again his thoughts transcended the limitations of time and space. When confronting the widespread despair that followed the news of the sack of Rome, he spoke of the universal human tendency to idolize the past and look on it as a golden age, though God was urging his people to live in the present and realize that judgment was at hand:

> You look back to former times which seem to you to have been happier. You were like olives hanging on the tree, swayed by the wind, enjoying your wandering desires in the freedom of the breeze. But now the time has come for the olives to be put in the press. They cannot always hang on the trees—the end of the year has come.[106]

Here the circumstances of the time are fused with a universal experience, making the illustration as vivid today as it was when he first delivered it. One of the main reasons for Augustine's success in this is that he believed that the subject matter for his sermons was given to him from the Bible,

---

[103] *Enarrationes in Psalmos* 99.1.
[104] *Sermones* 126.8.
[105] *Enarrationes in Psalmos* 138.1. Although he did not say so, Augustine was in fact behaving like an actor who has to pick up and carry on when one of his colleagues has fluffed his lines.
[106] *Enarrationes in Psalmos* 136.9.

which, as God's Word, contained all that was needed for the salvation of his people. Rather than speak directly to what he thought were their immediate needs, he looked for clues in the Scriptures that he could then apply to them. The Word of God is eternal because it speaks to the condition of mankind, which has remained unchanged since the fall of Adam and Eve, and offers the remedy of Christ, who likewise remains unchanged over time. As Augustine remarked on one occasion: "The holy Gospel which we have just heard read has spoken of the forgiveness of sins. This is what you must learn about from my sermon today. I am a minister of the Word, which is not my word but the Word of our God and Lord."[107]

As we still say today, the congregation was there to listen not to the words of the minister but to the ministry of the Word. Furthermore, the preacher himself had to listen to his own words, because God was speaking to him as much as to anyone else. Augustine knew that he was responsible for what he said, and that if he failed to practice what he preached, he would be in greater spiritual danger than anyone who heard him.[108] As he told his people: "I am bold to exhort you, but when I exhort you, I look into myself. The man who preaches God's Word without listening to it himself is wasting his time."[109]

True to his personal approach, Augustine did not hide the temptations that assailed him as a preacher, nor did he hesitate to recommend to others how they should deal with their temptations. Chief among the problems he faced was the danger of pride. As a man he wanted to be praised and appreciated, but as a child of God he knew that very often he would not be rewarded in that way, because his message, if faithful, would be painful to many.

> I like applause and it would be dishonest of me to say otherwise, but I do not want praise from people who lead wicked lives—that I hate and abominate. It gives me pain rather than pleasure. But praise from decent people [is something else]. . . . I do not want it, in the sense that I do not want to fall down spiritually because of human praise, but at the same time I do not want to be without it, because I do not want to have an audience that is totally unappreciative. I think of the burden of my responsibility, because I have to give account [to God] even for your applause. I am often praised, but I worry about the lifestyle of those who praise me.[110]

---

107 *Sermones* 114.1.
108 *Sermones* 179.7.
109 *Sermones* 179.1.
110 Frangipane, 6.2, in Morin, *Miscellanea Agostiniana*, 1:221–22.

Augustine preached because he felt he owed it to God to fulfill the mission that he had been given. As Christ had died for him, so he must give his life for the sake of his people. Even in his final illness he was concerned about this; it stayed with him and governed his thoughts right to the end of his life.[111] He had the rare gift of being able to identify with his people, even though in many ways he was not like them at all. He had had a relatively privileged upbringing, was well-educated, and after his conversion had devoted himself to a life of celibacy. Not many people in Hippo could have said that! But at the same time, he could legitimately claim to have stood and listened to others in the same way that his people were now standing and listening to him. He knew from experience how resistant they could be, and he appreciated that they would not find it easy to change their ways. Even more than many of his hearers, he had fallen into error and knew it. When his adversaries accused him of hypocrisy in preaching the Christ he had formerly denied, Augustine replied: "I was deluded and infatuated by a perverse error and do not deny it. . . . I judge my past conduct more harshly than you do. What you revile, I have condemned."[112]

One of Augustine's great strengths as a preacher was his ability to integrate what he had to say about any given text with what theologians call "the whole counsel of God" (Acts 20:27)—in other words, the teaching of the entire Bible. Unburdened by the overanalysis typical of so much modern scholarship, he saw nothing wrong with comparing one scriptural text with others, and sometimes with very many others. He knew that no text could be read in isolation, because every part of God's Word belonged to a greater whole. That whole could be described in various ways: it was Christ, it was our experience of God, it was the divine love at work in believers.[113] But where modern minds like to separate these out and detect different emphases in his preaching, in fact they are all ways of saying the same thing. God so loved the world that he gave his only Son to die for our salvation. Those who believed in Christ were born again of the Holy Spirit into a new life, which they then sought to live in union with him according to the teaching he has given us in Scripture. Augustine might refer to this reality by focusing on different parts of it, but he always had the whole in view.

Here, perhaps as much as anywhere, the modern preacher has much

---

[111] *Sermones* 133.1; Possidius, *Vita Augustini* 31.242.
[112] *Enarrationes in Psalmos* 76.10. His model here was the apostle Paul, who said much the same thing about his own pre-Christian antagonism to the gospel. See Gal. 1:13; Eph. 3:8.
[113] *Enarrationes in Psalmos* 98.4.

to learn from him. In examining one of the trees we must never lose sight of the wood to which it belongs. A verse of the Bible can be understood only against the backdrop of Scripture as a whole, and if we neglect that, the verse in question is liable to be misinterpreted by being taken out of context. In other words, preaching relies as much on systematic theological thinking as it does on acute exegesis, and to compartmentalize these is to lose the power of the Word to speak to us in the way that it spoke to Augustine and, through him, to his people.

One of the hardest things to appreciate when reading Augustine's sermons is his sense of humor and lightness of touch. Humor does not travel well, even among people who speak the same language. British people rely on word games and whimsical associations much more than Americans do, for example, which can lead to misunderstanding. Not so long ago I objected to the idea that a book of mine might be published on the first of April. My British friends understood immediately and were surprised that anyone would choose such a release date, but most of my American colleagues failed to see what I was getting at. To them, the first of April was simply the start of a new fiscal quarter, and what was wrong with that? Modern people face difficulties of this kind when approaching Augustine; often they do not understand where he is coming from and so do not get what he is saying. It is true that we can sometimes appreciate the joke even if the form of humor is new. For example, Augustine thought it quite fitting that coins should be round, because it reminds us of how easily money can roll away.[114] We may not find this all that funny today, but at least we understand that he was trying to be humorous.

It is harder for us to appreciate Augustine's language games, such as his remark that the Hebrew name Adam was composed of the points of the compass in Greek—*anatolē* (east), *dysis* (west), *arktos* (north), and *mesēmbria* (south). Augustine used this "fact" to illustrate that Adam is the ancestor of the entire human race, which was scattered to the four winds after he fell. Augustine was clearly playing a word game, and this does not appeal to the modern prosaic mind. But to his hearers this was the sort of cleverness they liked. To them, it was a wonderful way of remembering the point he was trying to make. The modern acronym TULIP for the five main points of Calvinism as expounded at the Synod of Dort is similar to this.[115] Dort

---

114 *Enarrationes in Psalmos* 83.3.
115 The points are Total depravity, Unconditional election, Limited atonement, Irresistible grace, and the final Perseverance of the saints, though the Synod of Dort did not use this terminology itself.

(Dordrecht) is in Holland, which we associate with tulips, and so the acronym seems to fit. Experts might quarrel that the synod approved the five point in the sequence not of TULIP but of ULTIP and that the Dutch word for tulip is actually *tulp*, but who cares? They are just spoiling the party and making life difficult, even if they are technically right.

It is only when we appreciate this that we can understand Augustine's mind and the methods he used. If technical accuracy got in the way of a good illustration, then that accuracy could be dispensed with. Augustine's congregations liked the way he created puzzles in the Bible and then solved them, and he was wise enough to use that inclination as a means of instilling truth into their otherwise resistant hearts.[116] At the same time, we must remember that Augustine always emphasized the need to begin with the literal and historical sense of the biblical text. If it contained hidden meanings, then these were to be sought in and through the words on the page, not beyond them.[117]

Much of what we learn from Augustine's approach to preaching comes from what he said to others who sought instruction from him. Augustine knew that because humor works only when those using it share a common frame of reference, a preacher has to know his audience. In private conversation it is usually not too difficult to work out what is and is not appropriate, but he explained:

> It is different when you are teaching publicly, surrounded by an audience of people who hold very different opinions. . . . These are bound to affect the man who is called to speak to them. His words will carry the stamp of his own mind, and this will affect the hearers in different ways, just as they also affect one another differently.[118]

Reaching out to others is more than just a matter of finding the right words. What we now call body language also counts for a great deal. Greek and Latin have different words for anger, but the phenomenon is the same, and everyone who sees the look of anger in a man's face understands what is going on, even if he uses different words to express it.[119] For this reason, audiences respond to the spirit of the person speaking to them more than to his actual words. People are turned on when "they see those minds

---

116 *Enarrationes in Psalmos* 49.9–10.
117 *Tractatus in Evangelium Ioannis* 50.6.
118 *De catechizandis rudibus* 15.23.
119 *De catechizandis rudibus* 2.3.

which are trying to affect them kindled by the same fire."[120] The love of God that inspires a speaker will confirm some hearers in that love and at the same time bring judgment on those who are trying to be Christians for something less than love's sake.[121]

Augustine also taught would-be preachers that they were to make themselves available to their people even when they thought they had better things to do; but he warned them not to reveal their private feelings about this in a way that might cause hurt and alienation.[122] A preacher also had to take care to communicate his message in the right way. If this meant ignoring the rules of grammar, then so be it. If he made a mistake and it was pointed out, then he needed to apologize, correct it, and move on.[123] Everything he said and did had to serve the ministry and not draw undue attention to himself. Above all, a preacher had to be engaged with his subject. Sometimes this involved having to say things several times over, which could seem quite tedious to do, but the preacher was never to let that show. In truth, Augustine said, repeating things could often bring them home to the speaker and make him rejoice in them even more than he had before.[124]

Whatever approach a preacher adopted, he was always to make sure that he was communicating with his audience. Sometimes people are too respectful and conceal their true opinions, giving the preacher the impression that they accept everything he says when in fact they disagree with most of it. On other occasions the audience may grow weary and stop listening, without saying anything to indicate that they have switched off.[125] The astute preacher will be on the lookout for signs of this and do what he can to counteract the negative effects. The best way, of course, is to deal with people individually, and even if that is possible only on a limited scale, it is worth pursuing. As always, the ultimate goal must be kept in view, and every legitimate means of getting there should be pursued.

To sum up Augustine's approach to preaching and his understanding of its importance, it is enough to recall that when God made the world he did so by speaking. By his Word the heavens were made, and by it too he gave his covenant and its promises to Abraham and his descendants.

---

120 *De catechizandis rudibus* 2.7.
121 *De catechizandis rudibus* 5.9.
122 *De catechizandis rudibus* 10.14.
123 *De catechizandis rudibus* 11.16.
124 *De catechizandis rudibus* 12.17.
125 *De catechizandis rudibus* 13.18–19.

Israel would eventually become a people of the book, but this was only because the nation started out as a people of the Word, given to them by the prophets, who were the privileged preachers of old. Above all, when the time came for the promises to be fulfilled, the Word became flesh. What God had *said* all along he now *did* once and for all in the life, death, and resurrection of his Son Jesus Christ. To preach the Word was therefore to bring Christ to the people. He was its author, its subject, and its reason for being. In his preaching, Augustine was proclaiming the lordship of Christ and calling on his hearers to submit to it in their lives. That is why it was so important. Without that submission there could be no salvation for them, and it was to seek and save the lost that the Word had come into the world in the first place.

Converting the World

Augustine knew that the heart of his ministry lay in proclaiming the Word of God and in winning men and women for Christ, but he also knew that there was a bigger battle against evil which he could not fight alone or in his own strength. It was not necessary to embrace the dualism of the Manichees to see that the force of evil in the world was more powerful than the will of a single individual. Those who turned to Christ found themselves living in an alien environment, because the prince of this world still controlled it. Even when most people were Christians, this negative power was at work, seeking to frustrate their spiritual progress and claim back whatever it could for the kingdom of darkness from which believers had been set free.

The world into which Augustine was born was going through a radical transformation. The pagan deities and beliefs that had governed it from time immemorial were gradually giving way to a message of election and salvation directly contrary to everything that people had always believed. The traditional religions and philosophies had emphasized the need to struggle against whatever was thought to be wrong and thereby achieve a higher kind of life. Whether this amounted to "salvation" or not depended on one's point of view, but it is safe to say that few people had any clear idea of what the world was for or where it was going. At most, they thought it was declining to a point where it would be destroyed (or self-destruct), only to be formed anew in an ongoing cycle of birth, life, and death. The lucky few might be rescued from this by becoming "gods" and joining the recognized pantheon of mythological heroes, but those who achieved this were themselves legendary—men like Achilles and Hercules, for example. The ordinary person hardly stood a chance.

Into this civilization, Christianity came like a shaft of light. It promised salvation to all who believed, regardless of their social standing or heroic achievements. There was certainly room for the latter—the cult of the martyrs testifies to that—but although martyrdom might have provided assurance that the victim had gone to his heavenly reward, it was by no means the only way of obtaining it. Fundamental to the Christian way of thinking was belief in an organized plan, established by a loving Creator God. Nothing happens by accident, because he is the Maker and Preserver of all things. But this belief was not a kind of fatalism; God is a personal being who has created humans in his image and likeness. It was therefore possible for men and women to work out their salvation in the context of a personal relationship with him that brought a sense of peace and fulfillment to believers in place of the fear or resignation of those who thought that they were subject to a blind and incomprehensible fate.

But if the Christian worldview brought a sense of security and assurance to believers where there had been none before, it also raised other questions. The most serious of these was the ongoing presence of evil in the world and its seeming power over the lives of all people, whether they were believers or not. The history of the world was a catalog of evil, or so it seemed. The Roman Empire, on the other hand, could be presented as the solution to this, at least as far as the civilized world was concerned. By conquering the entire known world, the Romans had brought a universal peace that permitted the development of trade and culture to a degree previously unknown. Christianity itself benefitted from this, because the gospel spread along the roads and sea routes that the Romans had either built or protected. Augustine in Hippo could correspond with Jerome in Bethlehem without difficulty, and a man like Pelagius could travel from his native Britain to Jerusalem in safety and complete freedom.

Unfortunately, in the course of the fourth century this great edifice of civilization was starting to crack, and during Augustine's lifetime it would gradually fall apart. The trouble began, or so it seemed to many, when Christianity was legalized in 313. Far from uniting the empire on the basis of a new and powerful religion, it led to divisions of a new and unfamiliar kind. Paganism was tolerant of different forms of belief, but

Christianity was not. There was one right way of thinking and behaving and any number of wrong ones, and it was the duty of the former to extirpate the latter if possible. The emperor Constantine I did his best to broaden the "right way" to include many options, which meant tolerating different forms of Arianism alongside the orthodoxy of the first council of Nicaea. This policy was adopted by most of his successors, though one of them, Julian "the Apostate," tried to restore paganism during his brief rule (361–363). When Augustine was a boy, it was still not clear what form of Christianity would take over the empire, if indeed it would.

The problem was resolved after a fashion in 380, when the emperor Theodosius I (r. 378–395) made Christianity the state religion and proscribed all other forms of belief. Pagan temples were closed or turned into churches, and pagan ceremonies, including the Olympic Games, were discontinued. Theodosius was the last man to rule the entire Roman Empire, and so his decree took effect everywhere, but after his death the whole edifice started to crumble. Gothic barbarians, who had been converted to a form of Arianism, were already marauding in the Balkans and making their way toward Italy. Their Germanic cousins were building up strength along the Rhine-Danube frontier, and at the very end of 406 they spilled over into the empire. Within a few years they had taken control of much of Gaul and Spain. Britain was abandoned (though not conquered by the Anglo-Saxons for another generation or more), and the old sense of security evaporated.

The climax came when Rome fell to the Goths and everyone was jolted into realizing that their world had fallen apart. Things were not actually as bad as they were made out to be, and Rome was to struggle on for another two generations or so, but the spell of the "eternal" city had been broken. Many people blamed this on Christianity. They argued that the pagan gods had protected the city and its empire for hundreds of years and that once they were rejected, their protection was withdrawn and the inevitable collapse occurred.[126] Christians could hardly accept that kind of explanation, but what could they put in its place? Events had overtaken their ability to explain them, and a new, more comprehensive approach to the question of God's plan of salvation was now required. How could the destruction of the world be part of the purpose of a loving God?

To answer this question, Augustine had to go back to the beginning of

---

[126] This had actually been predicted by the pagan senator Symmachus, when the altar of victory was removed from the Roman senate in 382. See the correspondence between Augustine and the governor Marcellinus, which can be dated to 412 (*Epistulae* 136, 138).

human history. Adam and Eve had fallen away from God as individuals, but their disobedience was part of a wider context of evil. They had not rebelled of their own initiative, but because they had been tempted by Satan, who had already fallen. They exchanged the rule of one kingdom (God's) for another (Satan's). In the Bible, these two kingdoms are described as "cities," a word that meant much more than it does today. To Augustine and his contemporaries, a city was what we would call a state.

Sometimes this relationship was obvious; both Babylon and Rome were empires that took the names of the cities from which they emanated. In other cases the connection was not so clear; Egypt and Assyria, for example, were not usually known by the name of their capital cities. But as Augustine came to see, these empires were merely different manifestations of the power of evil at work in the world.

In contrast to them there stood Jerusalem, the city of God. This was both a physical place—which had for a short time been the capital of a reasonably great empire—and a spiritual ideal. In the Old Testament it was difficult to sort out one from the other, though the frequent appeals to Zion in the Psalms strongly suggest that the spiritual idea was paramount in the mind of the psalmist, who in Augustine's eyes represented the voice of Christ. The apostle Paul was in no doubt about this. For him, Jerusalem was primarily the heavenly city that is the mother of us all, and its earthly counterpart was a kind of counterfeit.[127] Augustine believed that the Christian must therefore interpret history in a figurative sense, as Paul did, and concentrate on the eternal city of God, not on the earthly manifestations of good and evil powers that were at war with one another.

It was with this in mind that Augustine sat down to write his great book *The City of God*. It took him thirteen years to complete (413–426) and was the longest work that he ever wrote. In fact, apart from the Bible, it is the longest book to have come down to us from ancient times. *The City of God* is divided into twenty-two books, which can be grouped into those that attack paganism (the first ten) and those that expound the Christian life (the last twelve). The work as a whole therefore is not just a demolition job; it is also a constructive attempt to rebuild a coherent picture of the universe that can serve as a foundation for Christian thinking about the place of the self, the state, and society in the overall plan and purpose of God.

It is easy to criticize *The City of God* for its numerous digressions and

[127] Gal. 4:25–27.

apparent disorder in places, but Augustine was a busy man and did not have time to do the kind of editing that such a work would have demanded. In any case, its encyclopedic nature was appreciated by later generations, who often learned whatever history they knew from its pages. Its pockets of incoherence could be tolerated because its overall message was clear. Augustine wrote to reassure his readers that the sovereign Lord of the universe was in control of human history and that what had happened to Rome was no worse and no more preventable than what had happened to any number of cities before it and what would continue to happen until the end of time. Christians should not put their faith in earthly things, but lay up treasure for themselves in heaven, as Jesus had taught his disciples to do. In Augustine's words:

> As people hasten to a place of greater security when they see the walls of
> their houses starting to shake and spell impending ruin, so ought Chris-
> tians, the more that they see from their afflictions that the destruction of
> the world is at hand, rush to transfer to the treasury of heaven the goods
> that they were intending to store up on earth.[128]

In *The City of God* Augustine applied to world history the same spiritual principles that he had seen at work in his own life. The conflict of sin and grace in his own soul was mirrored in the struggle between the two cities on the world stage. Just as the soul was saved, but only by being put to death and raised again to a new and victorious life, so the world would be redeemed, but only by a similar process. In both cases, the final consummation would occur when Christ returns in judgment and history comes to an end.

In the meantime, the human race can be divided into two classes of people: "I classify the human race into two branches. One consists of those who live by human standards, the other of those who live according to God's will. I also call these two classes the two cities, speaking allegorically."[129] The community that shapes each of these cities was formed by a common interest. In the case of the earthly city, that was a self-love that reached the point of contempt for God. In the case of the heavenly city, it was formed by the love of God extending to the point of contempt of self.[130] The heavenly

---

128 *Epistulae* 122.2.
129 *De civitate Dei* 15.1.
130 *De civitate Dei* 14.28.

city was predestined to reign with God in eternity, but the earthly city is condemned to eternal punishment, along with the Devil.[131]

In the course of human history on earth, the two cities are intertwined and cannot be separated from one another. Members of both live and sometimes die for the honor of their country or family, and it may be impossible for observers to know the real motivations of each. But God knows the secrets of the heart, and when the final judgment comes, those secrets will be revealed for all to see. Thus it may happen that two people who have done exactly the same thing ostensibly for the same purpose (like give their lives for a cause) will go to different eternal rewards because their inner dispositions were completely different.[132]

There are times of course when behavior tells us which of the two cities a man belongs to. This was clear from the very beginning.

> Cain was the first son to be born of the parents of mankind, and he belonged to the city of man. The later son, Abel, belonged to the city of God. . . . Scripture tells us that Cain founded a city, whereas Abel, as a pilgrim, did not. For the city of the saints is up above, although it produces citizens here below, and in their persons the city is on pilgrimage until the time of its kingdom comes.[133]

In other words, we should expect the earthly city to appear to be stronger and more powerful to the naked eye, because those who belong to it are serving purely temporal ends and must therefore make their presence felt in this world. Given the nature of what motivates the members of the earthly city, we must not be surprised to discover that they are never satisfied. For this reason, "human society is usually divided against itself, and one part of it oppresses another when it finds itself to be the stronger. . . . The result has been that some nations have been entrusted with empire, while others have been subjected to foreign domination."[134]

Rome was a classic example of an empire and never really practiced justice, despite many claims to the contrary.[135] The peace that it brought to the world was part of the natural order created by God in which all human beings share but which is intended to last only as long as the world

---

[131] *De civitate Dei* 15.1.
[132] *De civitate Dei* 18.54.
[133] *De civitate Dei* 15.1.
[134] *De civitate Dei* 18.2. See also 19.17.
[135] *De civitate Dei* 19.21.

endures.[136] One of the functions of the earthly city is to promote the temporal welfare of its inhabitants, and although none does it perfectly, many make provision for giving assistance to those who are poor or in debt, and this is a good thing.[137] But economic prosperity is often based on oppression of others, in particular on slavery, which Augustine deplored even though he recognized that the institution existed by God's permission.[138] Nevertheless it was part of the fallen human condition, which he described in lurid terms:

> Men are plundered by their fellow-men and taken captive, they are chained and imprisoned, exiled and tortured, limbs are cut off and organs of sense destroyed, bodies are brutally misused to gratify the obscene lust of the oppressor, and many such horrors are of frequent occurrence. . . . From this life of misery, a kind of hell on earth, there is no liberation except through the grace of Christ our Savior, our God and our Lord.[139]

The parlous condition of mankind and the terrible likelihood that if an oppressor is left to his own devices, even greater evils will result—these inclined Augustine to adopt the so-called "just war" theory. This permitted hostilities when they were the lesser of two evils, and legitimated killing (for example) that would otherwise be unlawful. It should be noted in this context that while Augustine thought there were circumstances in which war could be *justified*, he never considered war *right* in itself. In the bigger picture, it was merely one way in which the earthly city managed to retain some semblance of order and justice in a fallen world.[140]

Members of the city of God, on the other hand, live in a different mental and spiritual universe, even though they are temporarily in exile in the earthly city as well. They are not concerned with leaving monuments behind; they are pilgrims on a journey elsewhere—a theme that would be taken up and immortalized by John Bunyan in *The Pilgrim's Progress* more than twelve hundred years later. The question for Christians was therefore clear. Do I spend my time and energy building up a kingdom in this world,

---

[136] *De civitate Dei* 19.13–14.
[137] *Epistulae* 113–15.
[138] *De civitate Dei* 19.15.
[139] *De civitate Dei* 22.22.
[140] *De civitate Dei* 1.20–21.

or do I place my affections elsewhere and suffer the consequences? Augustine supported his challenge to believers by referring to Paulinus of Nola, who, when tortured by barbarians, prayed, "Lord, let me not be tortured for gold and silver, for you know where my riches are."[141] The experience of Paulinus was arresting to those who read these words for the first time, and Augustine cited them with great power and effect.

The fact that the city of God is located in heaven did not mean, for Augustine, that life on earth is to be despised. The believer on earth lives in two worlds: at one level, he is a stranger on earth, living among the ungodly and trusting in God for his salvation, but at another level he is seated in the heavenly places, dwelling in the everlasting security of divine love.[142] In spiritual terms, this life is a childhood that will come to maturity when we get to heaven. Our life there will be different in many ways, but it will also be a continuation of what we experience now, yet in a richer and deeper way.[143]

If we embrace this vision as we ought to, the life we live here on earth will change profoundly. It will not be a question of choosing the church over against the state; that choice, and the conflict that it sometimes engenders, belongs to *this* world, not the next. The church on earth is a vehicle for preaching the kingdom of God, but it must not be identified with that kingdom itself. We can be servants of the state, but we must always reserve the right to speak against it if we have to. When it comes to ethical decisions, we cannot decide what is good and what is evil, but only what is right and what is wrong. The difference between these is that the former is an absolute distinction that cannot be made in a world of relativity, whereas the second is a call to practical action—what we must do in the present circumstances. We cannot know what the ultimate outcome of our actions will be, but that does not mean that we do not have to act according to our consciences and understanding.[144]

The fall of Rome gave Augustine an opportunity to examine the true worth of human life and action, and he was able to see just how ambiguous our existence is. The horrors of the twentieth century and the realization that it is now possible for one man to press a button and destroy the entire planet have brought this home to us in a new way. The optimism of

---

[141] *De civitate Dei* 1.10.
[142] *De civitate Dei* 1, preface.
[143] *De civitate Dei* 14.4.
[144] *Epistula* 138.

the nineteenth-century belief in "progress" has not disappeared, but like Rome, it has been ransacked, and its ultimate ruination is apparent for all to see. Those who are of the flesh resist this conclusion and cling to this fading world because they have no alternative. But the children of God know that if and when earthly destruction comes, it will not affect their eternal destiny. This is the hope of the gospel, the promise made by God to the sinners whom he loves, and the assurance that the gates of hell will not prevail (Matt. 16:18).

CHAPTER 5

AUGUSTINE TODAY

Augustine's Reputation

There can be no doubt that Augustine was the greatest of the Latin (or Western) church fathers. There had been giants before him, like Tertullian and Cyprian, though the former was of doubtful theological soundness and the latter's life had been cut short by martyrdom. Among Augustine's contemporaries, there were men like Hilary of Poitiers, through whom he learned of the Greek-language (or Eastern) Christian tradition, and Marius Victorinus, who taught him much about Neoplatonism and how it could be reconciled with Christian faith. Augustine himself knew Ambrose of Milan and corresponded with Jerome, the translator of the Latin Vulgate Bible. Whether he also knew the mysterious "Ambrosiaster," the man who wrote a superb commentary on the Pauline Epistles that has come down to us under the name of Ambrose, is uncertain, though some of the ideas Augustine expressed suggest that the two men moved in similar circles. Augustine was familiar with the writings of Pelagius, whose biblical commentaries were recycled under the names of Jerome and Cassiodorus in order to preserve them from destruction as the product of a heretic.[1] In the next generation there would be Leo I, surnamed "the Great," who as bishop of Rome would play a key role in resolving the christological questions that troubled the Eastern churches in Augustine's lifetime. Many other names could be added to this list: Novatian, Lactantius, Prudentius, Paulinus of

---

[1] It seems that both the third book of Augustine's *De peccatorum meritis et remissione* and his *De spiritu et littera* must be read as replies to Pelagius's commentary on Romans. For the arguments, see Isabelle Bochet, *"Le firmament de l'Écriture": L'herméneutique augustinienne* (Paris: Institut d'Études Augustiniennes, 2004), 54–85.

Nola, and so on. But however interesting and important their writings are, they pale in significance next to those of Augustine.

One reason for this is the sheer bulk of his output. Even allowing for losses over time, Augustine wrote an enormous amount. He also stands out by the breadth of his interests. In this respect, only Tertullian can approach him, though Tertullian—despite writing at length on many theological, philosophical, and social questions—did not venture into commentary on the Bible, nor did he leave us any letters or sermons. His books are highly personal in the sense that there can be no doubt who their author was, but they tell us little about the man himself. We know that he had a sharp tongue and could coin a memorable phrase, but we have no idea when (or how) he became a Christian, how long he lived, or whether he remained a member in good standing of the church at Carthage. Most people have thought that his evident sympathy with the Montanist movement from Asia Minor led him to break with his local church, but while there was a sect of Tertullianists in fourth-century Carthage (which Augustine reconciled to the mainline church), this is uncertain.

From our vantage point today, Tertullian is a powerful and original voice, but he lacks a body, so to speak; we hear him but cannot tell what he looked like. Augustine, on the other hand, comes across as a complete personality whom we know in intimate detail and whose mind is revealed to us in its context. We know not only what he said but also why he said it and (in many cases) how it was received by his congregation and contemporaries. He is, in short, the only ancient Christian writer of whom it is possible to write a serious biography, and in that sense he is accessible to us in a way that nobody else from the early church is.

Augustine also had the good fortune, if we can call it that, to have lived in the last generation of antiquity. After his death, it was still possible for some people in the Latin West to get a good classical education, as the careers of Boethius, Cassiodorus, and Gregory the Great remind us, but they were exceptions. The old Roman world no longer had urban centers where a large educated public eagerly debated philosophy and theology. Classical allusions fell on increasingly deaf ears as fewer and fewer people were brought up on the literary treasures of pre-Christian times. For many, Augustine—and especially *The City of God*—became the lens through which they read about what had gone before. He was the source, the encyclopedia of knowledge, through which the whole of antiquity, pagan and Christian, was distilled.

The chief evidence we have for the extent of his influence is the simple fact that his writings were widely copied. Some of them have been lost, to be sure, but given their bulk, what impresses us is how much has survived. In one or two cases, this may be the result of chance, but that cannot explain why his great works are still with us in their complete and unabridged form. They have come down to us because they were read for a thousand years before the invention of printing made their preservation so much easier. Even if it is not always clear how much later writers depended on Augustine directly, his thoughts were in the air, and his influence was impossible to escape. What codified this was the publication, around 1150, of the *Sentences* of Peter Lombard (ca. 1090–1160). Peter set out to compile a systematic theology, drawn from the writings of the Latin church fathers, and Augustine was his principal (though by no means his only) source. From then until the sixteenth century, every intending theology teacher in western Europe had to lecture on the *Sentences* and write a dissertation on them.

As a result, men who never read a complete tract of Augustine's became familiar with his ideas and could quote him—out of context perhaps, and to serve their own purposes, but nevertheless in a way that recognized his importance as an authority. The reader of John Calvin's *Institutes*, for example, realizes this immediately. Augustine is cited far more than any other ancient source apart from the Bible, though anyone who takes the trouble to consult the original texts may wonder whether Calvin was using them fairly. Like everyone else in his day, he plundered Augustine for what was useful to him and paid relatively little attention to the context in which he had written.

That awareness of context was to come only later, with the emergence of historical consciousness and "objective" scholarship in the eighteenth century. By then there were new authorities—Luther, Calvin, and Thomas Aquinas—who had supplanted Augustine, though they all drew heavily on his work and cannot be understood apart from him. It is fair to say that in the confessional debates of modern times, Augustine has been used by all branches of Western Christendom in support of their own doctrines and ecclesiology. Roman Catholic scholars are sometimes surprised to discover how much he relied on the Bible, and Protestants often find that he was more "Catholic" than they are comfortable with. But both sides have been prepared to use him and have found in him enough that they agree with to regard him as their ancestor in the faith.

At the same time, relatively few people have suggested that the divisions of the Christian world might be healed by returning to Augustine. The fact is that much of the debate between Protestants and Roman Catholics involves disputes over different aspects of his theology that raise questions which evidently never occurred to him and may reveal inner contradictions in his work of which he was blissfully unaware. That is a sign of his greatness, even if it is also a reminder that there can be no going back to a "golden age" that never was.

It should be said at this point that while Augustine's theology is foundational for the later Western tradition, which embraces both Protestants and Roman Catholics, it remains largely unknown in the East, where most modern Orthodox writers treat him (if at all) as something of an alien intruder. They claim that he had little knowledge of the Greek theology of his time, and that what he knew, he misunderstood. In *De Trinitate* Augustine confessed to being puzzled about what the Greeks meant by terms like *ousia* (being) and *hypostasis* (substance), which he thought were much the same thing but they evidently used differently. A Greek writer of the late fourth century could happily speak of the Trinity as one *ousia* in three *hypostases*, but for a Latin to say "one being in three substances" made no sense.[2] This was a terminological problem caused by the lack, in Augustine's day, of recognized definitions of the words used in christological discourse. It should not be inferred that he failed to understand what the Greeks were getting at; what was unclear to him was their choice of vocabulary. On the basic distinction of the Three and their unity in the One, there was no misunderstanding or disagreement of any real significance.

The problem arose only much later because, whereas Augustine had some knowledge of Greek theology, the Greeks knew nothing of his. They did not know about his concept that God is love, which governed his doctrine of Trinitarian relations. Neither did they have any idea about the psychological analogies he developed—for better or for worse. It was not until about 1282 that *De Trinitate* was finally translated into Greek, more than 850 years after it had been written, and then the context was very different. Greek theologians of the late thirteenth century were forced to deal with the problem of reuniting the churches of East and West, which meant coming to grips with what was by then a highly sophisticated Latin theology. It was because *modern* Latin theologians like Thomas Aquinas, with

---

2 *De Trinitate* 5.10.

whom they had to deal directly, relied so heavily on Augustine that they were forced to turn back to him and try to understand where he was coming from. The result was that Augustine suddenly became influential in the Greek-speaking world and remained so for much of the fourteenth century, though this fact is not readily acknowledged by the Eastern churches today.

Largely for political reasons, the reunion of East and West was doomed to failure, and with that came a rejection of Western theology, of which Augustine was seen to be the archetypal exponent. In other words, just as he was picked up in the East for largely political reasons, so he was also dropped—and criticized—for the same reasons. Only now, in the more irenic and ecumenical spirit of our own times, have some Eastern Orthodox theologians begun to reassess this attitude and in the process rediscovered a forgotten episode in their own history.[3]

Modern assessments of Augustine from a Western perspective are less likely to be mired in confessional debate, though this ecumenism is a recent phenomenon. For example, F. Van der Meer's otherwise excellent study *Augustine the Bishop*, which appeared in English translation in 1961, makes no distinction between the "Catholicism" of Augustine and that of his own Roman Catholic church. This leads Van der Meer to bracket Protestants with Manichees and Donatists and to compare Augustine to sixteenth- and seventeenth-century defenders of the papacy, of which he certainly was not one.[4] More recently, the Lutheran scholar Mark Ellingsen has tried to offer a way in which Augustine can legitimately be read by all branches of the church, though he relies on Augustine's "diversity" to make this possible.[5]

It is perhaps premature to pronounce on this ecumenical attempt one way or the other. But a survey of the recent literature on Augustine suggests that confessional issues have largely faded into the background and been replaced by something else—the divide between those who are openly Christian and those whose approach has been affected by what we now loosely call secularization.

On the one side are those who see Augustine for what he obviously was—a preacher and defender of the Christian faith—and who support this,

[3] See Aristotle Papanikolaou and George E. Demacopoulos, eds., *Orthodox Readings of Augustine* (Crestwood, NY: St Vladimir's Seminary Press, 2008).
[4] Frederik van der Meer, *Augustine the Bishop: The Life and Work of a Father of the Church* (London: Sheed and Ward, 1961).
[5] Mark Ellingsen, *The Richness of Augustine: His Contextual and Pastoral Theology* (Louisville, KY: Westminster John Knox, 2005).

even if they defend their views on an objective scholarly basis.[6] Roman Catholic influence on modern Augustinian studies is especially strong, thanks in part to the Institut d'Études Augustiniennes, which is linked to the Institut Catholique de Paris and publishes theses of outstanding quality on Augustine and related Patristic themes.

On the other side are those who find the religious dimension of Augustine something of an embarrassment, but who recognize that he must be taken seriously as a psychologist, as a political analyst, even as a historian. As a result, it has been possible to publish a portion of his *De Trinitate* as a text in the history of philosophy that leaves out the first seven books because they are too theological and therefore thought to be "irrelevant."[7] Poor Augustine must be rotating in his grave! More recently, there has even been a biography that treats him in much the same way, casting him in the mold of a modern seeker after truth rather than as he would have seen himself—a proclaimer of a Truth that had sought and found him.[8]

The drift of modern scholarship can be seen by comparing two companions to the study of Augustine that have appeared in the last generation. The first, edited by Roy W. Battenhouse, came out in 1955, and all but one of its sixteen contributors were clearly identified as teachers of theology or as practicing clergymen. They were also all Protestant—most of them Anglican, in fact—though that did not influence their presentation unduly.[9] More recently, the sixteen contributors to the first edition of *The Cambridge Companion to Augustine* cannot be so easily identified.[10] Only four can be called professors of theology or religion, most of the others being professors of philosophy instead. It is not clear how many could be called practicing Christians, though at least four are Roman Catholics and one is Lutheran. The total is probably higher, but it is significant that the subject is not mentioned in the brief biographies of the contributors. In the second edition, which appeared in 2014, nine of the fifteen contributors are clearly Roman Catholics, one is a Lutheran, and all but one of the others have a professional interest in Christian studies.[11] But although the evidence of

---

6 So for example, Michael Cameron, *Christ Meets Me Everywhere: Augustine's Early Figurative Exegesis* (Oxford: Oxford University Press, 2012). Dr. Cameron is a Roman Catholic, but (unlike F. Van der Meer) his confessional allegiance is generally kept in the background.

7 Augustine, *On the Trinity*, ed. Gareth B. Matthews, trans. Stephen McKenna (Cambridge: Cambridge University Press, 2002).

8 Miles Hollingworth, *Saint Augustine of Hippo: An Intellectual Biography* (Oxford: Oxford University Press, 2013).

9 Roy W. Battenhouse, *A Companion to the Study of St. Augustine* (New York: Oxford University Press, 1955).

10 Ed. Eleonore Stump and Norman Kretzmann (Cambridge: Cambridge University Press, 2001).

11 Ed. David Vincent Meconi and Eleonore Stump (Cambridge: Cambridge University Press, 2014).

personal religious commitment is higher than in the first edition, the second edition retains its "objective" approach, eschewing confessional bias. This approach now seems to be the norm. A recent international colloquium on the *De Trinitate* demonstrates this clearly. Although many of the contributors are known to be active Christians, either Protestant or Roman Catholic, this is nowhere mentioned in the published acts.[12]

This apparently "neutral" approach may have its advantages in avoiding the temptation that afflicts some in the churches who take issue with Augustine on, for example, predestination, original sin, or the "just war" theory and who criticize or try to sideline him as a result. Whether we like it or not, Augustine is one of the greatest figures in world history, and disagreeing with him on one point or another is not going to change that. The prevailing modern approach to him recognizes this and does not attempt to mount a theological case against his beliefs, being (usually) content to present them as they were and allow the reader to make up his or her own mind. Few will be inclined to adopt Augustine's positions wholesale, and it would be absurd if he were to become the focus of a new "fundamentalism," but neither is there anything to be gained by rejecting what he said and pretending that it is of little importance; too many people over too long a time have taken him too seriously for that to be a valid option. Augustine will continue to be read from a variety of different angles, and his works will not be consigned to oblivion. They are much too important for that.

Augustine's Legacy

What does Augustine mean to us now? What is there about his life and work that still speaks to the Christian life today, and to what extent are his thoughts original to him? Was he merely repeating what had gone before, or did he strike out on new pathways that have remained serviceable for the modern church?

There are doubtless many ways in which Augustine appears—or can be made to appear—strange and irrelevant to us. He spoke what is now a dead language and lived in a world far removed from our own. But if we dismiss him for that reason, we must dismiss the witness of the Bible too, since he was far closer to it (and particularly to the New Testament) than

---

[12] Emmanuel Bermon and Gerard J. P. O'Daly, eds., *Le De Trinitate de Saint Augustin. Exégèse, logique et noétique* (Paris: Institut d'Études Augustiniennes, 2012). Even the preface by Rowan Williams does not mention that he is a former archbishop of Canterbury!

we are. His social milieu strikes us as alien because it was hierarchically arranged. Questions of marriage and family were settled by parents, even among adults, as we can see from Augustine's own case. What man of thirty-two would now be expected to bow to his mother's wishes in such a matter? That may still happen in some third-world countries, but for most people in advanced industrial societies his lifestyle and family customs seem hopelessly strange and outdated. Above all, his conviction that celibacy was the way God had chosen for him, even though it meant abandoning his concubine of many years and the mother of his son, strikes most of us as bizarre—and cruel.

It is obvious that we cannot turn the clock back sixteen hundred years. The ruins of ancient Rome tell us a good deal about it, but they cannot substitute for living experience. We simply do not know what it felt like to be an ancient Roman in the last days of the empire and cannot know what we would have done in Augustine's shoes. We may like to think that we would have acted as modern people do, but that is extremely unlikely. Had we been his contemporaries, we would have been influenced by the same things that shaped him and would have behaved in ways much more like his than like ours now. Everyone is a child of his age and background, and it is unfair to judge someone so unlike us in these respects by the criteria that we would apply to ourselves and to our contemporaries. From a modern perspective, we may like what Augustine did, we may be indifferent to (or puzzled by) his behavior, and we may be hostile to some of the things he advocated. What we can never know is whether we would have felt that way at the time. We ought therefore to suspend judgment about things we cannot know and concentrate instead on principles we can share with him, however different the circumstances may be in which we have to apply them.

Relationship with God

The first thing we notice about Augustine is the emphasis he placed on *the relationship of the individual to God*. He lived in a world that was rapidly becoming Christian, at least in a formal and public sense. It would have been very easy for him to have gone with the flow, as many of his contemporaries did. After 380, when Christianity became the official state religion, conformity to it would have been expected from someone who had aspirations of being part of the governing class. But Augustine did not convert for that reason. He was already an adult making his own way in the world when formal Christianization was decreed, but he did not join in. He was not particularly hostile to the Christian faith, as many intellectuals of the time were. Nor was he spiritually indifferent. He was a man in search of truth and would go looking for it wherever his search took him, as his many years with the Manichees remind us. Strange doctrines (as Christian beliefs often seemed to traditional Romans) did not put him off simply because they were foreign.

Nor did Augustine despise his Christian upbringing or reject the church. He had learned a great deal from his pious mother, and in later life he could not thank her enough for that. He went to church from time to time and enjoyed the singing in particular. In Milan, he even sought out Ambrose, the leading Christian intellectual and preacher of his day, and sat at his feet. But in spite of all that, he did not become a Christian. It is true that he enrolled in catechism classes, hoping to learn more, and prepared himself for eventual baptism. The outward trappings of Christian faith and life had their place, forming a structure that would support and guide him when his eyes were finally opened. But they were not the cause of his conversion.

Augustine confessed that he became a Christian when the Holy Spirit of God moved in his heart, and not before. That movement was not an altogether pleasant one. He had to be brought face-to-face with his sinfulness and complete inability to save himself. He was forced to recognize that he had no hope other than to put his trust in Jesus Christ, who had died to pay the price of his sin. He had to learn that to be a Christian was to be in fellowship with the Son of God, to be united with him in a deeply individual union that rested on personal conviction, not on outward support or tradition. From beginning to end, his faith was a walk with God that could only be expressed as a dialogue between two spirits, which is how his *Confessions* are constructed. Take that away and there would be nothing to speak of—no faith to confess and no life to live.

In putting this personal relationship with God in Christ at the heart of his confession of faith, Augustine set a standard that has remained fundamental to the life of the church ever since. We can have all the superstructure we like, but without the transformed lives of individuals who know they have been saved by the grace of God, it is worth nothing. Our own experience may be very different from Augustine's, but all true believers will recognize the heart of the matter in his account of what happened to him. Nobody before or since has stated this with as much clarity and consistency as he did, and for this alone his witness remains of central importance for the entire Christian world.

The Church Universal

Next on the list comes *his adherence to the church*. Augustine knew that although every Christian must have a personal faith that is not dependent on outward rites and traditions, he also belongs to the universal church. In his day that was simpler than it is now, because there really was only one church spread throughout the world. Sects existed, to be sure, but they were localized. A Donatist could not find fellowship outside North Africa, but a member of Augustine's congregation could go anywhere and be accepted as a brother or sister in Christ. This sense of universality, or "catholicity," was (and still is) very important. Christians cannot leave the existing church and start one of their own, as if nobody else is good enough for them. There may be good reasons for establishing new congregations, but they ought to be in fellowship with others and not cut themselves off as if nobody else is quite as good or as pure as they are. Modern denominationalism complicates the picture, of course, and we must sadly admit that not everyone receives a warm welcome wherever they go. But it must also be said that in recent times the spirit of ecumenism (if not the official ecumenical movement) has made great strides, and that Christians of all kinds are now much more accepting of one another than they were even a generation or two ago.

Sectarianism of the Donatist kind is reprehensible, but the church must also guard itself against false teaching. Augustine did not believe that baptism or ordination was enough to make a person acceptable to others; whoever wanted to join or to minister in a congregation had to profess the orthodox faith as it was laid down in the Bible and stated succinctly in the creeds of the church. Heretics might baptize and claim all sorts of external qualifications for ministry, but if they did not preach the gospel, they were to be rejected.

Today the biggest problem with the mainline churches is that they have allowed themselves to become doctrinally diverse to the point where a significant number of their ministers no longer profess the faith once delivered to the saints (Jude 3). They may go through the motions, but they lack the mind of Christ that would make those motions meaningful and effective. From such ministers the true believer must turn away. But wracked by sin

and heresy as the mainline churches are, that is not an excuse for abandoning them altogether. There is no such thing as a pure or perfect congregation, as those who have tried to establish such things have discovered at
their own expense. In every place, the wheat and the tares grow together
until the harvest; the sheep and the goats will be separated only at the last
judgment. It was Augustine who first stated this clearly as the reason for not
breaking away from the church, and his logic is as valid today as it was then.

Sin and Inability

Augustine has also taught us more clearly than anyone else that *the human
race is united in sin and rebellion against God and cannot save itself.* This is a
biblical principle, of course, but for a number of reasons it was not emphasized as much in the early church as it should have been. There was a strong
sense that the promise of salvation given to the ancient Israelites had been
extended in Christ to the entire human race, so that everyone now has a
chance to be saved. In theory, of course, everybody agreed that this was a
work of God, but they tended to stress that human beings were able to respond to him in a cooperative fashion. The general message was that God
would help those who helped themselves, so that those who showed some
inclination to be saved would be rewarded accordingly. Human effort was
not to be derided but encouraged, and those who tried the hardest would
reap the greatest benefit.

This tendency was underscored by the cult of the martyrs, which by
Augustine's time was growing into a major element of Christian belief. A
martyr was someone who had sacrificed everything for Christ, and his
heavenly reward was guaranteed. In extreme cases, this had led some
people to seek martyrdom in order to be sure of their salvation. The legalization of Christianity had removed martyrdom from everyday experience,
thus creating a need for a substitute. That was found in asceticism, the ongoing "martyrdom" known as the mortification of the flesh. If a Christian
could not be put to death by a Roman executioner, he could at least fast,
give his worldly goods away, and live in celibacy, resisting the lusts of this
world in the hope of obtaining everlasting life.

Augustine did not disapprove of such behavior, but he rejected the
theological reasoning behind it. Asceticism might be good for the soul,
but could not save it any more than any other human effort could. Salvation was a gift of God bestowed by his grace on those whom he had chosen

from before the foundation of the world. We do not know who these chosen people are, and cannot explain why some people have been chosen but not others, but that is how God has exercised his sovereign will, and we must submit to his judgment.

Those who have met with Christ have learned that they must trust him completely and not rely on their own efforts, qualities, or inheritance for their salvation. The works they do as Christians are those commanded by God, but they make sense only within the context of the relationship that he has already established with his people in Christ. If that relationship is right, then everything a Christian does will be forgiven by God, however inadequate or unfruitful a person's life may be. But if that relationship is wrong, then even "good" works will be of no use, because the context and rationale for them are lacking.

This doctrine, as Augustine expounded it, was a radical challenge to much of the church of his day. Many people failed to see that every human being is born in a state of sinfulness, even if sinful acts come only later. What that means is that a baby is not innocent and does not go to heaven automatically—an important point in a world where infant mortality rates were extremely high. There is no possibility that anyone might grow up and avoid sinning. At the same time, sin is not an intrinsic part of human nature. If it were, the incarnation of the Son of God as the sinless man Jesus Christ would not have been possible. It follows that what we now think of as human nature is in fact unnatural and abnormal. Jesus showed by his life and death that it is possible for a man to be delivered from sin, but only if he dies to himself and is born again in union with the risen Christ. This deliverance does not mean that sin has been abolished; as long as we are in the flesh, we live as children of Adam in the earthly city that is the world. But it does mean that our sins are not held against us; they have been paid for by the blood of Christ, which for Augustine was the culmination of God's work in the world and is the true focus of our faith.

As a Christian, Augustine believed that he was saved not because of anything he had done, but because Christ had died for him. The Pelagian belief in some residue of goodness in fallen man that can respond to God's invitation sounds attractive, but it is false. Everything a human being does is affected by his inherent sinfulness, and there is no tribe or nation on earth that has escaped from this curse. Augustine did not go to strange places in search of primitive tribes that had been untouched by the corruption of civilization and might therefore be regarded as sinless. That had been the delusion of the Roman historian Tacitus, who thought the barbarians of Germany and Britain were far superior to the Romans because of their uncultured state. It would also be the delusion of Enlightenment thinkers like Jean-Jacques Rousseau, who applied a concept of the "noble savage" to North American Indians, among others. Even today there are those who claim that "Westernization" is a corrupting influence and that non-Western peoples should be left to their own devices.

Christian missionaries are often singled out as wrong-headed because they refuse to accept the inherent goodness of the people they are trying to reach. Christians are sometimes regarded as arrogant and as thinking that they are superior to others because of their beliefs. To this kind of criticism, Augustine's theology offers a clear and compelling answer. Christians are in no way superior to anyone else; all have sinned and fall short of the glory of God (Rom. 3:23). Non-Christians are worse off not because they are more wicked but because they have not heard or believed the good news of salvation. It is rather like saying that a cancer patient who is not receiving treatment is worse off than one who is. The underlying problem is the same, but one is being cured while the other is not. In this case, the only truly loving approach is to say that a cure is available to everyone without discrimination. Not everyone will want it, but that is a different problem that we cannot resolve. The spiritual struggle for the human soul is one that only God can win, and why he works the miracle of healing in some but not others remains a mystery. But our inability to understand it fully is no reason to reject it. For me to say that I do not want to be cured because some are not reveals a false humility that amounts to unbelief. The truly Christian approach is to accept the healing first and then proclaim it to the world. As flight attendants say while demonstrating safety precautions, "Put on your own mask first before helping others." It is not an either–or but a both–and, with those who have been saved called to reach out to those who are lost in the hope that they too might be redeemed.

Scripture, the Word of God

Augustine also taught the church that *the Word of God is to be found in the Bible and nowhere else*. This idea was not new to him and it can be found, at least implicitly, in Scripture itself. But until the canon was closed, and it was recognized that there would be no more sacred books forthcoming, it was hard to put this principle into practice. The apostles had the Hebrew Bible and used it for their preaching and teaching ministry, but before long the early church was using the apostles' writings for the same purpose. It can hardly be said that this was an apostolic practice, since Paul, for example, could not have used Gospels that he did not possess! But it was not long before a corpus of apostolic literature came to be canonized as the New Testament. This process was well underway in the second century, though it took more than two hundred years to complete. In fact, Augustine was one of the first people to draw up a list of the canonical books. His New Testament was the same as ours, but his Old Testament included what we now call the Apocrypha or deuterocanonical books that are preserved in the Greek Septuagint but are not found in the Hebrew Bible. He was wrong to do that and got into trouble for it with his contemporary Jerome, the great biblical scholar who made the definitive Latin translation we know as the Vulgate, but the notion that there was a fixed canon of revealed Scripture has remained the teaching of all the churches to this day.

Augustine suffered from an unfamiliarity with the original languages of Scripture and a lack of access to adequate textual resources. As a result, his exegesis is often faulty and cannot be trusted. But because he had a concept of the Bible as a single, overarching message from God, these faults of detail were less serious than they might otherwise have been. Augustine never appealed to an isolated verse in a way that would make it contradict the general witness of Scripture as a whole. For example, he did not use the assertion "God is love" in a way that would preclude eternal punishment in hell, of which Jesus himself warned his followers. However "God is love" was to be understood, it had to be consistent with the reality of eternal damnation, and on more than one occasion, this sense of "the whole counsel of God" preserved Augustine from errors into which he might otherwise have fallen. Occasionally, as we have seen, he even ended up twisting his erroneous text to make it fit the bigger picture, thereby interpreting it "correctly," even when the words in front of him suggested something else!

Augustine's sense of the bigger picture is of great importance to the church because there is a constant temptation to take Bible verses out of context and use them in ways that contradict the overall message of the gospel. There is also a temptation to introduce human traditions that are not in the Scriptures and make them tests of orthodoxy. For example, a Roman Catholic is expected to believe in the infallibility of the pope, a doctrine nowhere to be found in the Bible. Liberal Protestants claim that "gender equality" means that men and women are interchangeable in Christian ministry, which is contrary to the teaching of the New Testament but is often enforced as essential to "orthodoxy" in a way that belief in the bodily resurrection of Christ (for example) is not. Augustine's method was designed to prevent aberrations like these, and the miracle is that despite the limitations of the resources available to him, he succeeded as well as he did. We cannot always follow him, of course, and must correct his interpretations when we can show that he was wrong, but that is true of any interpreter of Scripture; nobody gets it right all the time! What we must not do is reject him because of his limitations and deny that he has anything to teach us. His conclusions may not always have been right, but his methods and principles remain surprisingly valid, even after so many centuries.

Inevitably, this raises the question of the allegorical interpretation of Scripture, which many modern exegetes believe is false but Augustine was prepared to embrace. There is a real problem here, and we must be honest enough to face up to it. Like most people in ancient and medieval times, Augustine was prepared to interpret difficult passages of Scripture by appealing to a higher, spiritual sense that supposedly lay behind the written text. Just as the divinity of Jesus Christ was not obvious to those who met him but had to be revealed by special divine intervention, as in the case of Peter,[13] so the divine message of the Bible is not apparent to everyone, but has to be revealed by the Holy Spirit.

That in itself is not objectionable. Plenty of people today, including a number of leading scholars, read the Bible but find nothing of spiritual value in it. To some it is a collection of tribal lore, mythology, and poetry—nothing else. They may comb it for clues about how the Israelites perceived themselves, or what the first Christians believed, but not because they think God is using it to speak to them. The result is that even when what they say may be technically correct, it is not a true interpretation of the Bible. The Old and New Testaments survive because they are used by either the synagogue (in the case of the Old Testament) or the church to hear what God is saying to them. The secrets of the Scriptures are revealed only to those who are submitted to them in the power of the Holy Spirit. To those who hear and obey, the Scriptures are the promise of eternal life; to others, they remain a closed book.

---

13 Matt. 16:17.

Christians agree on this basic truth today, even if they reject allegory as a means of discovering the spiritual truth of the Bible. But before we dismiss this method, we should at least have the humility to realize two things about it. First, men like Augustine did not use allegory in an uncontrolled way. They believed that the truths of the Christian faith were clearly stated in Scripture and that our doctrine must be based on what was revealed in the literal sense of the text. Allegory was valuable only as a supplement to this. It was a way of finding that literal truth in passages that seemed on the surface to conceal or deny it. In other words, no Christian doctrine was based on allegory. On the contrary, doctrine based on the literal sense is what created allegory. Creedal orthodoxy did not depend on allegory for its own existence or integrity. Second, texts that were almost always read allegorically, like the Song of Solomon, may have been intended to be read that way. Certainly it has to be admitted that no nonallegorical interpretation of the Song has won common consent. Perhaps someday one will, but it would be best to find it first before criticizing those who resorted to allegory in order to expound what they knew to be God's Word but could not interpret in any other way.

A Trinity of Love

Augustine taught the church that *God is a Trinity of love*. He certainly did not invent the idea that God is love; that is clearly stated in the New Testament (1 John 4:16). Nor did he construct the doctrine of the Trinity, which he inherited from both his Greek and his Latin forebears. But what he did, in a way that nobody before him had managed, was to bring the two things together. The early church had a problem in trying to work out how God could be one and three at the same time. By a long process of trial and error, it had come to the conclusion that the divine oneness describes God's nature and that the threeness expresses how he acts and relates to us. But did this mean that God's acts and relationality are just as eternal as his being? A century or so before Augustine started tackling the subject seriously, Arius had answered this question in the negative, and although his teaching had been condemned, there were still plenty of people around who subscribed to some version of his heresy. To them the unity of the mysterious and inaccessible divine being was more fundamental than the revelation of God as Father, Son, and Holy Spirit. They usually thought that the divine being was the same as the Father, and they argued about how the Son and the Spirit derived from him; but that was the context in which theology in the fourth century operated, with the defenders of biblical orthodoxy trying to show that the second and third persons were just as eternal and inherent in the divine being as the first person was.

Augustine inherited this situation and solved the problem it posed by resorting to the principle of love. Love cannot exist on its own because it is not a thing or an attribute possessed by a thing. In other words, God cannot be love unless there is something for him to love. But if that something were not part of himself, he would not be perfect. The Bible does not teach us that God needed the creation in order to have something to love; if he did, he could not be fully himself without it. So Augustine reasoned that God must be love inside himself. To his mind, the Father is the one who loves, the Son is the one who is loved—the "beloved Son" revealed in the baptism of Jesus—and the Holy Spirit is the love that flows between them and binds them together. It is in the Spirit, moreover, that we who are believers are bound to God and made partakers by adoption of that love which is intrinsic to his being.

By understanding God in this way, Augustine not only explained the Trinity but made it necessary to the divine being. Without the triune framework, God would not be the love that the New Testament said he was. Moreover, said Augustine, the inner necessity of a triune divinity can be seen in the composition of human beings, who are created in his image and likeness. The fact that our minds possess memory, intellect, and will, which can be distinguished but not separated, and which are all equally important if we are to love God, our neighbors, and ourselves as we are called to do, is additional evidence of the coherence of the Creator and his creation, which, if properly understood, reveals his own inner being to us.

Augustine's doctrine of the Trinity encompasses an entire philosophy of being in a way that none of his predecessors had managed to achieve. It is possible to criticize it of course, and his was not the last word on the subject. He wrote at a time when the word for *person* had not yet been defined with sufficient precision, and so he was able to question its appropriateness. Sometimes modern readers latch onto this as evidence that *person* is not the right term to use for the three members of the Godhead, but Augustine never went that far. He recognized that it had its limitations, but that some word had to be found, since the only alternative was to say nothing at all! There is also the problem of the Holy Spirit, who in Augustine's construction may appear to be less personal than the Father and the Son. This difficulty is rooted in the New Testament, of course, where Father and Son are a natural pair and the Holy Spirit does not seem to fit readily into the family structure implied by the other two. There is a sense in which both the Father and the Son are "holy" and "spirit," so to designate the third person in this way is to confess that he is really anonymous.

Modern critics, especially from the Eastern churches, have criticized Augustine on this point, saying that it leads to a subordination of the third person to the other two that distorts not only the Trinity but also the experience of the church, which finds itself relegated to the supposedly lower level of the Spirit. There may be something in this accusation, and perhaps it is necessary to rethink the whole question of the Spirit in relation to the other persons of the Godhead, but that should not detract from Augustine's overall vision. That the Trinity is a community of divine love and that we are integrated into that love, both because we were made for it in our creation and because it has been opened up for us in our redemption, seem to be incontrovertible and are immensely liberating truths to those who grasp their importance. If further refinement is needed, then so be it; Augustine himself would have accepted that. But as with his teaching on other subjects, let us not allow this leftover business to lead us to reject his achievement. Instead we should gratefully receive what he has given us and seek to define and develop it further in line with the teaching of Holy Scripture, on which his own reflections were based.

Created for a Purpose

Augustine further taught that *God created the world for a purpose*. The fact that God placed his own triune image in Adam, who was intended to be the crowning glory of his creation, teaches us that his otherwise mysterious act had a reason that we cannot fully understand or appreciate. Nobody can say why God made the world rather than do something else for his glory. It was not necessary for him to do so, and although we know that it was an act of love on his part, we do not know why he chose to express his love in this particular way. More importantly, we cannot say why he made creatures that were free to disobey his will and yet would not be annihilated as a result. Satan rebelled against God and was cast out of heaven, but he was not eliminated. Instead, he is still the prince of this world (John 12:31), and the human race has been tempted into subjecting itself to him. Why did this happen? Could God not have prevented it?

Presumably it would have been possible for God to have wound up the entire creation experiment as a failure, but he did not do so. Why not? Ultimately it must have been because his will and his love would not be thwarted by rebellion against him. Angels and men were given the freedom to reject him, presumably because God wanted fellowship with independent minds, not the slavery of robots who were incapable of entering into dialogue with him. That would also explain why the only way men could be saved was by the incarnation of one of the divine persons, who would offer himself as a sacrifice to satisfy the demands of divine justice. A God who did not want to be served by robots could not issue a decree that would cleanse and save the human race without any participation from them. There had to be some sort of engagement for the relationship to be real, but at the same time there could be no question of denying the ultimate sovereignty of God. Hence the incarnation, in which the divine Son came to do the will of his Father, a mission that was consummated by his death on the cross and expressed in the words "not my will, but yours be done."[14]

God resolved the mystery of human sin and suffering not by getting rid of it but by embracing it. He entered into our life, took our sin upon himself, suffered on our behalf, and rose again so that we might enjoy a new life in him. This does not resolve the ultimate questions mentioned above, but it does make sense of the world we live in and have to deal with. From our human standpoint we cannot understand many of the things we experience or see going on in the world around us, but we can know that there is a purpose in God's plan that will one day be revealed to us. Sometimes, as in the resurrection of Jesus, we see what that purpose is, because it is worked out within a time frame that we can grasp. But on other occasions, God's plans are not tied to our schedules. For him, a day is as a thousand years (2 Pet. 3:8), so the outworking of his will is hidden from our eyes. Augustine could not have known that his world would disappear and that a new Christian culture, based to a large extent on his ideas, would spring up centuries later in western Europe . He would probably have been astounded to think that people would still be reading not only his major works, but even his letters and sermons so many generations later. Yet he did know that there was a divine purpose at work in his

---

14 Luke 22:42. See also Matt. 26:39, 42.

life and that God was using him in ways that he could not fully appreciate. And that is what mattered to him.

Augustine also knew that what was true of his life was true in a broader sense of human history. The rise and fall of empires was part of an ongoing process that would ultimately triumph in the fulfillment of God's will for the world. None of us can say for sure what the future will bring, and prophets of doom abound today as they have done for centuries.

Not so long ago there was a real fear that the world would be overrun by Nazi Germany, or by Soviet communism. Yet we have lived to see both of these dangers disappear—one by violence and the other more or less peacefully. Who could have foreseen this? Christians cannot promise that life on earth will get better as time goes on; we have no assurance that it will. It is perfectly possible that our civilization will decline as ancient Rome did, and that our descendants will live through another dark age. The sinful passions of fallen man have not been defeated, and Satan is still active. We may be caught up in things that defy our imagination, and it is perhaps better that we do not know what will happen to us or to our children in this life. But what we can say for sure is that God is in control of events, that whatever happens will resound to his glory, and that no power in heaven or on earth can separate us from the love of God (Rom. 8:39).

By rewriting human history in the light of the Bible, Augustine brought this truth home to the perplexed men and women of his time, and his lesson remains with us still. We who have seen the outcome of the fall of Rome can live with the assurance that even if our earthly states collapse and disappear, God's will will be done in our lives, as it has been in the lives of those who have gone before us in the faith.

A Journey of Faith

Augustine also taught us that *the Christian's life is a journey that we walk by faith*. Again, this may seem obvious in one way, but we must not forget that our familiarity with this concept today owes largely to Augustine's emphasis on it. Within the context of his theology, his view of faith is an important complement to the doctrine of predestination, which, if not personalized, can easily look like a kind of fatalism. Augustine did not believe that a Christian should just sit back and let events take their course. To be in a relationship with God means to live with him, to share his thoughts, to have the mind of Christ, and to do his will in the power of the Holy Spirit on a day-to-day basis. From birth to death, every waking moment belongs to God, even if we are not believers. This is part of the message Augustine conveys in his *Confessions*, where he reviews different aspects of his pre-Christian life and points out how God was using them to further his purposes and how Augustine had already embarked on the Christian journey, even though he was not aware of it at the time.

What was true for him is true for every believer. We have all been called to walk with God, and if we have been chosen by him for salvation, we do so even though we may be far away from him at the time. Conversion is therefore not just the end of one thing and the beginning of another but also the fulfillment of what God has planned for us all along. It is only when we come to a deeper knowledge of him, however, that we are given the grace and insight we need to understand this. Things that meant little beforehand come into greater prominence, whereas other matters that we may have thought were very important at the time fade into the background. In short, we are given a new perspective that is vitally important for the way we live.

Once a person becomes a Christian, his or her priorities will be governed by a desire to please God. There is no prescription for what this might involve; each case is subtly different. Of course Augustine knew that as a Christian he could no longer engage in immoral activities, even if it took him some time to put that into practice. But this was not the point he was trying to make. More important was the lifestyle that he was called to live as a Christian. His mother simply assumed that he would marry and settle down—an obvious enough choice, one might think, but was it God's will for him? Augustine discovered that it was not and, through a combination of circumstances, came to realize that he was meant to lead a celibate life. He did not want to do that, but God made his will clear to him, and Augustine submitted to it. At first he tried to persuade his friends to follow him in a monastic lifestyle, but he soon discovered that it was not for them. This too was a learning experience for him. The way God chooses for his children is unique to each one of them, and no one can create a template that is valid for everyone. We all belong to the body of Christ, to be sure, but each individual is a different part of that body, and we must learn to respect that. It is a hard thing to do, but it is fundamental if we are to function in the wider society of the church. Not everyone is called to do the same thing, and room must be found for the great variety of gifts and callings.

At the same time, there is no excuse for idleness. Every Christian has a calling before God because every Christian has a personal relationship with him. We may not know at first what that calling is, and we may not particularly like it when we find out. But once we know what is right for us, we must pursue it because God has a place for us in his wider family. The people of this world look for fame, honor, and wealth, but the children of God seek only to serve him in whatever capacity he has chosen for them. Our heavenly reward is based not on achievement—the subtle deception of salvation by works again—but on obedience, and obedience is possible only when guided and governed by faith in the One who has called us to obey. With that perspective in view, we can go anywhere and do anything, knowing that God will be with us along our journey.

The Christian's goal is to please God, but at the same time to focus on the eternal reward laid up for us in heaven. What we do on earth has a direct bearing on that. It is not that we shall have a greater reward if we obey more, though that may be true. Rather it is that the glory of God is all the more revealed in us the more we are prepared to sacrifice for him. The traveler takes only what he needs on his journey and leaves the rest behind. This is what Augustine told his people they must do, and it is in this context that his devotion to ascetic ideals must be understood. He was not trying to earn his salvation through personal self-sacrifice but was seeking to discard what was nonessential in his journey to the heavenly city. Our circumstances are different from his, to be sure, but the message is still the same today as it was in his time.

A Mission and Legacy

Finally, Augustine taught us that *the Christian mission is important wherever it is exercised.* Augustine was a man schooled in philosophy and rhetoric. To pursue those interests it was necessary for him to go where the action was—to Carthage, Rome, and Milan, the seat of the western empire at that time. Had he stayed at home in Thagaste, such a career would have been inconceivable. Yet after he became a Christian, his fortunes changed. He retraced his steps—from Milan to Rome, then back to Carthage and even to Thagaste for a time. After a few years he was called to Hippo, a port city of medium importance commercially and unknown for any literary or academic achievement. He did not want to be a bishop, nor was he interested in spending the rest of his life in a backwater like Hippo. For over thirty years he was forced to preach to congregations that had little appreciation for his genius and would as soon go to the theater as listen to him. He had to write time and again against Donatism and Pelagianism, errors that his keen mind must have found risible at one level but that were disturbing the church to which he had to minister. Somehow or other he found the time to do other things as well, but there must have been many days when he was weary of the struggle and wished he could have been doing something else.

Augustine died in the knowledge that a few days later the barbarians would enter Hippo, which they were besieging at the time, and he must have feared that his life's work would go up in flames. Things did not turn out quite as badly as that, but there was to be no lasting legacy of his labors in Hippo—no great basilica with his name carved into it, no academic chair dedicated to his memory, not even a park bench with a plaque saying that his estate had paid for it. To the naked eye there was nothing. Yet as we know, what must have appeared then as a fairly insignificant ministry in a provincial town became the most productive life of any theologian in the Western world. Generations of Christians who would never go anywhere near Hippo would read what Augustine wrote in the hot and dusty chambers that were his earthly dwelling place, and would marvel at his gifts and intellect. More than that, they would be moved, as we still are, by his passion for Christ, and would go away from his writings more determined than ever to walk in the way mapped out for them by God.

That was, and still is, his abiding legacy. It is why, in spite of all the many things that separate us from him and make our lives so very different on the surface, we can still hear his voice and feel his encouragement as we seek to live for God in the world today. God is love, as Augustine reminds us, and those who walk in love walk with God and will be blessed by him with a reward that no earthly power can bestow.

FOR FURTHER READING

Works

Latin

There is no complete edition of Augustine's works in Latin. The most comprehensive collection of them is still

> *Patrologiae cursus completus. Series Latina.* Edited by J.-P. Migne. 221 vols. Paris, 1841–1864. Vols. 32–47.

To this may be added the following:

> *Corpus Christianorum, Series Latina.* Turnhout: Brepols, 1953–. Vols. 27–50.
> *Corpus Scriptorum Ecclesiasticorum Latinorum.* Vienna, 1866–.

Neither of these two is complete, though further volumes in each series are projected.

English

The most widely used translation is that found in the first eight volumes of the *Library of Nicene and Post-Nicene Fathers*, ed. Philip Schaff (New York: The Christian Literature Company, 1886–1890). The series is now out of copyright and readily available online.

The New City Press of New York is sponsoring *The Works of Saint Augustine: A New Translation for the 21st Century.* Several volumes are now available, and more are forthcoming. Two volumes of his works have also been published in the Library of Christian Classics, available from Westminster John Knox Press.

Some individual works of Augustine have been published in popular editions, of which the most common are these:

Confessions. Translated by Henry Chadwick. Oxford: Oxford University Press, 1991.
The City of God. Translated by Henry Bettenson. London: Penguin, 1972.
On Christian Teaching. Translated by R. P. H. Green. Oxford: Oxford University Press, 2008.

A number of his anti-Donatist writings can be found in

Atkins, E. M., and R. J. Dodaro, eds. *Augustine: Political Writings.* Cambridge: Cambridge University Press, 2001.

Studies

General

For any student of Augustine today, two basic reference works are essential:

Fitzgerald, Allan D., ed. *Augustine through the Ages: An Encyclopedia.* Grand Rapids: Eerdmans, 1999.
Di Berardino, Angelo, ed. *Patrology.* Vol. 4. Westminster, MD: Christian Classics, 1986. Translated from the original Italian edition published as *Patrologia.* Vol. 3. Turin: Marietti, 1978. 342–462.

Also valuable are the following:

Battenhouse, Roy W., ed. *A Companion to the Study of St. Augustine.* New York: Oxford University Press, 1955.
Stump, Eleonore, and Norman Kretzmann, eds. *The Cambridge Companion to Augustine.* Cambridge: Cambridge University Press, 2001. This volume has recently been replaced by Meconi, David Vincent, and Eleonore Stump, eds. *The Cambridge Companion to Augustine.* 2nd ed. Cambridge: Cambridge University Press, 2014. It contains a number of new and thoroughly revised essays.

Biographies

Brown, Peter Robert Lamont. *Augustine of Hippo: A New Biography.* Berkeley, CA: University of California Press, 2000.

Hollingworth, Miles. *Saint Augustine of Hippo: An Intellectual Biography.* Oxford: Oxford University Press, 2013.

His Philosophy

Gilson, Etienne. *The Christian Philosophy of Saint Augustine.* London: Gallancz, 1960.

Rist, John M. *Augustine.* Cambridge: Cambridge University Press, 1994.

Evans, G. R. *Augustine on Evil.* Cambridge: Cambridge University Press, 1982.

Harrison, Carol. *Beauty and Revelation in the Thought of Saint Augustine.* Oxford: Oxford University Press, 1992.

His Theology

Markus, R. A. *Saeculum: History and Society in the Theology of St Augustine.* Cambridge: Cambridge University Press, 1970.

Ayres, Lewis. *Augustine and the Trinity.* Oxford: Oxford University Press, 2010.

Sullivan, John E. *The Image of God: The Doctrine of St. Augustine and Its Influence.* Dubuque, IA: Priory, 1963.

Papanikolaou, Aristotle, and George E. Demacopoulos. *Orthodox Readings of Augustine.* Crestwood, NY: St Vladimir's Seminary Press, 2008.

His Interpretation of the Bible

Bright, Pamela, ed. *Augustine and the Bible.* Notre Dame, IN: University of Notre Dame Press, 1999. Translated and adapted from La Bonnardière, A. M., ed. *Saint Augustin et la Bible.* Paris: Beauchesne, 1986.

Patte, Daniel, and Eugene TeSelle, eds. *Engaging Augustine on Romans: Self, Context, and Theology in Interpretation.* Harrisburg, PA: Trinity Press International, 2002.

Cameron, Michael. *Christ Meets Me Everywhere: Augustine's Early Figurative Exegesis.* Oxford: Oxford University Press, 2012.

Arnold, Duane W. H., and Pamela Bright, eds. De doctrina Christiana: *A Classic of Western Culture.* Notre Dame, IN; University of Notre Dame Press, 1995.

English, Edward D., ed. *Reading and Wisdom: The* De doctrina Christiana *of Augustine in the Middle Ages.* Notre Dame, IN: University of Notre Dame Press, 1995.

For those who read French, the indispensable work on this subject is the following:

Bochet, Isabelle. *"Le firmament de l'Écriture": L'herméneutique augustinienne.* Paris: Institut d'Études Augustiniennes, 2004.

His Pastoral Practice

van der Meer, Frederik. *Augustine the Bishop: The Life and Work of a Father of the Church.* London: Sheed and Ward, 1961. Translated from the Dutch *Augustinus de zielzorger.* Utrecht: Het Spectrum, 1947.

Ellingsen, Mark. *The Richness of Augustine: His Contextual and Pastoral Theology.* Louisville, KY: Westminster John Knox, 2005.

Rist, John M. *Augustine Deformed: Love, Sin, and Freedom in the Western Moral Tradition.* Cambridge: Cambridge University Press, 2014.

Rowe, Trevor. *Saint Augustine, Pastoral Theologian.* London: Epworth, 1974.

A NOTE ON THE NUMBERING
OF THE PSALMS

Augustine used an Old Latin translation of the Psalms that had been made from the Greek, not from the original Hebrew, which in many places is quite different. One difference is the numbering of the psalms, and Augustine follows the Greek numbering. Since the Reformation, Protestants have followed the Hebrew text and numbering, which have now become standard in almost all modern translations, but this creates a difficulty in reference to ancient Patristic texts. If a verse from the Psalter is quoted in isolation, it can be referenced according to the modern standard, though not all translations of Augustine do this. But when one quotes the *Enarrationes in Psalmos*, in which Augustine goes through each of the psalms in turn, a real difficulty arises. Should his text be referenced as it stands, or should it be adapted to the modern norm?

The general tendency today is to cite the Latin text in its original form, using the Greek numbers for the individual psalms and ignoring verse divisions, which were not introduced until the sixteenth century. The traditional sentence and paragraph numbering is thus retained, which usually bears no resemblance to the modern verse division. With translations of the *Enarrationes*, things are more complicated. The most commonly used English translation is that of the *Library of Nicene and Post-Nicene Fathers*, produced by nineteenth-century Protestants who made Augustine's text correspond to the modern (Hebrew) numbering of the psalms. More recently however, a new translation produced by the New City Press has retained Augustine's original numbering!

In this volume, all quotations of individual verses and translations have been given according to the Hebrew style, but references to the *Enarrationes* themselves have preserved their original (Greek) numbering. To help the reader sort this out, the following is a table of correspondences between the two systems:

Greek/Latin	Hebrew/Modern
1–8	1–8
9	9–10
10–112	11–113
113	114–115
114	116:1–9
115	116:10–19
116–145	117–146
146	147:1–11
147	147:12–20
148–150	148–150

GENERAL INDEX

SCRIPTURE INDEX

WISDOM FROM THE PAST
FOR LIFE IN THE PRESENT

Theologians on the Christian Life

AUGUSTINE by GERALD BRAY

BAVINCK by JOHN BOLT

BONHOEFFER by STEPHEN J. NICHOLS

CALVIN by MICHAEL HORTON

EDWARDS by DANE C. ORTLUND

LEWIS by JOE RIGNEY

LLOYD-JONES by JASON MEYER

LUTHER by CARL R. TRUEMAN

NEWTON by TONY REINKE

OWEN by MATTHEW BARRETT & MICHAEL A. G. HAYKIN

PACKER by SAM STORMS

SCHAEFFER by WILLIAM EDGAR

SPURGEON by MICHAEL REEVES

WARFIELD by FRED G. ZASPEL

WESLEY by FRED SANDERS

The Theologians on the Christian Life series provides accessible introductions to the great teachers on the Christian life, exploring their personal lives and writings, especially as they pertain to the walk of faith.

Visit crossway.org/TOCL for more information.